TEACHING

Course Offerings and Class Projects

GRAPHIC

from the Leading Graduate

DESIGN

and Undergraduate Programs

edited by Steven Heller

ALLWORTH PRESS
NEW YORK

School of
VISUAL ARTS

11   10   09   08   07   7   6   5   4   3

Published by Allworth Press
An imprint of Allworth Communications, Inc.
10 East 23rd Street, New York, NY 10010

Cover and interior design by James Victore Inc.

Page composition/typography by SR Desktop Services, Ridge, NY

Library of Congress Cataloging-in-Publication Data
Heller, Steven.
    Teaching graphic design : course offerings and class projects from the
leading graduate and undergraduate programs / Steven Heller.
        p.   cm.
    ISBN-10: 1-58115-305-8 (pbk.)
    ISBN-13: 978-1-58115-305-7

    1. Commercial art—Study and teaching (Higher)—United States.
    2. Graphic arts—Study and teaching (Higher)—United States.   I. Title.

NC1000.H45   2003
741.6'071'173–dc22
2003015463

Printed in Canada

To Martin Fox, former editor-in-chief of PRINT magazine, who has made a lifelong contribution to design journalism, and to my professional life.

contents

Part 1: Undergraduate

First Year

Second Year

Third Year

Fourth Year

Part 2: Undergraduate/Graduate

Part 3: Graduate

acknowledgments

I want to thank all of the great teachers I have had, known, worked with, and those I wish I could have had, known, and worked with: without you there would be no design pedagogy.

Thanks to the contributors to this book: without you there would be no book. I hope that your methods will serve the community in which you practice and the students who you are preparing for a life in design.

Sincere gratitude goes to Nicole Potter, my editor on this (and other) books, for her devotion to this project and those persistent queries that served to improve the entire presentation. Also thanks to Jessica Rozler, assistant editor, and Tad Crawford, publisher, for his continued support. Tip of the hat to James Victore for his splendid design.

Steven Heller

introduction

Those Who Teach

xi

The old Woody Allen line "Those who can't do, teach; and those who can't teach, teach gym" is not applicable to graphic design education. I don't know of any design schools that even have a gym. I also don't know of many graphic design teachers who became educators because they could not hack it in the work-a-day world.

Teaching is dedicated work, and I've learned that being a good teacher is not as easy as simply passing on one's knowledge base to others. Some great designers with formidable experience are pathetic teachers. Good design educators must have the ability to relate to students, engender trust, show compassion, and instill ideas, techniques, and abilities.

A teacher must be generous to a fault, but not entirely selfless. A teacher must have the courage and confidence of her convictions, yet know when to bend if necessary. A teacher must create a program that will encourage his students to learn how to learn, and then know when to leave the rest up to them. Incidentally, a teacher must be a mentor, which is easy to say but difficult to be.

I have "taught" in design and illustration programs for over two decades, but until I became co-chair of the School of Visual Arts MFA/Design program in 1996, I had not realized that I was not the kind of teacher I have described above. Rather, I am a lecturer, and the distinction is significant. Although a teacher must also give lectures, a lecturer is not always a teacher in the Platonic, Socratic, or any sense of the word. Frankly, as an administrator I have to juggle many balls, but as a lecturer all I have to do is stand in front of a class and confidently and enthusiastically convey my material as the students passively listen. They certainly get a lot of information, but I do not take them to the next stage of discovery. That's the job of a teacher. What I provide is the raw data, while a true teacher uses this material as a foundation for building knowledge and experience. As a lecturer I may leave the students interested, but a good teacher then guides them into immersion, analysis, and critique, which leaves them inspired and hungry for more.

I have watched inspiring teachers teach and it is a grueling mental *and* physical activity (not to watch, mind you, but to teach). To do it correctly a teacher must balance the requisites of the class, needs of the students, and expectations of the school, and still have a fresh result. An individual educator's energy and charisma is essential to the fulfillment of this process, but the syllabus is her blueprint, roadmap, and manifesto rolled into one. I don't have to stress the role of a syllabus to anyone reading this book, but it is nonetheless necessary to emphasize the unsung cumulative importance of this document as a building block in all design education.

In all but one of the earlier volumes in the Allworth Press *Education of . . .* series, which I have edited, I included sections devoted to syllabi because they provide indelible, concrete examples of the education process. It was also fascinating to read the unique variations on fundamental classes and ideas behind new and innovative ones. In addition, the syllabi in these books were presented as models for any teachers in need of inspiring ideas for teaching their classes. Of course, these syllabi alone are not panaceas for ailing departments; how the teacher presents his material makes all the difference, but the ideas and methodologies in these syllabi from all parts of the world and at all levels of experience can be valuable in structuring pedagogy.

Given the large number of truly winning syllabi found in hundreds of university programs and art/design schools, I felt it would be beneficial to have a volume entirely dedicated to collecting as many as possible in the form that they are presented to students. I was not at a loss.

Divided into three sections—undergraduate, undergraduate/graduate, and graduate—are over fifty such examples of courses ranging from basic to intermediate to advanced to eccentric. The focus is on graphic design studio classes with examples of multimedia (Web, film, and games) courses. Design history and professional practice is also included.

Most syllabi follow the same fundamental structure (introduction/purpose, requirements, weekly breakdown, projects, selected reading, etc.), which is how they appear here. Some are more detailed than others, but I have only edited them to eliminate redundancies. Although all of the syllabi came with examples of student work, owing to space constraints I am showing only a few visuals where necessary.

When asked to submit to this volume, not one teacher balked; in fact, they were all extremely anxious to share their methods with others in the education community. Some critics argue that standardized curricula should be instituted throughout design education, and maybe this idea has merit. But judging from the diverse syllabi, even the most rudimentary type class benefits from a modicum of individuality. While suggesting ways of developing standard curricula, the syllabi presented here indicate that it takes a great teacher to inspire and a great course to expand a student's horizons.

Steven Heller

part 1

undergraduate

1st year

COURSE TITLE _ INTRODUCTION TO GRAPHIC DESIGN
INSTRUCTOR _ Julie Mader-Meersman
SCHOOL _ Minnesota State University, Moorhead
FREQUENCY _ One semester (16 weeks plus finals week), twice weekly
CREDITS _ Four
LEVEL _ Undergraduate

purpose

This course is the first (beyond foundation studies in two- and three-dimensional design and drawing) in a program of courses leading to a BFA* in graphic design, tailored to prepare a student for professional practice in the graphic design field.

description

This is an introductory course for majors in our department of art and design's graphic design program. It involves studio inquiry into the nature of graphic design and visual problem solving. Topics introduced in the course are symbols, typography, information design, visual concepts, and three-dimensional graphic design. The course also introduces the student to studio operations and procedures, client-designer relations, production processes for print media, and graphic design history. Lectures, readings, demonstrations, slide presentations, group exercises, class discussions, and one-on-one meetings with students are used.

Our BFA degree has selective admission; a BA in graphic design is also offered.

description of classes

Week 1
Introductions. Syllabus review. What is graphic design?

Week 2
Symbol show-and-tell; Symbol lecture; Slides; Timed sketchbook exercise;
Introduce symbol project; Studio
Session 2: Group research review; Studio

Week 3
Review thumbnails and roughs; Studio
Session 2: Studio; Mounting demo

Week 4
Preliminary design review
Session 2: Studio

Week 5
Symbol critique
Session 2: Anatomy of typography lecture (read Craig, pp. 12–23; 28–35);
Introduce three-part type project; Group exercise (Koberg & Bagnall,
pp. 52–65)

Week 6
Research and thumbnail review
Session 2: Twentieth-century typography slide presentation; Studio

Week 7
Preliminary design review
Session 2: Open studio

Week 8
Typography critique
Session 2: Visual concepts and creative process lecture (read Koberg & Bagnall,
pp. 8–34 and 78–91); Slides; Introduce project; Group brainstorming exercise

Week 9
Research review; Studio
Session 2: Thumbnail review; Studio

Week 10
Spring break, no class

Week 11
Preliminary design review
  Session 2: Open studio

Week 12
Visual concepts critique
  Session 2: Information design lecture; Slides; Introduce project; Group
  exercise (read Koberg & Bagnall, pp. 66–77)

Week 13
Research and thumbnail review; Studio
  Session 2: Professional practice lecture (2:00–2:30 P.M.); Field trip to printer
  (2:45–4:30 P.M.)

Week 14
Preliminary design review
  Session 2: Departmental portfolio reviews, no class

Week 15
Information design critique; Introduce 3D project; Slides
  Session 2: Design firm field trips, no class

Week 16
Research and thumbnail review; Studio
  Session 2: Open studio

Week 17
Preliminary design review
  Session 2: Study day, no class
  Final Critique (3D Project): Tuesday, May 7, 3:00–5:00 P.M.

assignments
Samplings of two projects used in the course follow.

Typography: Playing with Type
A three-part assignment follows.

Part I. Warming Up: Crafting Letterforms

Choose one of the two attached fonts to trace. Trace the font until the tracing looks and feels natural to do. Adhere your tracing(s) into your sketchbook.

Objective: This is a preliminary exercise that begins to develop your ability to craft typography and improve your ability to draw letterforms.

Part II. Brainstorming Exercise: 100 Thumbnails**

Choose a letter from the alphabet. Use both upper- and lowercase forms of this letter (real or invented) and visually interpret it one hundred different ways. Consider cropping, touching, overlapping, intersecting, positive/negative space, composition, texture, scale, color, etc. You can use any kind of writing or drawing instrument for this, but no computer.

Use the grid template provided. Cleanly and squarely blow it up 160 percent on a black-and-white copier to fit on 11" × 17" paper. Do your design sketches directly on the 11" × 17" copy—not on the 8.5" × 11" template.

Objective: To encourage compositional play, risk-taking, and experimentation in form; and to test endurance and resourcefulness. The requirement of trying to find so many preliminary ideas can be exhausting. This is the critical point, when attention tends to wander and impatience begins to set in. By simply completing this demanding task, you will begin to believe in your own infinite possibilities.

6

Part III. Design: An Interpretive Composition

Generate a composition using typography to express a specific emotional state. Each person will have a different emotion to express in his or her composition. We'll draw those out of a hat today. For your design, you may work with found type, computer-generated type, and/or photocopied type elements. Use color if the concept dictates it. The size of the composition is to be 11" × 17". Develop a minimum of fifteen thumbnails for concepts by the time of the thumbnail review.

Objective: To use type as an artistic element, to emphasize the interpretive potential of typographic form, and to communicate a specific meaning (the feeling of an emotion) through design.

Specs: Mount Parts II and III separately, each on a 15" × 20" photo-gray mat board with cover sheets. Turn in all preliminary work (neatly and chronologically packaged), as well as sufficient, documented evidence of research with your final designs. All parts are due at the time of the final critique.

Designing for Three Dimensions: Project Aerofont

Together we will design a three-dimensional font called "Aerofont," based on the theme of flying. Each person is individually responsible for designing and building two characters of the font (which we will draw from a hat today). As a group, your letters will form the whole font. The characters will be tied together solely by the theme.

**This part is a modification of an exercise in Wilde & Wilde's Visual Literacy.

Thoughts: You can express an interpretation of the theme through the design of the letter itself and/or through type and images applied to the surface of a form. The letterforms can be entirely invented by you, or you can use or manipulate an existing typeface. Many aspects of the meaning of "flying" as a concept should be explored in the developmental stages. Incorporate model building and experimenting with materials early in your process.

Specifications:

Color. Use whatever supports your concept (polychromatic, monochromatic, black and white, etc.).

Size. Student's choice, but no smaller than 12" high and 6" deep. Again, design your form to support your concept. Keep in mind that it may be easier to manage the forms if they are larger.

Medium/Materials. The forms can (but do not have to) use digital imagery. Use whatever materials it takes to successfully render your interpretation of the theme. Some possible materials: cardboard, foam core, handmade papers, newspaper, wire, metal, found objects, fabric, floral foam, dowel rods, t-pins, glue, paint, images to collage, digital output, balsa wood, chip board. . . .

Final presentation. Three-dimensional forms. Neatly compile and turn in all preliminary work and evidence of research at the final.

description of critique

Critiques are conducted for all five of the main projects. Students are required to participate in a mandatory "preliminary design review" (a highly refined work-in-progress critique) that precedes the final critique for each project. The emphasis at the preliminary design review is on affirming the validity of the students' concepts and analyzing form. The final critique is used to evaluate the evolution and resolution of the designs. In all critiques, students are expected to come prepared to present their concepts, discuss how the forms of their designs support their concepts, as well as describe the ways they arrived at their ideas/forms.

conclusion

The course structure and content is designed to emphasize design as a noun and a verb. Students learn from the outset that *how* they make/think is as important as *what* they make. The process-oriented emphasis of this course is used to prepare students to function on an increasingly independent basis as they move through the intermediate and advanced levels of the program. Art/design students often have difficulty distinguishing between the many processes that affect their progress: their own individual creative process, the process of design as it relates to a professional environment, and various production processes related to the physical making of art/design. By structuring the sequence of studio activities and grading criteria to emphasize these distinctions, students are able to comprehend and perform more effectively, efficiently, and successfully.

Students are expected to move through specific phases of projects, which are scheduled in a cyclical fashion to provide a methodical means for navigating varied subject matter. Grading criteria is broken down to reveal strengths and weaknesses in specific areas of performance, which correspond with the phases of the process we use.

COURSE TITLE _ GRAPHIC DESIGN I
INSTRUCTORS _ Stephanie Tevonian and Sondra Graff,
   Joan Lombardi, Graphic Design Curriculum Advisor
SCHOOL _ Communication Design Department, Fashion Institute
   of Technology
FREQUENCY _ Four weeks, twice a week.
CREDITS _ Three (six studio hours per week)
LEVEL _ Undergraduate
PREREQUISITES _ AD 214 Corporate Image, AD 272 Computer
   Typesetting and Design

purpose

To:

Understand that visual relationships hold relevant proportion to the substance of the idea(s) conveyed.

Organize research procedures to solve graphic design problems.

Learn to create a concept to amplify content, while also developing sensitivity to typography, symbolism, language, and text.

Define the hierarchy of information through the ordering of elements into a comprehensive visual unity.

Harmonize the integration of all elements with a conscious understanding of the intention with which elements are chosen, organized, and created.

Work with formal design principles in the approach to solutions.

Emphasize analysis and process in the development of visual ideas.

Teach a professional and objective approach to design, following specifications, deadlines, and presentation.

Anticipate and plan for emergencies in relation to today's technology.

Reinforce the human potential in varied approaches to design with regards to the integration of technology.

Create excellent portfolio pieces that visually communicate through the embodiment of form and function.

description

A comprehensive approach to the study of graphic communication. Three units are used to develop an understanding of the inventive potential of form and message to create a visual language. The emphasis will focus on developing this understanding through analysis, research, and organizing information. The creation of solutions based on content and the use of formal design principles will be developed.

evaluation

Evaluation will be based on the development and demonstration of clear intent in all levels of approach to each project. These include research, analysis, and visual exploration, from thumbnails through to completion. Class attendance, participation, effort, adherence to deadlines, improvement, and striving toward professionalism and design excellence will all contribute to the final grade:

40 percent class projects, including work done outside of class; 20 percent final portfolio; 20 percent participation; 20 percent process notebooks

description of classes

Week 1: Session 1

Introduction: Discuss the objectives and requirements of the course. Topics for each assignment are introduced to give the students an overview of the semester's projects.

Clarification of grading, attendance, and classroom policy.

Students are to keep a photographic journal of graphic design as found in their everyday environments.

Students are also to keep a process notebook with thumbnails, concept sketches, research, and written analysis of each project throughout the semester.

Supplies: typographic reference, dictionary, thesaurus, tracing pad, black markers (various weights), schaedler rules, tape (white and transparent), exacto knife and blades, straight edge, triangle, pencils, and white paper.

Week 1: Session 2

Lecture: What is graphic design? How does it function in relation to culture? Discuss the development of visual communication through the embodiment of the concept that "form follows function." Introduce "events," as the journey through which we will experience the methodology to develop highly refined graphic design solutions.

Unit I: A Personal Event
Objective: To translate a personal event into a unique graphic solution. To stretch one's range by designing with specific intent (i.e., use of three

approaches.) To explore how we communicate through the use of symbols, color, and language (both visual and typographic).

Introduction of First Assignment: Discuss industry-related issues involved in creating/printing an invitation or announcement with matching envelope. Show samples of printed pieces. Emphasize the importance of designing an exterior that draws a viewer in. Analyze content and the hierarchy of information. Discuss varied approaches to design, such as transformation, surprise, and the use of analogy.

Assignment: Choose a personal event. Create an invitation or announcement to commemorate this event.

Final will also include a matching envelope.

Present three different approaches to your "event":

   1. humor or contrast
   2. a strange perspective
   3. color

Weeks 2–4: Sessions 3–8

Students begin working in class. Process will go from thumbnails, roughs, refined roughs, through to finish. Final must fit inside an existing envelope size. Text is to be written by each student. Experimentation with die-cuts and/or interesting folds and stock is encouraged.

Studio Sessions

Consultations with individual students. They will present their "event" and discuss how they will portray it conceptually to the professor. One solution is chosen, and the students then focus on determining the physical parameters of this piece (i.e., size, shape, folds, color, and style of execution).

Sessions will continue with students working individually in class, creating comps, and refining solutions. The writing and organization of text is explored and resolved. The students will also experience working as design teams. They are instructed to present professionally and also practice art direction. Emphasis is placed on moving past the obvious and on how to think beyond literal interpretations.

Final due: the eighth class. Each student will present his or her project formally to the class.

Students are also to submit process sketches and include full documentation of the development of their solutions. A written analysis/assessment of the student's intent and concept will also be required in conjunction with the finished project.

Week 5: Session 9

Unit II: An Historic Event

Objective: To research and analyze an historic event. To develop an arresting visual image that communicates a unique perspective. To integrate the visual and typographic to convey an intended message. To learn how to determine the placement of information in proportion to its relevance. To create a concept to amplify content.

Introduction of Second Assignment: Discuss poster design and the function of a poster. Show samples of posters designed in different countries and time periods. Survey political posters and link these to those that we have encountered in our lives.

Assignment: Choose one of three historic events. Create a triptych in the form of a poster (or series of posters) to convey a unique perspective of the event. Students will write the text as well as create the visual language for the poster(s).

Choose one of the following:

The first heart transplant (a symposium)

The bombings of Hiroshima and Nagasaki (a commemoration)

The first flying machines (an exhibition)

(Topics may vary at instructor's discretion from semester to semester.)

Students begin working in class using three different approaches to the "event":

1. type as design personification

2. repetition

3. manipulated symbols

Students bring in research on the chosen subject along with a written synopsis based on their analysis. Students use this report as a departure point to determine the perspective that will be portrayed. They will develop the text for their poster with ten different potential headlines and create a grid for the triptych. Students should determine whether they will be creating one poster or a series of posters. They are to begin with the chosen title and develop a variety of thumbnails.

Bring the text for your poster(s) to the next class organized in the order that it should be perceived. Students are asked to find visual reference of art created in the form of a triptych. The students will proceed with analysis and discussion of these forms.

Typographic reference should also be brought to this class.

12

Weeks 6–10: Sessions 10–19

Studio Sessions
Consultations with individual students. They will present their poster topic and show concept sketches for each approach to their series. One concept will be chosen and executed. Students will be encouraged to explore and develop a distinctive visual approach to designing the triptych. The students are asked to create a series of grids that could be applied to the triptych. Roughs focusing on proportion, relationship of elements, sequential viewing, and the organization of information are requested. Their poster(s) will be developed from these studies.

Week 10: Session 20
Final due: the twentieth class. Each student will present his or her finished poster(s) to the class. If possible, all sections should come together for this final critique. Outside guests may be invited.

Again, students are to submit process sketches, a written page discussing their intention and conceptual development and should also include full documentation of this process along with their finished poster(s).

The strongest pieces will be submitted to the Junior Design Show.

Week 11: Session 21

Unit III: An Ethical Event
Objective: To expand our perspective by reflecting on the present and projecting into the future. To increase awareness of how design functions in, speaks to, and reflects our culture. To encompass the principles of cause and effect and our relationship to what has come before us. To encourage students that as designers, they have a powerful voice and can develop the tools to communicate and affect their future world.

Introduction of Third Assignment: Discuss design as a reflection of the times. Encourage analysis of how history, invention, and world events affect our lives. Discuss the roles designers play in responding to these events.

Assignment: Select an event that has been defined or limited by the First Amendment of the United States Constitution. This event can be chosen from past as well as present history. The goal is to design a brochure or booklet to bring awareness to this situation. Students must determine their audience and client. Research of an organization that would produce this piece is essential.

This solution must be type dominant and include no fewer than 1,500 words of text. Students are encouraged to design using typographic sensitivity with emphasis placed on font choices, scale, weight, tonal value, positioning, and contrast.

Students are encouraged to read alternative periodicals, such as *The Utne Reader, Sphere, Metropolis, Mother Jones, On the Issues, The AIGA Journal of Graphic Design, Red Herring, Whole Earth News,* and *The Flatiron News.* The St. Marks Bookshop (31 Third Avenue, New York) is recommended as an excellent resource.

Weeks 11–14: Sessions 22–28

Studio Sessions

Consultations with individual students. This project will progress with the systematic development of a concept, format, and final. The structure of this piece, including the integration of content and form, is emphasized. Students will work progressively, synthesizing the use of typography, analysis, defining the hierarchy of information, conceptual thinking, and aesthetic refinement to fulfill this final project.

Week 15: Session 29

Final due: the twenty-ninth class. Review, critique, and final evaluations.

This session will include a discussion of the semester's objectives and the students' growth.

Students are to submit:

1. process notebook, which will include all concept sketches, research, and the visual development of each project
2. photographic journal of graphic design as found in their everyday environments
3. a portfolio of their finished projects
4. a written analysis of "events" and how this has impacted their approach to graphic design

Week 15: Session 30

Portfolio Review

Faculty review of the semester's coursework.

Faculty discuss the student's coursework one on one.

COURSE TITLE _ DESIGN ISSUES: WHAT IS THIS THING CALLED
   GRAPHIC DESIGN?
INSTRUCTOR _ Terry Stone
SCHOOL _ CalArts
FREQUENCY _ One semester, fourteen sessions (once a week)
CREDITS _ Two
LEVEL _ Undergraduate

purpose

This course covers a range of answers to the question, and may generate more questions, as we look at various aspects of graphic design and the people who practice it. Included will be a survey of the design profession, basic components of the design, as well as methods of evaluating, discussing, and presenting graphic design. An off-campus studio tour of a graphic design firm in greater Los Angeles will provide a real-world examination of the topics covered in the classroom.

grading

Students will be evaluated on the following:
   Completion of assignments/presentations
   Participation in class discussions
   Final Exam (based primarily on required readings)
   Attendance

course requirements

Class assignments will include finding designed artifacts, doing research, reading from textbooks, writing reports, and making presentations. Class time will be based on the assignments, and all students are expected to participate.

description of classes

Session 1: Graphic Design

Introductions and Course Overview: What Is Graphic Design?
   Presentation: The basic definition of graphic design is that it is a commercial art form that uses words and imagery to represent or communicate ideas for a purpose.

Discussion: Design is all around us. A look at graphic design in the real world; review/discussion of candy mints packaging and cookbook design samples.

Homework: Bring in retail store shopping bags and discuss the design ideas represented (basic research and analysis project to evaluate design awareness).

Session 2: The Design Profession

Guest speaker: TBA.

Presentation: Overview of the graphic design profession.

Discussion: Graphic design in the real world; the shopping bag exercise, discussion of the ideas represented, a preliminary discussion of design elements visible.

Homework: Students typeset their names in two ways: one that couldn't possibly represent them and one that definitely does represent them. Also, bring in a logo that is meaningful to the student.

Session 3: Type as Idea

Exercise: On a 3" × 5" card, each student quickly writes three words that describe themselves. Put name on the reverse side. (Later in class these get matched up to the typeset student names, and we evaluate if the typography represents the descriptive words.)

Presentation: History of corporate identity. What is branding? Where did logos come from? Brief introduction to the profession of identity design.

Discussion: A look at identity design, by reviewing the logos brought in by students, as well as the typesetting of their names. Introduce the idea that design has repercussions; read from *Culture Jam: How to Reverse America's Suicidal Consumer Binge—Any Way We Must* by Kalle Lasn (Quill, 1997). Designer as responsible citizen.

Homework: Bring in book covers; find animate and inanimate imagery that represents the concept/idea of "good" and another cover that represents "evil." Read textbook chapters from *Becoming a Graphic Designer: A Guide to Careers in Design* by Steven Heller and Teresa Fernandez, Second Edition (John Wiley & Sons, 2002) on type design and book design.

Session 4: Image as Idea

Discussion: Review of book covers. Imagery as representational of ideas. Designers are responsible for making choices and should understand that certain images are loaded with meaning in our culture. Discussion of the profession of book designer. Review a series of image styles and represented ideas taken from recent books and publications. Also discussion of inspirational source material—encouragement to look at the vernacular, the original texts, fine arts, and not be derivative of other designers'/art directors' work.

Homework: Students begin thinking about a graphic designer that they would like to make a presentation about.

Session 5: Design Research

Tour of the library and assets.

Discussion: Introduce design trade magazines and design annuals. Discuss the reasons for archiving design and studying graphic design history. Introduce *A History of Graphic Design* by Philip Meggs, Second Edition (John Wiley & Sons, 1992).

Assign: Graphic designers and outline presentation requirements. Students to begin work on their designer.

Homework: Prepare presentations.

Graphic Designer Project

Each student will be making a presentation on a graphic designer in order to better understand the variety of people who practice design and the types of work they produce. Each student will select one designer to prepare a presentation on.

Using three 20" × 30" black illustration boards and color printouts/photocopies, include the following:

A short bio of the designer (forty to seventy-five words)

The designer's firm's logo/identity

A photo of the designer

A photo of his or her staff and/or office

Client list

Mission statement and/or philosophy (according to designer)

Three to five projects (samples of the designer's work) that are representative of the designer

Your comments on the designer and his or her work (fifty words)

17

Session 6: Designer Presentations

Guest speaker: TBA.

Presentations: Students present their graphic designers.

Homework: Read *Understanding Comics*, reprint edition, by Scott McCloud (Kitchen Sink Press, 1994), Chapter 7: The Six Steps. Also bring back the graphic designer presentation boards to class for continued discussions and evaluations.

Session 7: The Six Steps

Discussion: Presentation of "The Six Steps" ideas so that students will have criteria and language by which to begin to evaluate graphic design objectively. Review last week's designer presentations to begin to reevaluate each designer using the standards learned in "The Six Steps."

Written assignment in class: Students revise their written comments about the graphic designer they researched.

Homework: Students to bring in their three favorite CDs and be prepared to discuss the designs. Read chapter in *Becoming a Graphic Designer* about music business design.

Session 8: Design for the Entertainment Business

Guest speaker: TBA.

Presentation: An overview of design for the entertainment business, including music, TV, and films. How do designers work? Who hires them? How do they get their ideas? What is it like to work with music clients?

Discussion: Students present their three CDs and discuss the design, the ideas represented, and review whether or not these CDs have any relation to the three words the students used to describe themselves. Introduce the concept of connotative/denotative design.

Homework: Students each get a partner and choose a magazine category. Bring in two magazines (show cover, TOC, standing column, and feature.) Be prepared to discuss how the idea of "beauty" is represented (beauty of the subject, beauty of the design, objectification) in the publication. Read chapter in *Becoming a Graphic Designer* about editorial design.

18

Session 9: Editorial Design

Presentations: Student presentations of the various publications.

Discussion: Life as a publication designer. Review design of magazines over time, a look at publications from different eras, and a discussion of trends. Introduce ethics, particularly the concept of copyright and plagiarism.

Homework: Prep for studio tour. Students to research the firm we are visiting by going to their Web site online. Read chapter in *Becoming a Graphic Designer* about environmental and exhibition design.

Session 10: Design Studio

Studio tour.

Session 11: Design Language

Guest speaker: TBA.

Discussion: Observations/reactions regarding the studio tour.

Presentation: Discussion of design and production terms, as well as slang. Additional review of "The Six Steps" from *Understanding Comics* and further discussion of successful use of language in design presentations. Brief introduction to design criticism and the sources of critical writings on graphic design. Introduce the concept of the value of being well read, as well as culturally literate, as a designer.

Class Assignment: Students to go online and find a sample fifty to seventy words of "design speak," print it out, return to class, then read their samples. Discuss the meaning in class.

Homework: Students to bring in a favorite movie DVD and be prepared to discuss the opening titles in class. Read chapter in *Becoming a Graphic Designer* about motion graphics design.

Session 12: Motion Design

Presentation: Students present their movie titles and discuss the design. Screen an Eames and Saul Bass film.

Discussion: Motion graphics trends. The difference between motion graphics and print or online design. What issues arise visually and technically when design moves? A brief introduction to the profession of motion graphics design.

Homework: Students to choose a beverage company to research on the Web. Bring in color printouts of four pages from the site (top page, two feature pages, an e-commerce page.) Be prepared to discuss the design. Read chapter in *Becoming a Graphic Designer* about Web design.

Session 13: Web Design

Guest Speaker: TBA.

Presentation: Students present their beverage Web site and discuss the design.

19

Discussion: Web design trends. The difference between Web design and other design for the screen. A brief introduction to the profession of Web design.

Homework: Students to review required readings and class notes in preparation for final exam.

Session 14: Final Exam

COURSE TITLE _ VISUAL COMMUNICATIONS I AND II

INSTRUCTOR _ Joseph Roberts

(Original syllabus by Professor Emeritus David Gates.)

SCHOOL _ Pratt Institute, Brooklyn, New York

FREQUENCY _ Two semesters

CREDITS _ 2 BFA credits for each course

LEVEL _ Undergraduate

PREREQUISITES _ All art and design or architecture foundation courses. Required of all graphic design, illustration, advertising, and computer graphics majors.

purpose

In the Visual Communication I and II courses you will explore the creative process of making images that can move ideas and information to the minds of others.

The general principles studied and practiced in these courses are the foundation of creative thinking and successful solutions for graphic design, illustration, and advertising art direction communications problems. These are not courses in mere page layout, media techniques, or the making of beautiful pictures.

Understanding how we respond to imagery is the key to creating pictures and words that communicate a message. Responses can be varied and complex, but can be described basically as conceptual or perceptual.

A perceptual response deals primarily with aesthetic qualities of an image such as pattern of form, color, and beauty of execution.

Conceptual response concerns the significance of imagery. In order for us to respond conceptually, it is not enough for the image to be simply appropriate or beautiful—the picture elements must stand for something, and they must be represented in a new or invented relationship. If they are merely a representation of life as it exists, we not only don't need to ideate, but also respond with "I've seen it before."

Since we are already somewhat familiar with perceptual forms of art and design, these courses will stress conceptual solutions to assignments. If such an emphasis isn't made, solutions tend to be pretty but mindless, with major emphasis on technique.

Each assignment covers a different aspect of the creative communication process and generally presents visual problems that can be solved in any media—from painting to photography to computer graphics. Most assignments are three weeks in duration: (1) roughs, (2) revised sketches, and (3) finished comps. There will be four to five assignments each semester.

Class time is devoted to lectures and critiques where students are asked to critique their classmates' displayed work. Such evaluations are very important in the development of self-analytical judgment.

description

Goals

The primary course goal is to develop an understanding of the methods employed in solving communications problems in graphic design, advertising, illustration, computer graphics, photography, film, and video professions. It is also a goal of the courses to develop the understanding that communication is an active process between people and not just a statement of the artist's self-expression or the passive appreciation of it. It will be shown that in order for us to act, we must interpret the significance of the information before us and therefore participate in the communication process.

Objectives

1. To define the scope of the imagery, both real and mental—visual, verbal, aural, and even tactile—and its impact on human behavior.
2. To gain a rudimentary understanding of semiotics.
3. To demonstrate the power of simultaneous presentation of pictorial elements with conflicting or contrasting meanings.
4. To explore the use and usefulness of various production and dissemination media in the communication process.
5. To dispel the tenacious rumor that communication artists use devious and covert methods to entice reaction. There is nothing covert about the communication process. It is all up-front, with no apologies—the ultimate achievement of the communicator is to persuade others.

Rationale

The creative process of problem solving through imagery does not come instinctively or equally to everyone. These courses lay solid foundations and dependable methods for creating meaningful, imaginative, communication solutions through research and analysis of communication tasks and their target audiences.

Evaluation

Each assignment is evaluated on:

1. Effectiveness of the imagery to provide a thoughtful response (50 percent).
2. Skill of execution of finished imagery (20 percent).
3. Fulfillment of assignment physical specifications (10 percent).
4. Neatness of presentation (10 percent).
5. Deadline adherence (10 percent).

Materials

Most assignments are designed to challenge students with problems that can be solved using the full range of production media—collage, computer graphics, illustration, photography, typographics, etc.

Materials necessary for this course include any media and supplies that you prefer to use for the production of sketches and finished presentations. Mounting materials will also be required for each finish.

You may use any technical (computer or optical) tools or materials to produce finished comps—but these technical aids do not include computer clip art or stock photographs and illustrations, even when copied in a different graphic treatment. All of your visuals and copy must be original. Use of existing source material as your own is plagiarism. An exception to this rule would be a case in which material is used because of its recognizability and no attempt is made to claim it as original. But if this is the case, existing copyrights must not be violated.

Required at Each Class

1. Weekly assignment to be completed by deadline date.
2. All work completed for previous classes on that assignment.
3. Drawing pencil and pen with tracing or visualizing pad.
4. Class participation.

Attendance

There are no excused cuts. Students are expected to attend all classes. Any unexcused absences may affect your final grade. Three unexcused absences will result in failure for the semester.

Grades

Your final grade for the course is based on the performance evaluation criteria listed as well as your attendance, punctuality, and class conduct. A grade of Incomplete (Inc) will be considered only for medical reasons or other serious reasons beyond your control. Last-minute service bureau problems or loss of files because you did not back them up are not legitimate reasons for an incomplete grade.

If you are majoring in advertising art direction, graphic design, or illustration, you are required to participate in a semester-end survey. Failure to do so will result in a grade of F for the course.

Supplemental Assignments

Other assignments may prove valuable in exploring other nonliteral solutions to visual communication problems. Most do not use the montage theory. They do, however, put visual elements in a new or invented relationship, thus invoking a conceptual response.

Derived from sophisticated literary devices, they also work as visual analogues. They are symbolism, visual metaphor, irony, and visual puns.

COURSE TITLE _ TYPOGRAPHY I
INSTRUCTOR _ Kali Nikitas
SCHOOL _ Minneapolis College of Art and Design
FREQUENCY _ One semester
CREDITS _ Three
LEVEL _ Undergraduate

purpose

This class will examine basic typography as a compositional tool; the architecture of type from the single letterform to an entire page layout.

objective

Upon completion of this class, students should have a clear understanding of hierarchy and typographic formalism.

Development of functional and visually engaging compositions using any volume of type within any given space.

methodology

Lectures, demonstrations, group critiques, one-on-one critiques, working in both classroom and computer labs, formal exercises leading up to projects. Projects building off of one another. Critique and evaluation of success/failure.

In the beginning, typography is very intimidating (does that ever go away?). What is not intimidating and what is not "unfamiliar"? It is all that students have done leading up to the class. For years, they have worked with line and shape, both structured and organic. My goal is to teach them typography through their understanding of those elements. I have included slides and photocopies of some of the results. By the end of the semester, students have a common lexicon, structure for critiquing, and hopefully an understanding, love, and appreciation for typography.

description

Week-to-week description of classes: contingent upon the development and rate of development for each class.

assignments and projects

1. Research and presentation on assigned typographers
2. A logotype
3. Introduction to the grid and a series of formal and typographic exercises

Stage One: working strictly with a grid and limited freedom; all information must be horizontal.
Rules for Stage One:
- Form: compositions using only line, dots, and dashes
- Typography: one font, in point sizes ranging from 7 to 12

Stage Two: begin to break the grid. Show that it exists but loosen up; change in orientation allowed.
Rules for Stage Two:
- Form: compositions using larger shapes and lines, issues of scale, greater hierarchy, positive and negative space
- Typography: one serif, one sans serif, in point sizes ranging from 5 to 200.

Stage Three: ignore the grid, use your own type, go mad!
Rules for Stage Three:
- Form: no rules
- Typography: no rules

Final Project
Redesign two train schedules: one very legible, using a grid, style sheets, rules, and tabs (on the computer, of course).

The second schedule is experimental and done by hand (cut and paste). Students challenge legibility but capture the spirit of travel or movement.

Readings
Students research two typographers: one contemporary, one historical. The department provides a bibliography for all of the design students. From there, they find most information and research additional texts.

Description of Critique
Class begins with work from all students hung on the wall. There are three styles of critiquing that occur over the course of the semester:

The first: Traditional, all-class discussion where the student begins by talking about the work and asking his fellow classmates and instructor for guidance on improving. The length of the crit is four to five hours—rigorous but fruitful. Most work is discussed and reworked several times so that application of the comments are made and seen. *All students have notes taken by a classmate so that they may focus on the discussion.*

The second: Students choose a work on the wall and write a critique, which they read to a fellow classmate. The purpose of this exercise is to assist the student in finding the confidence to speak clearly and articulately about design.

The third: One-on-one with the instructor. Many times, other students from the class will sit in and hear what is being said.

NOTE: When discussing the work, students are given some suggested guidelines so that they have a context for critiquing. For example composition, craft, hierarchy, positive and negative space, attention to detail such as letterspacing, and the bigger picture of "traditional rules of type."

NOTE: The students do not work on the computer except in two instances: (1) to generate type (they are given nine to ten fonts to use, with the exception of the experimental applications); and (2) to produce one of their final projects, which is done on the computer and is used to introduce the students to tabs, rules, and style sheets.

NOTE: In the fall, I teach two sections of this course. Both classes become involved with one another, working together in and out of classes, stopping in to see what is hanging on the wall on their "off day."

conclusion

This is a very important class in terms of building a foundation of typographic understanding, commitment to fellow classmates, self-confidence, ability to critique, and pride in seeing that one can produce, by the end of the semester, something that they never imagined being able to do.

2nd year

COURSE TITLE _ GRAPHIC DESIGN II

INSTRUCTOR _ Louise Sandhaus

SCHOOL _ Graphic Design Program at California Institute of the Arts

FREQUENCY _ Two semesters; Fall: 14 weeks, Spring: 17 weeks;
   meets 2 times per week, 3 hours per session

CREDITS _ Six units per semester

LEVEL _ Undergraduate

overview

The second year of study in the program is concerned with developing confidence and competence in creating form and concepts. Students are encouraged to take risks, to develop their own voices as designers, as well as to expand the vocabulary with which they express ideas by employing visual rhetorical strategies such as metaphors, puns, irony, metonymy, etc.

Students are simultaneously encouraged to explore formal possibilities while developing work that communicates an intended message, resulting in work that is meaningful, compelling, and engaging. Classroom discussion allows students to recognize potential meanings and ways of understanding and developing form. Students are required to keep a sketchbook in order to develop a practice of notating and testing ideas visually. A workbook keeps track of the development of each project and encourages a consciousness of process and organization.

The sequential steps of a design process are quantified and used to structure the first projects: research, ideation, thumbnails, roughs, design development, and final presentation.

The second semester of Graphic Design II encourages an understanding of style as it relates to culture and technology. Students are also encouraged to explore their own unique interests while utilizing the skills acquired from their elective classes: Typography I and II, Photography for Designers, and Imagemaking.

description of classes

Fall Semester
14 weeks

Self-Portrait: How the Visual Speaks
2 weeks

Description: Through a series of self-portraits we'll investigate (compare and contrast) various ways to engage visual language.

Key issues: Reading images. Connotation; denotation; iconic versus symbolic representations; types of abstractions (visual rhetoric): metaphor, metonymy, synecdoche, and irony; audience; and media.

Assignment 1: Readings on reading images. Make a portrait of yourself to convey something important about you that you want me to know.

Assignment 2: Readings on visual rhetoric. Find or make images that represent you metaphorically, metonymically, and ironically.

Political Poster: How Words and Images Work Together
3.5 weeks

Description: In this series of assignments you'll take a stand on a political issue. Using factual data and symbolic imagery you'll develop your intended message in a way that engages the audience, provides information, and convinces the viewer to seriously consider your point of view.

Key issues: Visual and verbal messages, types of messages, addressing an audience.

Assignment 1: Research the issues and political posters. Determine the message: What do you want to say to your peers?

Assignment 2: Find factual data.

Assignment 3: Find different types of metaphoric images.

Assignment 4: Composition: structuring words and images.

Assignment 5: Design refinement.

Assignment 6: Final design.

Symbol, Logotype, and Application: Abstracting Ideas and Visual Form
5 weeks

Description: In this series of assignments we'll look at the different ways ideas can be represented through concept, form, and style. We'll also connect design to contemporary culture and look at how culture influences meaning. In the first part of the assignment you'll research an animal as icon. Next, you'll develop the identity for a store that will take the form of a symbol and then as a logotype. For the final assignment, you'll apply the identity you've developed to a t-shirt.

Key issues: Visual and conceptual abstraction; type and connotation; cultural influence; style; composition and space.

Assignment 1: Animal assigned. Create a morphology of animal images, both iconic and symbolic, as well as a range of styles and techniques.

Assignment 2: Go shopping. Decide what kind of shop might be appropriate.

Assignment 3: Have the name of your animal.

Assignment 4: Brainstorm symbols.

Assignment 5: Symbol design development.

Assignment 6: Symbol refined design.

Assignment 7: Logotype typefaces studies.

Assignment 8: Develop logotype.

Assignment 9: Refine logotype.

Assignment 10: Final refinement of symbol and logotype.

Assignment 11: Design a t-shirt applying the symbol and logotype.

Assignment 12: Create a t-shirt.

Presentation: Present t-shirts.

Motion Project: Make Meaning through Time-Based Narrative
3.5 weeks

Description: In this last quick, fun project you'll be introduced to the basics of making meaning through narrative and time.

Key issues: Narrative in space and time; sound and structure

Assignment 1: Intro to After Effects and sound program. Pick or make a ten-second piece of sound. Create sound file. Determine structure of sound.

Assignment 2 and Assignment 3: Using your store symbol from the last assignment, create a narrative about the symbol.

Assignment 4: Storyboard the narrative based on the sound structure.

Assignment 5: Create rough animation of your narrative.

Assignment 6: Refine animation.

Assignment 7: Final animation.

Spring Semester
17 weeks

Graphic Design History Presentation
2 weeks

Description: Five- to seven-minute digital slide presentation on assigned design movement, ranging from William Morris to "Encyclopedic Typography." Discuss the reasons behind the movement and describe the formal and conceptual characteristics of design from the movement.

Key issues: Increase awareness of design history; exposure to stylistic vocabulary; development of ability to understand and analyze design; development of presentation skills.

Assignment 1: Prepare rough of presentation.

Assignment 2: Describe stylistic characteristics, including motifs, colors, typefaces, presentation.

Graphic Design History Timeline
2.5 weeks

Description: Create a timeline for assigned design movement in the style of that movement. Include movement name, dates, description of movement, additional data as needed, and at least six examples of graphic design.

Key issues: Develop greater awareness of style; exposure to information design—organizing informational elements (text and pictures) using hierarchy, spatial relationships, and levels of reading.

Assignment 1: Roughs of timeline, including all text and stylistic characteristics.

Assignment 2: Refine design.

Presentation: Final design.

Book Covers
5 weeks

Description: Design a book cover using two different approaches: (1) image and type (image predominates) and (2) type only. Class divided into thirds, and one short story out of three options is assigned to each third of the class. Sum up the story and come up with something from the story to represent. Use denotation, connotation, and metaphor.

Key issues: Review of denotation, connotation, and metaphor; review of composition and process; creating and working with images; creating and working with type.

Assignment 1: Read story and determine things to represent. Brainstorm denotative, connotative, and metaphoric images.

Assignment 2: Image cover: idea thumbnails and image research.
Assignment 3: Image research and roughs of several directions.
Field trip and holiday
Assignment 4: Image cover design development (develop typography).
Assignment 5: Image cover design development (composition studies).
Assignment 6: Image cover final design.
Assignment 7: Type cover roughs of several directions (typefaces, both made and found, and compositions).
Assignment 8: Type cover design development (typefaces and compositions).
Assignment 9: Type cover design development (color studies).
Assignment 10: Type cover final design.
Presentation: Type and image covers final refined design.

Magazine
7.5 weeks
Description: Conceive, edit, and design a magazine based on your interests. Create a "proof-of-concept" campaign consisting of cover (including masthead) and three spreads.

Key issues: Learning to develop one's own ideas. Developing and working with systems and structures. Using and applying typography. Exposure to publication design.

Assignment 1: Review magazine concepts and story ideas.
Assignment 2: Grid and typography studies
Assignment 3: Cover. Roughs for masthead (logotype developed from existing typeface).
Assignment 4: Cover. Masthead development and roughs of cover, including images.
Assignment 5: Cover. Design development.
Assignment 6: Inside. Rough layouts of articles including image sketches.
Assignment 7: Inside. Image research and development.
Assignment 8: Inside. Design development of articles.
Assignment 9: Inside. Final design development of articles and cover.
Assignment 10: Final magazine.
Presentation: Final refined magazine.

COURSE TITLE _ VISUALIZATIONS
INSTRUCTOR _ Christopher Ozubko
SCHOOL _ University of Washington School of Art, Division of Design,
   Visual Communication Design Program
FREQUENCY _ One quarter, 11 weeks
CREDITS _ Five
LEVEL _ Undergraduate

purpose and goal

To examine the ways in which complex ideas and messages can be interpreted
and represented in visual form, thus offering clarity or deeper meaning and
understanding to the intended receiver.

description

Interpretation, conceptualization, and visualization are basic to the practice
of design. This class is intended to address these issues through a series
of problems stressing visual representation and expression in visual
communications.

Experimenting with a variety of different image generating techniques, students will interpret and produce visual solutions based upon specific assigned
problems. Emphasis will be placed upon original concept development and the
exploration of diverse processes, techniques, and methods. Drawing, photography, xerography, abstraction, color, typography, collage, and photo mechanical
methods are stressed. The computer and other electronic illustration and image
development systems are not encouraged but experimentation in traditional
medium is. In order to develop greater originality, students may not use existing (source) photography or images that preexist as finished art. This does not
exclude "found art."

Students will be expected to experiment and explore, thereby expanding
upon their visualizing skills. Problem solutions are expected to transcend mere
object representation and expressively communicate subjects and ideas. There
will be three projects, each differing in scale and format—this is intended to
accommodate possible limitations related to specific processes or materials.

Grades will be based upon: class participation/interaction, project preparatory development, final project concept development and project execution
/presentation.

The problems this quarter are intended to address different circumstances faced by designers as visualizers:

1. Visualizations that represent or symbolize a subject through presenting its attributes or character.
2. Visualizations that express a topic or issue and are intended to evoke a desired response.
3. Visualizations that explain a topic and are intended to inform the audience.

assignments and projects

Project One

The first exercise is to design a series of covers for an educational journal/magazine (any level) that deals with science/nature and our current world. The solution requires identification of the subject matter with at least one word (specific name or topic) and a periodical number (arbitrary) integrated into the composition. Develop an image/concept that presents this subject in an exciting and original way. The final format is 9" × 12" (vertical). You select and research a subject area—any topic related to science or nature, i.e., geology, earthquakes, bio-technology, archaeology, astronomy, nano-technology, etc.

Three solutions are required for your series. Establish a visual format for continuity.

Project Two

With this exercise you must visually interpret a common form of emotional ailment/malady, mental disorder/dysfunction. In the translation, express the essence of the problem/disorder to the general audience through clarity of idea and not complexity of composition. Use an arresting image to stimulate interest. Choose from the following or select another, but no two students should duplicate a topic.

Anxiety, panic disorder, schizophrenia, anorexia, agoraphobia, shyness, insomnia, postpartum depression, grief, autism, fear, alzheimers, codependence, narcolepsy, acrophobia, dyslexia, bulimia, depression, attention deficit disorder (ADD), obsessive compulsive disorder (OCD).

The final format is 10" × 16" (vertical or horizontal).

Only incorporate essential word or words (if necessary).

Project Three

The last problem will address a subject of your choosing within the broad category of current national and international events or topics. Your interpretation may have a neutral or biased slant to stimulate the viewer to take action. Keep headline text to a minimum. If you include statistics, be sure to correctly credit the source.

Topics could address social, political, or economic issues. Subjects of interest may include: child airbag safety, illiteracy, homelessness, terrorism, racism, airline safety, floods, earthquakes, etc. Topics will require prior approval following class discussion.

The format will be a one-half-page black-and-white newspaper ad.

COURSE TITLE _ TYPOGRAPHY I

INSTRUCTOR _ Ellen Lupton

SCHOOL _ Maryland Institute College of Art

FREQUENCY _ Fifteen weeks, once a week, five hours

CREDITS _ Three

LEVEL _ Undergraduate, sophomore level

purpose

The students' first formal exposure to typography.

description of classes

Week 1: Letter

Class exercise: Drawing letterforms/letterform terminology

Project: Typeface drawings and research (due next week). Select one of the typefaces. Make a six-inch-tall pencil drawing of the lowercase *a*. Position the letter on a sheet of 8.5" × 11" paper; label with the name of the typeface and its designer and date. Portray the "spirit" of the typeface—its weight, curves, openings and endings, and internal relationships.

You must also research a contemporary typeface. The typeface must have been designed after 1985. Choose a typeface that you like, and think about why you like it. Note the designer's name and the date of introduction. Visit the Web sites listed on our class's Blackboard site (blackboard.mica.edu) for your research. You can also consult books in the library. Bring to class a printout or photocopy of the font, as many letters as possible. Make a six-inch drawing of the lowercase *a*; label your drawing.

Reading (for next week): "Letter," from *Thinking with Type* [editor's note: this is from the prototype of Ellen Lupton's forthcoming book, *Thinking with Type from Page to Screen*, forthcoming, Princeton Architectural Press, 2004].

Week 2: Letter

Lecture: History of typography/typeface terminology.

Pin-up: Typeface drawings.

Project: Type prototype (begin sketching during class; complete design due next week). Develop a concept for a new font whose forms relate to an 8" × 8" square grid. Each box in the grid must be either "on" or "off." You have no curves or true diagonals. Represent the letters A, B, C, P, Q, R, in capitals only. Draw your letterforms on graph paper. Consider proportion, weight, and structural features such as height of cross bars, how elements end, how to accommodate curves and diagonals within the grid of squares, etc. Give your typeface a name.

Week 3: Word

Critique: Type prototype.

Project: Word compositions. Choose two pairs of words from the list provided. Create two compositions (one for each pair) that express the meaning of the words. (See details on project sheet.) Begin work in class.

Week 4: Word

Critique: Word compositions.

Project: Choose one of your word pairs and make it into the identity of a business or organization (café, theater, store). Apply your identity to an object (t-shirt, mug, building, van). Represent your object within a six-inch square.

Reading (for next week): "Text," from *Thinking with Type*.

Week 5: Text

Critique: Word compositions/identity.

Discussion: Text terminology.

Project: Text composition (first draft due next week; final due the following week). Within a 6" × 6" square, compose the text in a manner that expresses its meaning. Use 9 point Adobe Garamond only. Use variations in alignment, leading, line length, orientation, and spacing. Avoid variations in weight, style, or size.

Week 6: Text

Critique: Text composition (first draft).

Due after break: Revised version of text composition. I will mark final corrections on your printout.

During break: Prepare for quiz on recognizing fonts. You must also be able to distinguish real Adobe Garamond from the default/substitution font inserted by the MICA system.

Week 7: Page

Quiz: Typefaces (don't worry; it's multiple choice).

Class project: Paragraphs. Working singly or in teams of two, devise at least six different ways to break the text provided into paragraphs. Work in QuarkXPress. Be creative! Win valuable prizes!

Project: Poster/hierarchy. Design an 11" × 17" poster for a lecture series about contemporary design, using the text provided. Your poster may include typography, blocks of color, lines, and abstract shapes. It may not include images.

Week 9: Page

Critique: Poster/hierarchy.

Exercise in class: Missing square. Open up the document "04 Missing Square File," a six-inch-square document with a two-inch white box at the center. Make the box visible by arranging the text provided in a purposeful way.

Project: Continue working on your poster.

Week 10: Page

Critique: Poster/hierarchy.

Class exercise: Grid. Using the printed grid provided, cut and paste type and images from magazines to create two interesting layouts.

Project: Book (concept presentations due next week). All students will design and produce two copies of a sixteen-page book. Create your own content, or use the text provided. For initial presentation, be prepared to discuss your book idea.

What is the content? How will you approach the design?

Week 11: Book

Discussion: "Eight Strategies"/contemporary book design.

Discussion: Book concepts.

Project: Begin designing your book. The format of your book is 7 × 7 inches. You can choose a different shape or size if you have a reason. Bring in at least four sample spreads.

Week 12: Book

Workshop: Bookbinding. Hands-on bookbinding workshop will show a few simple bookbinding techniques.

Project: Continue working on your book.

Week 13: Book

Individual critiques: Book.

Project: Prepare a complete dummy for the interior of your book, in full-scale double-page spreads, trimmed to the edge and taped together in sequence.

Week 14: Book

Individual critiques: Book.

Week 15: Final Reviews

I will meet with each student individually; bring all projects.

COURSE TITLE _ IMAGE DESIGN
INSTRUCTOR _ Cedomir Kostovic
SCHOOL _ Southwest Missouri State University,
    Art and Design Department
FREQUENCY _ Sixteen weeks
CREDITS _ Three
LEVEL _ Undergraduate

purpose

Imagery is integral to visual communication. In many graphic design problems, it is a vital part in the effective transmission of content. This course will explore the communication of ideas through imagery. Class problems for the term will include the following:

1. Sound problem
2. World record problem
3. Fiction—spread; two pages problem
4. T-shirt problem
5. Visual diary problem
6. Movie poster problem
7. Cube and rectangle problem

objectives

Through this course you will:

- Develop your technical skills, analytical, visual, and creative thinking
- Develop sound and exhaustive methods in visual problem solving
- Explore the relationships between imagery and other elements of visual and nonvisual communication
- Promote and strengthen visual thinking and image generation as integral parts of the design process

description

Course Regulations

This course is based on group and independent studio instruction and individual work at home. (Six hours per week in the classroom and a matching minimum six hours per week of work at home.) Specific information for each assignment will be given with a due date and schedule for class critiques and presentations. Class critiques are part of the teaching process, therefore active participation is required. Lectures and demonstrations will be held during class periods without special notice, therefore tardiness and absence must be avoided. Attendance will be taken at the beginning of every class period. If late to class, it is the student's responsibility to make sure he or she has been marked as present. After three unexcused absences a student may anticipate a lower final grade due to a lack of participation—excessive absences (six or more) may result in failure of the course due to missed individual and class critiques. Scheduled deadlines for each project must be observed. Any project that is not included in the final critique will result in an F grade for the project.

All projects assigned during the semester must be completed. Failure to complete any assigned project will result in an F grade for the semester.

Readiness for each individual and class critique is required and progress on the project must be shown.

Cheating and/or plagiarism may also result in an "F" grade for a given project, or may result in failure of the course.

Make-up projects (re-dos) will be accepted, but only if the deadline has been met and the project exhibited for final critique. (A combined grade of the original solution and redone project will be given as a final project grade in such cases.)

Each student must maintain a notebook (one-inch three-ring binder) where concept sketches will be kept. The main purpose of these notebooks will be to document the design process of each project. Documentation of the design process will be assessed and included as part of the final grade. The final grade will be based on an average of all grades (points) received during the semester in combination with grade modifiers such as participation, growth, progress, etc.

For the final exam you have to submit a printed portfolio and a CD with TIFF or PDF files of finished projects.

Grading
Student achievement will be evaluated according to the following criteria:
- Ability to define concepts
- Research
- Constructive use of studio time
- Problem development
- Formal and conceptual aspects
- Growth and perceptual aspects
- Homework
- Craftsmanship/presentation
- Final outcome of each project

Students will be expected to present their projects at each stage of development, including verbal and written articulation of their decisions and solutions, as well as discussing and questioning the work of their peers.

Students may receive extra credit by writing reaction papers to cultural and arts events, such as critiques of foreign or art films (University Film Series), concerts, plays, literary readings, etc. Papers should be approximately one page long, typed with one-inch margins in standard-size text, double-spaced (12/24).

All grades are based on the scale:

A—excellent, B—good, C—average, D—poor, and F—failing.

This scale will be applied according to the quality of presented work. In order for a student to receive an A grade, work must be exceptional in all aspects. Final grade is based on average grades received during the semester along with a final evaluation of the student's growth and progress.

Materials

This may be a somewhat expensive course; however, it should be understood that it is the goal of these projects to prepare you for future profession. I also expect that you have basic graphic design tools and supplies.

High-quality output of finished projects will be required. Lower-quality prints will be acceptable for sketches only. PMTs are acceptable, and a variety of other methods of creating comprehensives or mock-ups. 16 × 20 inches will be the size of presentation board used for all projects. A paper portfolio that can accommodate 16 × 20 inches is required.

I recommend a book, *Thinking Creatively: New Ways to Unlock Your Visual Imagination* by Robin Landa, Second Edition (How Books, 2002), as well as a subscription to *Print* magazine. You should also join the Graphic Design Book Club (look for an offer in *Print* or other graphic design magazines).

Visit the library as often as you can. Besides books about graphic design and illustration, there are periodicals like *Communication Arts, How, Eye*, etc.

If you have any question about your progress or grade during the semester, please feel free to speak with me, either in class or during office hours.

COURSE TITLE _ POSTER DESIGN
INSTRUCTOR _ Elizabeth Resnick
SCHOOL _ Massachusetts College of Art, Communication Design
   Department (Boston, Massachusetts)
FREQUENCY _ One semester, once a week for three hours
CREDITS _ Three
LEVEL _ Undergraduate

purpose

Poster design is the point at which graphic design and fine art meet. Posters function best when communicating a simple idea, in a way that is visually arresting. This course will seek to extend the poster's utilitarian goal with an aesthetic experience. Students will be encouraged to explore different media and techniques used in both art and design. Conceptualization, employing type and image, and the conflicts that arise between the need to communicate and artistic self-expression will be addressed.

41

objectives

The emphasis of poster design will be to explore and expand upon the basics of visual language, enabling the student to create strong, powerful visual statements. The class will consist of critiques, slide lectures, and weekly homework assignments. Guest critics and/or field trips as time allows. Assignments will include designing posters for social and cultural issues. Slide lectures on the history of modern poster making—from Chéret, Toulouse-Lautrec, and Mucha to contemporary movements, artists, and designers—will inform students of the continuing history and relevance of this medium.

description of classes

Week 1

- Introduction to the course content and expectations.
- Slide lecture: Chéret, Toulouse-Lautrec, Ukiyo-e. The posters of French artists Jules Chéret and Henri Toulouse-Lautrec, and the influence of Japanese Ukiyo-e woodblock prints of 1600–1800 on European Western art and poster making.

Assignment 1: Word and Image Poster
A visual idea is a pictorial response to an abstract problem. Through the marriage of word and image, a designer can create an alluring shorthand to engage
a viewer or convey information. Using skillful manipulation, interpretation,
and juxtaposition of different images/elements and typography, a designer can
create new images that either literally or figuratively suggest a specific meaning. In this first assignment, students will be asked to select one of the following words—*culture, check, vote, consume, exercise, diverse, revive, return*—and convey a conceptual message by the integration and/or juxtaposition of type and
image, possibly in a new or unexpected way. Students can use magazines or
books to locate images whose formal aspects add another layer of meaning or
enhance the meaning of the selected word from the word list given on the
assignment sheet.

Objective: To visually and conceptually create meaning with one image and
one word placed in an engaging compositional format.

Homework: Create two word and image compositions for critique; read
pages 7–28 (mainly reproductions of posters) in *Posters: A Concise History*, by
John Barnicoat (London/New York: Thames & Hudson, 1985).

Week 2

• Critique of sketches for Assignment 1, word and image poster.
• Lecture: Mucha, Art Nouveau, Beggarstaffs. Turn-of-the-century Art
  Nouveau in France and England will be explored in the poster art of
  Alphonse Mucha and the Beggarstaffs.
• Homework: Based on the feedback received in the class critique,
  students are to incorporate the critical commentary into their fin-
  ished poster. Read pages 29–47 in *Posters: A Concise History*.

Week 3

• Critique of Assignment 1, word and image poster.
• Lecture: Beardsley and Bradley. Turn-of-the-century Art Nouveau in
  England and America will be explored in the poster art of Aubrey
  Beardsley, Will Bradley, and others.

Assignment 2: Literacy Poster: Learn to Read
How has the definition of literacy changed in the last several years? How
does television affect literacy? The Internet? Is literacy rising, declining, or
just changing? Do we now communicate with images rather than words?
Should the definition of literacy include the quality of being visually literate? Does *Ray Gun* magazine and MTV signal the beginning of the end

of written literacy? Could this actually be a good thing or a bad thing? Pondering these questions, students will voice their opinions on this subject by creating a visual, conceptual statement directed to a general audience using the integration and/or juxtaposition of type and image, possibly in a new or unexpected way.

Objective: To convey, using photocollage, the student's point-of-view while encouraging literacy to the general audience.

Homework: Two half-size or full-size sketches will be completed for homework and brought to class for critique. Read pages 47–63 in *Posters: A Concise History*.

Week 4

- Critique of sketches for Assignment 2, the literacy poster.
- Lecture: Bernhard and Hohlwein. Exploration of the "object poster," which developed at the beginning of the twentieth century in the work of German poster artists Lucien Bernhard and Ludwig Hohlwein.
- Homework: Based on the feedback received, students are to incorporate the commentary into their finished posters. Read pages 103–108 in *Posters: A Concise History*, and article handouts.

Week 5

- Critique of Assignment 2, the literacy poster.
- Slide discussion of contemporary posters, with an emphasis on theatre posters.

Assignment 3: Theatre Poster: Death of a Salesman

In this assignment students will be asked to design and produce a poster to advertise a current production of the Arthur Miller play *Death of a Salesman*.

Objective: To capture the essence of idea within the creation of a strong, simple graphic statement that can be understood by general audiences.

Homework: Students will read/research the play and then create two half-size or full-size sketch concepts for their poster due for critique.

Week 6

- Critique of sketches for Assignment 3, the theatre poster.
- Lecture: Futurism and Dada. The influence of the modern art movements Futurism and Dada on poster art of the 1910s and 1920s.
- Homework: Students are to incorporate the critical commentary received in critique into a full-size working rough. Read pages 158–172 in *Posters: A Concise History*.

Week 7

• Vacation week.

Week 8

• Critique of tight rough for Assignment 3, the theatre poster: *Death of a Salesman.*
• Lecture: The poster goes to war. Propaganda posters of World War 1 in England, America, and revolutionary Russia.
• Homework: Students are to incorporate the critical commentary received in critique into a finished poster. Read about World War 1 posters in your text, *Posters: A Concise History.*

Week 9

• Critique of finished poster for Assignment 3: the theatre poster.
• Slides of posters with a human rights theme will be shown in class.

Assignment 4: Declaration of Human Rights Poster
This assignment will ask the student to choose one of the thirty-one "rights" from Amnesty International's "Declaration of Common Rights of Humanity" and create a statement that visualizes this "right" in any medium. [See assignment "handout" at the end of this syllabus for more information.]
   Homework: Students will be asked to deliver a short written statement about their "rights" selection with the presentation of two large sketch concepts.

Week 10

• Review sketches for Assignment 4, declaration of human rights poster.
• Lecture: Stenberg Bros., Klutsis. The influence of early Russian poster design on twentieth-century graphic design.
• Homework: Based on the feedback received in the class critique, students are to incorporate the critical commentary into their next round of roughs for the poster.

Week 11

• Critique of tight roughs for Assignment 4, declaration of human rights poster.
• Lecture: A.M. Cassandre and Lester Beall. The 1930s and 1940s in Europe and America.
• Homework: Based on the feedback received in the class critique, students are to incorporate the critical commentary into their finished poster. Read about 1930s and 1940s in Europe and America in your text, *Posters: A Concise History.*

Week 12

- Critique of finished poster for Assignment 4, declaration of human rights poster.
- Slides on posters that fit the subject matter.
- Assignment 5, series poster. To be announced. [See assignment "handout" at the end of this syllabus for more information.]
- Homework: Students will do research on the topics assigned.

Week 13

- Critique of sketches for Assignment 5: series poster.
- Homework: Based on the feedback received in the class critique, students are to incorporate the critical commentary into their sketches.

Week 14

- Critique of tough roughs for Assignment 5: series poster.
- Lecture: Early Swiss, Armin Hofmann, Josef Müller-Brockman, and Wolfgang Weingart. The Swiss contribution to the legacy of early and modern poster design.
- Homework: Based on the feedback received, students are to incorporate the critical commentary into the finished posters due for critique.

Week 15

- Critique of finished posters for Assignment 5, series poster.
- Last class, all work is due for grading.

Assignment 4: The Human Rights Poster

Your assignment is to create a visual statement in the form of a poster that illustrates one of the thirty-one Rights of Humanity in any medium. Research Amnesty International and other human rights organizations to understand their mission and motivations.

Choose one of the thirty-one rights listed in the handout. [Editor's note: hand out recreated at the end of this syllabus.] Think of ways in which you can create a strong, effective, meaningful message that supports the right you have chosen and can be understood by a general audience.

How does the effective poster achieve its aim? Remember, by its very nature, the poster has the ability to seize the immediate attention of the viewer, and then to retain it for what is usually a brief but intense period. During that span of attention, it can provoke and motivate its audience. It can make the viewer gasp, laugh, reflect, question, assent, protest, recoil, or otherwise react. This is part of the process by which the message is conveyed and, in successful cases, ultimately acted upon. At its most effective, the poster is a dynamic force for change.

Specifications
Size: 18" × 24" or 20" × 30".
Color: Any.
Media: Try to use a different media or technique than you have used so far (although always consider what might be the best media to articulate your concept).
Copy: Wording for the "right" you choose. It can be edited for brevity.

Assignment 5: The Lecture Series Posters

Your assignment is to design and produce a series of three posters for a lecture series entitled: "Children of the Twenty-First Century: What Do They Need to Know about _____?"

This three-part lecture series is aimed at middle-school children who will attend the lectures as part of an educational out-reach program sponsored by the Museum of Science in Boston and the City of Boston. The lectures will take place over a three-week period on Saturday mornings.

Each poster will take as its subject matter the following topics: astronomy, biology, and chemistry.

Objective: To announce this educational out-reach lecture series to the children of Boston and their parents. The posters will be distributed through a direct-mail campaign to parents of school-age children and through postings at the area schools and libraries.

Specifications
Size: 15" × 22" vertical or horizontal.
Media and color: Any
Title: "Our Children of the Twenty-First Century: What Do They Need to Know about _____?"
When: Three consecutive Saturday mornings.
Where: Museum of Science.
What:

- Astronomy. The Earth is a tiny speck in space. If you imagine it shrunk down to a diameter of a twenty-fifth of an inch (1 millimeter), the Sun's nearest neighboring star would be 1,800 miles (3000 kilometers) away. The remotest visible galaxies are so distant that the light they send out takes about 10 billion years to reach us, even though light can travel to the Moon in just over a second. Astronomers survey this huge volume of space. Our nearest star, the Sun, sends out light and heat to make life on Earth possible.

46

- Biology. The word *biology* is derived from Greek and means "knowledge of life." Originally biologists studied the structure or anatomy of animals and plants, and tried to describe their relationships with each other. The study of anatomy of animals and humans led quickly to the development of surgery and to medicine becoming a science in its own right. Some of the most important work in biology is directed toward finding out how cells work. This type of study could lead to the prevention or cure of many diseases.

- Chemistry. Ever since our earliest ancestors began using fire one and a half million years ago, we have been able to produce and control chemical reactions to help us observe, investigate, and change the properties of substances. Today, chemical substances of all kinds are mined and manufactured, used for research and for the production of detergents, dyes, cosmetics, drugs, food additives, glass, paints, paper, and plastics.

- Homework: You will do research on the three different topics. Create an appropriate visual aimed primarily to attract and excite school children ages eleven to fourteen. Think Nickelodeon, MTV, etc. Unify the posters through a visual language system, format, or structure. Write two to four lines as a general text statement or use the "blurbs" suggested above.

Finish in this order:

1. Concept sketches of all three posters (at least half-size) due for class critique.
2. Large roughs for each poster due for critique.
3. Finished posters due for critique. Last class.

Declaration of the Common Rights of Humanity

We hold these truths to be self-evident, that all humans are created equal, that they are endowed with certain unalienable Rights, that among these are life, Liberty, and the Pursuit of Happiness.

Yet there are those who would attempt to abridge and condemn these fundamental Rights. Let this Declaration be read by all such tyrants, that they may realize their wrongs; let this Declaration be inspiration and hope to all under the rule of such tyrants, that they may regain their basic Rights; and let this Declaration be a precaution to the rest of humanity, that those Rights are never usurped once more.

Let this Declaration go forth to the world and serve its Goal on this day, the eleventh of October in the year of the Common Era one thousand nine hundred and ninety seven.

1. All people deserve the Right to free press and free broadcast in all its forms, the Right to freely assemble in a peaceful fashion, the

Right to free speech and free expression, the Right to debate and discussion, the Right to express grievances to governments and institutions, and the Right to peacefully challenge those governments or institutions without fear of persecution or retaliation.

2. All people deserve the Right to freely practice any religion and its beliefs, rituals, and practices, the Right to refuse to practice any religion and the Right to challenge religious institutions without fear of persecution or retaliation.

3. All people deserve the Right to be free from persecution or discrimination based on any physical feature or quality, including race, gender, disability, age, sexual orientation, or any other physical feature or aspect, and the Right to be free from persecution or discrimination based on any sentient feature or quality, including nationality, social status, wealth, or religious belief.

4. All people deserve the Right to do what they wish with their own bodies, be it beneficial or harmful as long as what they wish does not physically hurt another who does not wish it.

5. All people deserve the Right to be tried for violating the Law by an independent, impartial group of peers in a speedy but fair fashion, the Right to appeal punishments for such violations of the law, the Right to be free from execution, torture, or denial of basic human necessities for such punishment, and the Right during such punishment to exercise free speech, free practice of religion, and the ability to address grievances.

6. All people deserve the Right to debate and challenge any Law, Decree, Treaty, or any other similar official action, without fear of persecution or retaliation.

7. All people deserve the Right to be free from search and seizure of any property without an official warrant, the Right to be sure that the warrant is issued only under the recommendation of a witness with reasonable suspicion, and the Right to be sure that any property seized is not damaged and destroyed and is returned to the owner once established to be legal.

8. All people deserve the Right to be free from coercion, threats, or bribery while serving any function of the Law, and the Right to protest those who attempt to do so.

9. All people deserve the Right to be given, when arrested or detained for violating the law, a list of legal rights, including the opportunity for legal representation, protection from coercion and threats, and the ability to conduct personal matters while in custody.

10. All people deserve the Right to an equal education, and the Right to this education without propaganda or excessive bias.

11. All people deserve the Right to make money in any fashion that does not cheat or otherwise harm another, the Right to keep and invest money freely, the Right to taxation only with representation, the Right to appeal unfair or excessive taxes without fear of persecution or retaliation, and the Right to protect their money from coercion, bribery, or fraud.

12. All people deserve the Right to possess weapons for self-protection without fear of persecution or retaliation.

13. All people deserve the Right to refuse to quarter, join, supply, or otherwise assist any army or armed faction in peacetime or war without fear of retaliation or punishment.

14. All people deserve the Right to be free from execution, torture, denial of basic human necessities, or detainment by any army or armed faction, the Right to refuse to reveal any information, official or personal, to any army or armed faction without fear of retaliation, and the Right to be able to protest an armed faction's decisions without fear of retaliation or punishment.

15. All people deserve the Right to be free from attack weapons of mass destruction, including nuclear, chemical, and biological weapons, the Right to be free from indiscriminate or long-lived weapons, including land mines and booby traps, the Right to be free from poisoned or contaminated food, water, and air, and the Right to protest such actions without fear of persecution or retaliation.

16. All people deserve the Right to peacefully obtain basic human necessities in times of dire need, including food, water, and basic shelter, even if it violates the Law.

17. All people deserve the Right of free travel, free commerce, and the free exchange of information, regardless of nationality or political affiliation, and the Right to apply for and to receive citizenship in any country, regardless of nationality.

18. All people deserve the Right to be able to receive truthful, uncensored, information, such as public records, laws, budgets, and judicial decisions, from any government or institution.

19. All people deserve the Right to be treated equally in social situations, regardless of any physical or sentient feature or aspect, the Right to freely engage in conversation, the Right to engage in humorous dialogue, even if considered offensive by some, and the Right to be respected by others.

20. All people deserve the Right to form their own opinions, thoughts, and convictions, the Right to express those beliefs, even if those beliefs are considered offensive by others, and the Right to challenge and debate other's beliefs.

21. All people deserve the Right to express themselves freely, as long as that expression does not physically hurt others.

22. All people deserve the Right to be treated in a fair and humanitarian way, without undue risk of injury or death, in their work, the Right to refuse to do such dangerous work without fear of retaliation, the Right to freely form independent trade unions and organizations, the Right to peacefully protest and challenge the decisions or policies of their superiors, the Right to be paid reasonable wages, and the Right to be judged only on merit for jobs and social positions, not by any physical or sentient feature or aspect.

23. All people deserve the Right to be fairly represented in government, the Right to a secret ballot vote for representatives, heads of states, and important policy issues regularly without discrimination due to any physical or sentient feature or aspect, and the Right to such voting without coercion, threats, or bribery.

24. All people deserve the Right to be protected from ex post facto laws and to be protected from the execution of laws to deeds done before the passage of the law.

25. All people deserve the Right to not be denied privileges due to a lack of nobility or any other power or status based on heredity.

26. All people deserve the Right to own any property, regardless of any physical or sentient quality, the Right to refuse to buy or sell property without fear of persecution or retaliation, and the Right to challenge unreasonable prices and monopolies without fear of persecution or retaliation.

27. All people deserve the Right to charge other persons or parties for violation of the Law without fear of persecution or retaliation.

28. All people deserve the Right to make sure that their governmental representatives and heads of state submit to the results of elections and that they do not hold their positions for undue periods of time.

29. All people deserve the Right to make sure that any martial law or emergency dictatorship will be swiftly disbanded and replaced with their original government once the crises is gone.

30. All people deserve the Right to defend their rights in any peaceful manner possible, the Right to call on governments and institutions to follow these Common Rights, and the Right to, when all else fails, overthrow any government who does not give basic, fundamental Rights to their citizens.

31. All people deserve the Right to Life, the Right to Liberty, and the Right of the Pursuit of Happiness.

As I write these words, let the Universe be my witness.
Jeff Stansbury, October 11, 1997

3rd year

COURSE TITLE _ GRAPHIC DESIGN III

INSTRUCTOR _ Charles Hively

SCHOOL _ Parsons School of Design

FREQUENCY _ One semester (seventeen weeks)

CREDITS _ Six

LEVEL _ Undergraduate

51

purpose

Increase proficiency in page layout for applications in publishing, advertising, and Web design.

description

Students will study and apply their knowledge of page layout coupled with extensive use of typography with specific applications in page design for advertising and collateral projects. Students will be expected to draw, write, and illustrate projects in addition to using the full components of Quark, Photoshop, and Illustrator.

Class work will consist of typographic assignments, critiques of off-site projects, as well as lectures and visiting speakers.

- Typography. Students will explore typographic solutions starting from the simple and graduating to the complex.
- Page layout. Students will learn the basics of page design incorporating the grid concept into their projects.

- Photography. Students will explore basic photography concepts and cropping techniques for use in two special projects.
- Special projects. Students will research and develop two booklets incorporating page design, photography, and typography.

Students will be assigned projects during each class period including in-class assignments; assigned projects will be reviewed at the following scheduled class unless otherwise noted. Students must come to class with their assignments, even if they are in sketch form. If your assignment cannot be printed in time for class presentation, you must bring your work on a disk to class, which I will review off-site. Failure to present an assignment will result in an F for that assignment. Students must engage in the formal critique and will be judged by their comments. There will be a final exam judging the student's understanding of design principles, design theory, and history.

Materials for some class projects will be furnished online. Students must have the list of required typefaces on their computers and use only those faces for assignments unless otherwise indicated. Photos, headlines, manuscripts, and logos will be sent via e-mail for all projects.

You are required to keep a sketchbook that will be reviewed once a month. This is not a place for sketching, or for working on class projects. This is a place to start collecting advertising and design ephemera, such as interesting typefaces you find, graphic design pieces—everything from matchbook covers to reproductions of posters—ads, packages, photographic images, and illustrations that catch your eye. The sketchbook will be judged on how well you cover each of the categories, and the quality of the work you select.

description of classes

Week One

Class introduction, fill out forms, class overview, and schedule.
In-class assignment: Fill out forms.
In-class assignment: First test, type identifier, page layouts.
Type assignment: Design 3 × 5 inch nametag using favorite typeface.
Page design assignment: Bring in three favorite ads.
Project assignment: Research Eames, Corbusier, Rand, and Brodovitch.
    Write paragraph on each.

Week One: Class Two

Lecture: Designers.
Critique: Nametag designs, review portfolio samples.

In-class assignment: Review typeface (Bodoni).
Type assignment: Set headline in Bodoni.
Page-design assignment: Bring in three favorite ads, postcard.
Project assignment: Assign designer, booklet due.
Review: Weiss Stagliano, DDB.

Week Two

Lecture: Advertising design.
Critique: Postcard.
In-class assignment: Review typeface (Cheltenham).
Type assignment: Set headline in Cheltenham.
Page-design assignment: Target ad.
Review: Goodby Silverstein, Bartle Bogle Hegarty.

Week Two: Class Two

Lecture: Personality Types.
Critique: Target ad.
In-class assignment: Draw capital letter and lowercase letter from memory.
Type assignment: Use type to illustrate the word *fire*.
Page-design assignment: Refine Target ad, LeCorbusier poster.
Review: Progress on designer booklet.
Research paper: Adolf Loos.
Writing: Walking tour.

Week Three

Lecture: Holga.
Critique: *Fire*, LeCorbusier poster.
Pop Quiz.
In-class assignment: Review typeface (Futura).
Type assignment: Use type to illustrate the word *baby*.
Ad assignment: Copia ad series.
Project assignment: Develop booklet.
Photography: Research Holga, bring examples to class.

Week Three: Class Two

Lecture: Holga.
Pop quiz (Cheltenham/Futura).
Critique: *Baby*, Copia ads, walking tour.
Type assignment: Use type to illustrate the words *love* and *hate*. Set and kern
   the words *round, stone, going, more, young.*
Page-design assignment: Refine Copia ads.
Project assignment: Begin NY, NY book.
Research: Paul Strand, Alfred Steiglitz.

Week Four

Designer booklet due.
Critique: *Love, hate.* Kerning. Designer booklet.
Designer quiz.
Lecture: Alexy Brodovitch.
Page-design assignment: *InformationWeek* ad series.

Week Four: Class Two

Lecture: 1, 5, 10.
Critique: Ads, booklets, kerning.
In-class assignment: Review typeface (Goudy Old Style).
Type assignment: Set headline in Goudy Old Style.
Page-design assignment: Refine *InformationWeek* ads, Eames poster.
Review: AIGA 365.
Photography: Frustration, Tony Stone.

Week Five

Visiting lecturer: Art director.
Review contact sheets.
Pop quiz (Goudy).

Critique: Ads, Frustration, Eames poster.
In class: View film by Eames.
Page design: Refine Eames poster.
Photography: Continue photography.

Week Five: Class Two

Lecture: Circle, square.
Sketchbooks due.
Critique: Eames poster.
In-class assignment: Review NYADC annual—poster category.
Type assignment: Illustrate the words *mother and child*.
Page-design assignment: Optimize ad.
Review: Chermayeff & Geismer Web site.
Research: Tibor Kalman.

Week Six

Photography booklet due.
Critique: Poster, optimize ad, *mother and child*, NY, NY booklet.
In-class assignment: Review NYADC annual—Package-design category.
Type assignment: Review typeface (Torino).

Page-design assignment: Develop package design using furnished elements, logo first.
Research: Allen Hurlbert.
Review: SPD site.

Week Six: Class Two
Lecture: "Extra Ordinary."
Pop quiz (Torino).
Critique: Package design—logo.
Type assignment: Refine logo, package design.
Project assignment: Begin SPD magazine spreads.
Research: Franco Maria Ricci.

Week Seven
Visiting lecturer: Packaging designer.
Critique: Package design.
In-class assignment: Review NYADC annual—editorial section.
Page-design assignment: Continue SPD magazine spreads.

Week Seven: Class Two
Critique: Magazine spreads, package design.
In-class assignment: Review NYADC annual—identity section.
Type assignment: Create logo.
Page-design assignment: Paul Rand poster.
Research: Bruce Mau.
Review: SVA exhibit.

Week Eight
Critique: Logo, Rand poster.
Research: Wolfgang Weingart.

Week Eight: Class Two
Lecture: Portfolio.
Critique: Logo, Rand poster.
Film.

Week Nine
Spring break.

Week Ten

Visiting lecturer: Web designer.
Critique: Logo, Rand poster.
Page-design assignment: Develop book cover, home page.
Research: Chip Kidd.

Week Ten: Class Two

Lecture: Profile test.
Sketchbooks due.
Critique: Book cover, home page.
Page-design assignment: Newspaper ad.
Research: Cassandre.

Week Eleven

Critique: Newspaper ad, book cover, home page.
Page design: Home page, refine book cover.

Week Eleven: Class Two

Visiting lecturer: Graphic designer
Critique: Home page, book cover.
Project assignment: Lyle Lovett CD packaging.

Week Twelve

Critique: Lyle Lovett CD.
Page design: Refine CD.
Film.
Read: Chapter 9.

Week Twelve: Class Two

Lecture: Job market.
Critique: CD.
Project assignment: Le Cremaillere packaging.

Week Thirteen

Critique: Le Cremaillere.
Page-design assignment: Refine packaging.

Week Thirteen: Class Two

Lecture: Clients.
Critique: Le Cremaillere.
In-class assignment: Review collateral section of NYADC annual.
Page-design assignment: Produce brochure cover and spread.

Week Fourteen
Critique: Brochure cover and spread.
Page-design assignment: Refine packaging, cover, and spreads.

Week Fourteen: Class Two
Lecture: "Dare Mighty Things"
Sketchbooks due.
Critique: Brochure cover and spread.

Week Fifteen
Critique: Brochure.
Page-design assignment: Newspaper ad.

Week Fifteen: Class Two
Critique: Newspaper ad.
Assignment: Prepare semester-end portfolio.

Week Sixteen
Review portfolios.
Film.

Week Seventeen
Final.

57

assignments and projects

1. Students are encouraged to use the resources of the library to explore all forms of design applications. Students will be given one of the following assignments to research and then layout and produce an eight-page booklet (minimum) including photography and page layout done in the style of one of the following designers:
    Charles and Ray Eames
    Le Corbusier
    Paul Rand
    Alexy Brodovitch
2. Students will be introduced to the use of photography in design and complete a booklet of their photographs. Subject matter: Light and shadow on the streets of New York. Time permitting, a second assignment will explore the Metropolitan Museum of Art, with the end result being an exhibit booklet with selected examples of the student's photography.

3. Students will create poster designs for Eames, Le Corbusier, and Rand. Packaging assignments for a food product, CD cover, and book cover. In addition there will be an editorial assignment and various type design assignments.

description of critique

Students are encouraged to present their work as if they were in an actual client presentation. Class crits consist of students presenting their work to the entire class and then selecting one student to critique all of the work. If time permits, everyone in the class will get to critique the work—this works best with simple assignments. In larger assignments, after all the students have presented, I then select the first student to critique one piece, usually starting at either the left or right of the board, then follow that with the student whose work was just critiqued critiquing the next piece, followed by the next piece until all work is critiqued. At the end of the critique, we might as a group select what we think are the best pieces, compare and contrast the work, and finally I give my individual critique of all the work pointing out the good and the bad. During the critique, students are encouraged to tell the class why they like something and why they don't; students are graded on how well they critique.

conclusion

What I've attempted to do in my class is bring in actual examples of projects that I am involved in at work, or projects that have real-world scenarios. I strive to get students to think about how to solve problems and make the assignments more than just pretty type and clean designs.

COURSE TITLE _ BFA III

INSTRUCTOR _ Michael Worthington

SCHOOL _ Graphic Design Program at California Institute of the Arts

FREQUENCY _ Two semesters: Fall—fourteen weeks; Spring—seventeen
    weeks; two times per week, three hours per session

LEVEL _ Undergraduate

CREDITS _ Six units per semester

purpose

The third year concentrates on visual sophistication and the development of a personal voice. Superior skills in typography and image-making are consistently demanded. Projects in Graphic Design III are complex and require solutions that are well considered and visually sophisticated. Projects take the form of movie titles, booklets, music CDs, posters, and books. Design processes and methodologies are closely scrutinized; both the pragmatic and poetic aspects of design are examined and discussed.

Students are expected to have confidence in their formal and conceptual abilities and the projects allow for freedom (and responsibility) for the designer to make editorial and content decisions. The timeline of projects becomes accelerated as students learn how to produce high-quality work under tight deadlines and to manage a number of projects at once.

Graphic Design III is complemented by a series of other required skill-building classes, including Typography III and IV, Historical Survey of Graphic Design, Beginning and Advanced Motion Graphics, Advanced Web Design, Advanced Image-making, Social Design, Writing for Designers, and Information Design.

59

description of classes

Fall Semester

14 weeks

Self-Improvement
1.5 weeks

If you could have any one thing to improve your life (on any scale), what would it be? The "miracle addition" could be abstract or practical, physical or emotional, unambitious or life altering. Name your invention, and design a package to contain that missing thing.

The packaging should let the audience know what the product is but also let them know what your attitude is as the designer/manufacturer/marketer.

Students present: Verbal ideas, black-and-white mock-up, color mock-up.

Form-Making-Form
4 weeks

The project examines processes and methodologies related to form-making.

Students are given a complex piece of music, they choose three descriptive words that have an associative relationship with the music.

Students create twenty-four compact visual images for each of the three words: eight for each word made by hand (two line drawings, two nonlinear paintings, two by a printing method, two with unorthodox materials); eight made on the computer (two in Illustrator, two in Photoshop, two with scanned objects, two in a program of your choice); eight made by photographic means (two unaltered photos of your own, two unaltered found photos, two collages with found photos, two collages with your own photos).

Students are then given complex and varied sets of instructions (methodologies) for combining and crossbreeding their images to create hybrids, metas, hypers, and one über symbol. They also create several methodologies of their own.

At the end of the project students will each have made 125 images.

Form-Making-Form-Making-Motion
Students use their 125 images to create a 20- to 30-second animation, using a segment of their original piece of music as the soundtrack.

Students present: Verbal ideas, storyboards, key frames, animation tests, rough edit, final edit.

Movie Poster and Titles
6 weeks

Students create a movie poster and title sequence for a film drawn from a list of contemporary and classic independent cinema.

The goal is to communicate the ambience, mood, concepts, and emotions of the film through its graphic representation. The poster should tell the audience something about the film. No headshots, no star names, no Saul Bass rip-offs. Complexity, multiple narratives, suitability, and controlled hierarchy are among the major issues discussed.

Students present: general research, verbal ideas, 30 different ideas, 100 formal sketches, 3 black-and-white half-size posters, 1 full-size black and white, and 2 rounds of the final full-size color poster.

Students create a title sequence of at least sixty seconds in the same visual style as their poster. An emphasis is placed on typography in motion, as well as image-based footage.

Students present: Written ideas and sketches, storyboards, key frames, animation/footage tests, rough edit, final edit.

Titles are shown in a public screening of motion graphics, in the Institute cinema at the end of the year.

CalArts Jazz CD

1.5 weeks

Students design and produce highly finished mock-ups for the CalArts Jazz CD. The program director from the jazz program acts as the client.

Students present: Verbal ideas, initial sketches, mock-ups, color mock-ups, final CD package.

One design is chosen to be produced commercially.

Spring Semester

17 weeks

Design History Project

4 weeks

This project looks at the importance of history and research, how to use historical models, understand the context design was produced in, and understand the influence on contemporary designers by looking at connections between the past, present, and future, formally and conceptually.

Students produce a design zine about a historical design figure and a poster that traces their influence on contemporary design. Students make black-and-white copies of their zines for all of their classmates so that at the end of the project everyone has a full set of zines to keep.

Students present: Research, rough designs, developed roughs, mock-ups, color mock-ups, and final posters and zines in color.

Science Project

3.5 weeks

Students create graphic solutions to illustrate supplied scientific problems/theories (e.g., gravity, x-rays, blood, boomerangs, hearing) in both pragmatic and poetic fashions. In both cases there is a need to explain and understand complex subject matter in order to convey it graphically to the audience. The problem is supplied, but not the "form" for the solution. Format is an intrinsic part of the design solution.

The pragmatic solutions encourage clear communication, structured information graphics, and readable image-making.

The poetic solutions encourage creative thinking, experiential design, lively graphics, and performative results.

Students present: Thorough verbal knowledge of research, rough designs, black-and-white mock-ups, color mock-ups, and final presentations of both pragmatic and poetic solutions for comparison.

Art Catalog Project
3.5 weeks

Students produce a twenty-four-page catalog for an imaginary art show. They take on the role of "curator" as well as designer, curating three to ten artists into a group show. Students are responsible for concept, artists, the text, and the images they use.

Students present: Research, rough designs, selective pages, pagination, black-and-white dummy, color dummy.

Project Folders

Students keep a workbook that documents the process of each project, from rough ideas to finished design pieces, usually a folder or binder is used to file any odd bits of paper, research, sketches, influences, etc.

Sketch Books

Students are encouraged to keep a personal sketchbook of interests, notes, found objects, drawings, etc.

Designer Presentations

During the year students make one presentation to the rest of the class about the work of a living contemporary practicing graphic designer (or design group) whose work they admire. They cannot select anyone who is part of the CalArts faculty. Presentations are for twenty minutes in front of the class.

Book Review

Each semester students are given a book list and asked to write a review of one design book. The review is typed, and at least 1,000 words.

COURSE TITLE _ GRAPHIC DESIGN 367:
    COMMUNICATIONS PROGRAMS
INSTRUCTOR _ Douglas Wadden
SCHOOL _ Division of Design, School of Art, University of Washington
FREQUENCY _ Winter quarter, twice a week for three hours
    per meeting
CREDITS _ Five
LEVEL _ Undergraduate

purpose

This course will investigate the development of a communication design program, using an international architecture conference as an occasion to implement an array of related printed elements that establishes the definition of the theme as well as a form of graphic identity. The class will base their investigations on the theme of "The Future of Cities and Architecture: Monuments and Shelters, Aesthetics, and Sustainability." (You may create any title for the conference that addresses the theme or uses this working title.)

63

method

This subject is to be researched broadly and thoroughly from the point of view of the history of design, architectural education, building materials, urban planning, transportation, open spaces, community and population issues, and the social, economic, political, and legislative issues related to any of these areas. These can all be addressed from a national and global point of view. Your audience will be architects, educators, planners, community activists, researchers, and municipal, state, and federal government officials. The program design requirements will include: a program announcement (poster/mailer), a press release package consisting of a letterhead, two envelopes, label, application form, a computer disk/case, a prototype for a Web site on conference information/registration, and at least one other element such as a prototype for a calendar of events, or site banners, signage, commemorative items, etc.

requirements

A design program entails several concerns: an innovative interpretation of the theme; establishing a definitive and memorable visual presence through typography, image, format, and color; the effective and sometimes systematic application of design; as well as the comprehensive organization of information. Each program solution includes an explanation of the theme, a title, and a conference program outline that includes site, travel, promotional, and registration information. A chairperson's statement and a list of speakers with their biographies are required for the sessions, which would span approximately three days. You must identify a logical sponsoring institute, foundation, or agency and an appropriate site. If undecided, use the American Institute of Architects as your sponsor.

While you research your topics and theme, we will collectively discuss and explore typographic issues, organizational systems, and client/user concerns. You are encouraged to collaborate on your research and documentation and can share "team" information and copy. This is especially true of the more mechanical or functional parts of the copy. However, all images, designs, maps, and/or supporting elements must be original as well as independent. This is especially true of images. There are no restrictions on the visual medium you use or production methods, but you must request approval to deviate from approximately 24" × 36" poster dimensions. These posters may be self-mailers or simply use 9" × 12" envelopes. Final presentation requirements will be discussed and collectively agreed to as the class develops.

Your grade will be based upon your definition of the theme, thoroughness of your subject research, the originality of your interpretation, and your final design presentation. Particular emphasis will be based on your contribution as a "team critic," as we will discuss each student's efforts in detail throughout the quarter.

COURSE TITLE _ VISUAL COMMUNICATION DESIGN:
   INTERMEDIATE JUNIOR STUDIO (Visual Narrative)
INSTRUCTOR _ R. Brian Stone
SCHOOL _ The Ohio State University, Department of Industrial,
   Interior, and Visual Communication Design
FREQUENCY _ Ten weeks (spring quarter), twice weekly
CREDITS _ Five
LEVEL _ Undergraduate

purpose

This course aims to provide students with an opportunity to learn and apply the important principles of information design, visual translation, and interface design. Design solutions should carefully address the specific requirements and abilities of the user audience, be easy to understand, and support the structure, meaning, and purpose of the information.

description

This course is structured to provide information and experience in the area of visual problem solving. This problem solving will involve the conscious integration of humanistic factors, technology, and aesthetics. It is intended to optimize function and value. Students apply course principles by creating a series of visual narratives involving a sequence, evolution, or cycle.

This is a progress-oriented course that requires active student participation. Students meet twice per week for approximately five hours each day. Class sessions are comprised of lectures, demonstrations, and assignments. An equal balance between theory and application is expected.

Students are evaluated on participation in class discussions, presentations, their ability to apply course material to projects, their ability to create professional quality work, and their ability to exchange ideas and accept constructive criticism. The highest standard of quality visual work is expected.

description of classes

Week 1

Lecture: "I can't understand why people are frightened by new ideas. I'm frightened of old ones" (quote from John Cage).

Introduction of project: Sequence, cycle, or evolution.

Class discussion: Developing a visual narrative, designers as translators, the continuum of translation media, the importance of observation.

Week 2

Presentation of preliminary project proposals.

Group discussion: The concept of sequence = linear; the concept of evolution = structure; the concept of cycle = continuity.

Studio activity: Research, sketching, concepting.

Class discussion: How to avoid flatness; the concept of layering and separation.

Studio activity: Research, sketching, concepting.

Week 3

Our four areas of concern: information, visual translation, interface, and interactivity.

Studio activity: Further consider project topics; build primary and secondary research (books, Web sites, magazines, periodicals, pamphlets).

Class discussion: Intended narrative.

Loose, pencil sketches deliverable on tracing paper.

Week 4

Class discussion: Are there universally understood symbols?

Studio activity: Further develop concepts; organize levels of comparison.

Class discussion: Are there universally understood aesthetics? The use of diagrams to explain complex problems.

Studio activity: Work toward clarity, precision, and efficiency.

Week 5

Class discussion: Metaphors, indexical signs, icons, and pictograms.

Studio activity: Purposefully integrate statistical, verbal, visual language.

Group critique: Poster pairs, concepts, information organization.

Week 6

Midterm evaluations: Individual meetings with students discussing their performance in the following areas—research, imagination, representation of ideas, personal initiative, use of time, communication with faculty, attitude, appropriateness to problem, and presentation form.

Studio activity: Appropriately consider and apply feedback from critique.

Studio activity: Prepare material for formal presentation; consider how information changes in scale (half-size to full-size mock ups); review proportions, textual and visual language.

Week 7

Studio activity: Hone visual language.

Group critique (half scale): Incorporating real text; poster pairs should be equally resolved; narrow and commit to concepts.

Week 8

Studio activity: Consider dimension, color, communication, and order.

Studio activity: Consider accessibility, clarity, and connection.

Week 9

Group critique (full-scale posters/tiled).

Studio activity: Building a holistic view . . . no verbal explanation needed; composition of poster pairs.

Week 10

No class.

Studio activity: Final refinements; text editing, proofreading; production/output issues

Week 11

Final presentation.

67

project

"A graphic designer maintains a perspective based upon an awareness of fundamental principles, self-criticism, and a process-oriented approach to his or her work. From this vantage point, he or she understands the implications and connections between form, media, and information, and possesses the flexibility and inventiveness to address the ever-expanding body of knowledge and complexity of our culture." (Paul Rand)

When conveying information, it is our mission to develop a clear and effective picture for our audience. As with music, design can set a mood, generate tension, surprise, or calm; it can startle or seduce. We must communicate information through form, color, texture, and visual symbols.

The assignment is to develop a series (pair) of visual narratives depicting sequence, evolution, or cycles. A pair of posters are developed focusing on one of these themes. Posters can contrast or compliment one another. Final posters should clearly express student concepts and demonstrate one of the following processes:

Sequence: the following of one thing after another in an orderly or continuous way.

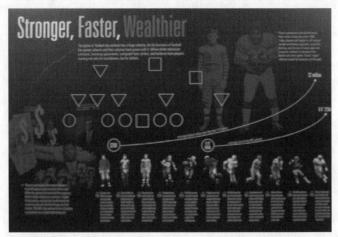

Les Lehman, Stronger, Faster, and Wealthier Football Players

Jisun An, A Perfect Replica

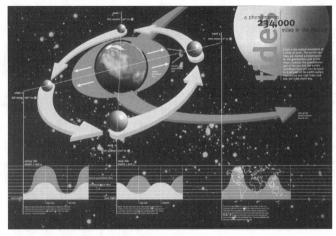

Laura Kaluza, The Cycle of Tides

Evolution: the process by which something develops gradually into a different form.

Cycles: a series of events or operations that repeat regularly in the same order.

description of critique

Critiques during the first half of the quarter are lead by the instructor. Student designers are not identified; however, student comments are encouraged. During the second half of the quarter, students present their work. The instructor then offers constructive criticism. Student comments are welcome, which typically leads to an interesting class dialogue.

conclusion

The course has been extremely well received by faculty and students. It has quickly become one of the most anticipated projects of our visual communication junior class. The results have been exhibited in our university president's office, and several have been awarded merit in student design competitions. We have found it an excellent bridge moving into the senior year, by integrating exposure to research, information design, visual narrative, and poster design.

COURSE TITLE _ PROFESSIONAL PRACTICES IN DESIGN:
THE ART OF THE BUSINESS OF DESIGN
INSTRUCTOR _ Terry Stone
SCHOOL _ CalArts
FREQUENCY _ One semester, thirteen to sixteen sessions, depending
on holidays and breaks, weekly, three hours in length
CREDITS _ Two
LEVEL _ Undergraduate

purpose

Building a successful career requires not only creative talent and a great portfolio, but an understanding of best practices and the standards governing the ever-evolving business of graphic design. This course is a guide to the business aspects of design. Included will be an exploration of creative business processes, marketing and self-promotion, negotiation and pricing, ethical standards of practice, and professional relationships in design. Numerous off-campus studio tours of graphic design firms in greater Los Angeles will provide a real-world examination of the professional practice topics covered in the classroom. A portfolio review event concludes the course.

description of classes

NOTE: I often invite professionals into the classroom to team teach with me on the topic they are expert in.

Session 1

Introductions
Course overview
Career options/job descriptions
Work culture
Job search/recruitment (in general terms)
Choose the firms we will visit on class studio tours

Session 2

The working process
Project flow and management
Time and record keeping
Forms (explanation and samples)

Session 3

Studio tour

Session 4

Marketing strategies
Marketing plans
Self-promotion programs
Sales process overview

Session 5

Proposals
Contracts
Rights and usage
Terms and conditions

Session 6

Studio tour

Session 7

Pricing
Estimating
Exercises in determining fees and expenses

71

Session 8

Presentation skills
Negotiation
Communication
Relationships with clients

Session 9

Studio tour

Session 10

Financial/legal operations of a design firm
Basic financial management
Personal finances exercises and worksheets

Session 11

Working with suppliers
Specifying jobs accurately for pricing and estimating projects
Building creative teams

Session 12
Studio tour

Session 13
Job search preparation
Hiring process
Interviews and portfolio presentations

Session 14
Portfolio review event (sometimes we do an ethics discussion with our reviewers)

Required Textbook
AIGA Professional Practices in Graphic Design. New York: Allworth Press, 1998.

Assignments/Projects

1. Read textbook chapters related to lecture topics.
2. One short quiz on contract language.
3. Pricing game, "How much would you charge for this project?" done in class.
4. All students must develop an estimate for a job, with terms and conditions on their own letterhead or form.

COURSE TITLE _ TYPOGRAPHY III
INSTRUCTOR _ Sean Adams
SCHOOL _ CalArts
FREQUENCY _ One semester
CREDITS _ Three
LEVEL _ Undergraduate, third year

purpose

This class continues the typographic education from Type I and II. At this point, the students explore issues of typographic form, history, and concept. Type III begins the exploration of personal expression and experimentation typographically.

The goal is to broaden the vernacular of typographic exploration, refine the craft of typography, and rethink existing constructs and ideas.

description

The class uses a sequence of assignments that concentrate on issues of denotation, connotation, hierarchy, context and theme, image-type relationships, and interaction and typographic history and expression. Lectures, critiques, and individual in-class explorations are used to further these ideas. Lectures, presentations of examples by students, written reports on various subject matter and in-class individual working sessions are also employed.

assignments and projects

Class 1: CD Assignment

Connotation and Denotation
Design two versions of a CD package for *Songs from Liquid Days* by Philip Glass: cover, sample spread of booklet, using typography only, black and white.

Version 1, Denotative: To refer to specifically, mean explicitly; present the information in the most clear, most legible way.

Version 2, Connotative: To suggest or imply in addition to the literal meaning; present the information and emotional characteristics of the content.

Class 2: CD Assignment

Critique, make corrections. Unmounted printouts are acceptable for critique.

Class 3: CD Assignment

Final assignment due. Final color printouts for each version mounted on 15" × 20" blackboard, one board for the connotative packaging, one board for the denotative packaging.

Class 4: Recipe Assignment

Hierarchy

Design a recipe brochure featuring four unrelated recipes (meats, soups, desserts, appetizers, main dishes, etc.). Cover at least three panels. Each panel must be 7" × 11", black and white, plus one color.

Class 5: Recipe Assignment

Critique, composition, hierarchy, basic typographic craftsmanship, make corrections. Unmounted printouts are acceptable for critique.

Class 6: No Class

Class 7: Recipe Assignment

Final color printouts for each version trimmed to correct size, accordion fold.

Book Assignment

Hierarchy, Image-Type Relationships

Design a monograph of the work of David Salle. Explore ideas central to his themes and concepts using type and image only 9" × 12" page size, two double-page spreads.

Spread 1: Introduction or essay copy.

Spread 2: Image pages with captions and other pertinent information. Black plus one PMS color, four-color process images.

Include: running feet (or heads), page numbers (folios).

Class 8: Book Assignment

Critique, composition, hierarchy, basic typographic craftsmanship, pacing, image-type relationships.

Make corrections.

Unmounted printouts are acceptable for critique.

Class 9: Book Assignment

Color printouts mounted to boards due.

Type Movement Poster Assignment

Current Practice
Design an information poster about a typographic movement or style. Incorporate your personal response to the movement.

Choose one: Dada, De Stijl, Bauhaus, Constructivism, American typographic expressionism, American Modernism. The content should be clear to first-year design students who know nothing about typography or design history. 20" × 30". Black plus three PMS colors.

Class 10: Type Movement Poster Assignment
Critique, information, composition, hierarchy, basic typographic craftsmanship. Can we distinguish between the typographic style or movement and your personal response to it?

Make corrections. Unmounted printouts are acceptable for crit.

Class 11: Type Movement Poster Assignment
Color printouts mounted to boards due.

Invitation Postcard Assignment
Using supplied type and images, design an invitation to Ryoanji, the Japanese garden. Incorporate Japanese rock garden proportions and ideas. 7" × 10", black and white.

Be prepared to cut type and paste down multiple versions of the invitation.

Class 12: Invitation Postcard Assignment
Critique, information, composition, hierarchy, basic typographic craftsmanship.

Three versions: (1) type and image, (2) image is replaced with words and shapes, and (3) words and shapes are replaced with type only, no shapes.

Unmounted printouts are acceptable for crit.

Class 13: Invitation Postcard Assignment
Color printouts mounted to boards due.

COURSE TITLE _ THE HISTORY OF GRAPHIC DESIGN: MEANING
   AND VALUE IN COMMERCIAL IMAGE-MAKING
INSTRUCTOR _ John Calvelli
SCHOOL _ The Art Institute of Portland
FREQUENCY _ Eleven weeks
CREDITS _ Three
LEVEL _ Undergraduate

purpose

This survey course will examine the history of graphic design. Upon completion of this course, students will be able to recognize and describe major designers, their work, and specific design movements. Illustration and other media will be discussed as they relate to the field of graphic design.

course outcomes

Students will be able to identify major designers and design movements.
   They will be able to recognize key illustrators who collaborated with designers.
   Students will gain a broader understanding of how design affects and is affected by the culture we live in.
   Supporting competencies:

- Identify major movements in graphic design history.
- Identify individual artists, illustrators, graphic designers, etc.
- Recognize specific styles and individual works.
- Recognize the impact that visual design and advertising have on society.

course philosophy

When considered telescopically within an historical framework, graphic design becomes a cultural artifact. By considering it as artifact, we can look at the larger meaning that the practice of graphic design has on culture and society; and we can also analyze how it has created value for the culture at large. By understanding how meaning and value operate historically within the practice we call "graphic design," we are more able to understand our own contemporary practice: solving communication in a *meaningful* way that has *value* for our client and the audience or end-user.

required reading

Philip B. Meggs, *A History of Graphic Design*. New York: Van Nostrand Reinhold, 1983.

You will be responsible for and tested on any material covered in class, including that which appears in Meggs. This means individual works of design, the work of designers or other artists and authors covered in class, design movements, genres and periods, and visual analysis of works of design illustration, or fine art as it relates to design. Although each student is encouraged to read Meggs in depth, it is suggested that the student use Meggs as an ongoing resource, for preparation for upcoming lectures, and for review. Reading assignments given in Meggs are recommended as the best preparation for the lectures, and ensure that the complete book and history of design are covered within the eleven-week period. Other texts will be handed out in class or available on the Internet.

description of classes

Lesson 1

Graphic design is a practice of creating visual form using words and/or pictures for the purpose of communication. This communication must have meaning (otherwise it is not understandable), and it must create value (it must be worth something to somebody). In this lecture, we will expose ourselves to an overview of the prehistory and history of graphic design to the present day, looking to see how these terms "meaning" and "value" can illuminate the design of the past and present.

Assignment

Select a contemporary work of graphic design and write two paragraphs on how meaning and value operate within it. Post image and caption data on server.

Reading: Meggs, part 1, chapters 1–4 (54 pages); "The Power of Memes": *www.memes.org.uk/ByAuthor/SusanBlackmore/THES19990226.html.*

Lesson 2

Graphic design originated in the primal past, as humans became capable of analyzing their visual environments and creating symbolic visual representations for the purpose of understanding, communication, recording, and effecting change within their lives in some way. On the one hand, it is surmised that images were used magically—as divination, or for exerting some kind of psychic control on the environment (as in a hunt, for example). On the other hand, it became a way to record value; for instance, in creating "a line in the sand" to distinguish what is "mine" from "yours." Later, in Sumerian times, a system of writing developed for the purpose of recording purchases or taxation. From these beginnings, we will look at the development of writing and illustration through Roman times, when both our modern alphabet became standardized, and also when the first visual representations of individuals became a cultural occurrence.

Periods: Prehistory, Sumerian, Egyptian, [Mesoamerican], Ancient China, Greek, Roman.

Assignment
Select and post image from periods covered but not shown in class, writing two paragraphs on how meaning and value operate within it. Post image and caption data on server.

Reading: Meggs, part 2, chapters 5–8; part 3, chapter 9 (77 pages); handout: chapter from Roland Barthes, *Mythologies* (Noonday Press, 1973).

Lesson 3

During the Middle Ages, words and pictures were used almost exclusively in the service of a religious worldview—that of Catholicism. That began to change due primarily to the Protestant Reformation in northern Europe and the rise of a secular and scientific humanism. As the patronage structure of religious commissions changed within a more mercantile economy, and as the invention of the printing press brought a revolutionary new technology to society, the role of visual artists changed to accommodate these new conditions. By taking a close look at these changes, we can better understand what the roles of the graphic designer, illustrator, and Web artist are today, and how the distinction between fine artist and professional artist informs our practice.

Periods: Early Christian, Medieval, Renaissance, Reformation, Revolutionary Era.

Assignment
Select and post image from periods covered but not shown in class, writing two paragraphs on how meaning and value operate within it. Post image and caption data on server.

Reading: Meggs, part 3, chapters 10–13; part 4, chapter 1 (96 pages).

Lesson 4

The machine changed everything. It created new opportunities for disseminating visual work. It created huge "mass" audiences, especially in urban centers, to receive the work. There were powerful incentives for artists and designers to create work: fame and money. The Industrial Age, with the increasing centralization of capital needed for large-scale productive investments, also helped shift the role of the graphic designer from that of an independent scholar-artist toward the increasingly professionalized and specialized role of a visual form-giver. We will explore the repercussions of the early machine age on individual designers, artists, and movements in the decades leading up to the twentieth century.

Periods: Industrial Revolution, Westward Expansion, Arts and Crafts, Art Nouveau, Vienna Secession.

Assignment

Select and post image from periods covered but not shown in class, writing two paragraphs on how meaning and value operate within it. Post image and caption data on server. Review for test.

Reading: Meggs, part 4, chapters 15–18 (69 pages).

Lesson 5

What modern was—or is—the big bang of the twentieth century. Reacting to war, to inhuman conditions in cities and the factories of industry, and to new opportunities provided by the Machine Age, designers and artists created a new worldview in visual form, at once both monumental in its ambition and revolutionary in its visual form and effects. From negation and nonsense to propaganda and social activism, from visual theology to industrial idealism, what was achieved in the first few decades of the last century provided a set of possibilities that we still pick from today.

Midterm quiz.

Periods: Dada, Futurism and Surrealism, Russian Constructivism, De Stijl, Bauhaus.

Assignment

Select and post image from periods covered but not shown in class, writing two paragraphs on how meaning and value operate within it. Post image and caption data on server.

Reading: Meggs, part 4, chapter 19; part 5, chapter 20 (37 pages).

Lesson 6

Graphic design, especially in America, played a huge role in the development and growth of consumer society, beginning in the early part of the twentieth century and continuing, unmitigatedly, through the present. Along the way, its power of persuasion was used to unite a country during economic difficulties and through a second world war. The binding of identity to image on a collective and cultural level—which begins in the United States at this time through advertising, packaging, branding, and style-making—was surpassed in history only by the influence of the visual artists, sculptors, and architects of the Catholic Middle Ages.

Periods: Art Deco, Early Consumerism, WPA and Depression, World War II.

Assignment
Assignment

Select and post image from periods covered but not shown in class, writing two paragraphs on how meaning and value operate within it. Post image and caption data on server.

Reading: Meggs, part 5, chapters 21–22 (53 pages); handout: chapter 3, "The Marriage between Art and Commerce," from *All Consuming Images: The Politics of Style in Contemporary Culture* by Stuart Ewen (New York: Basic Books, 1999).

Lesson 7

A world war was won by America and its allies, and economic and cultural power crossed the Atlantic. Technology developed during the war provided the basis for forward-looking optimism; and cultural currents that had originated in Europe before the war found powerful, though mutated, expression in American postwar consumer culture. The social idealism of European Modernist designers became the basis for a universal visual language of corporate might, worldly influence, and individual hedonism. Designers created the spectacle, and drove into the ever-progressing future in their fancy Detroit automobiles.

Periods: American Modernism, Pop Futurism, Swiss Modernism, the early sixties.

Assignment

Select and post image from periods covered but not shown in class, writing two paragraphs on how meaning and value operate within it. Post image and caption data on server.

Reading: Meggs, part 5, chapters 23–25 (65 pages); excerpt from *Society of the Spectacle* by Guy DeBord (Zone Books, 1995).

Lesson 8

The vision of ever-expanding progress in a universal society of consumer conquest splintered under the weight of military defeat of the United States in Vietnam, a war begun by a generation shaped by the hardships of the Depression and the victory of a just war, and to be fought by the first full-fledged consumer generation, educated in individualism and self-fulfillment. Graphic language mutated into hybrid forms of protest and sub-cultural dialects, as well as reincorporated into new consumer forms of historical revisionism and the challenged but still potent form of high corporate modernism.

Periods: Counterculture, American seventies and New York School, Punk, American and Swiss New Wave.

Assignment

Select and post image from periods covered but not shown in class, writing two paragraphs on how meaning and value operate within it. Post image and caption data on server.

Reading: Meggs, part 5, chapter 26, epilogue; excerpt from "First Things First" manifesto in *Looking Closer IV*, Beirut et al., eds. (New York: Allworth Press, 2002).

Lesson 9

Technology—hardware and software—developed initially through obscure mathematical theory and built into de-encryption machines (which helped win the mid-century world war) filtered their way down to the consumer masses by 1984, signaled by the famous television ad by Apple Computer. Hypersensitized to cultural difference and aware of the power of information to persuade and control, graphic designers seized these new tools, dismantling the old universals and creating hyper-individual idiolects in their place. In the process, typefaces proliferated amidst an increasingly branded world, calling into question both the limits of individualism, and the corporation as designers' patron and consumers' refuge.

Periods: Early Digital, Deconstruction, Raves and the New Vernacular, current visual culture.

Assignment

Select a Web site, do a screen capture of its home page, and post it as well as its URL. Do a meaning/value analysis.

Reading: handout on memes (Susan Blackmore, "The Power of Memes," in *Scientific American* 283, no. 4 (October 2000), pp. 52–61).

Bonus Assignment

Review your first-assignment slide selection of a contemporary image. Either write a one-page defense and/or analysis of your selection using skills and understanding learned in the course; or pick a new image and write a one-page analysis, including meaning/value. New image selection and posting due in one week, paper due in two weeks.

Lesson 10

In an odd historical quirk, a computer network devised by the American military for post-Doomsday survival gave birth to the new decentralized media of the Internet. Both highly technological in origins—yet still in its infancy as a medium of communications—designers, authors, and technologists collaborated—sometimes in the same person—to give visual and cultural expression to a real-time global community. A creative culture of specialized producers developed for the Web, which businesses relied on when the technology this time filtered up, and the Internet became a required competitive tool for business. The era of e-commerce began and with it developed new and innovative forms of multimedia graphics, instant branding, as well as new design disciplines of information architecture and user experience. A collapse of the high-tech and e-commerce sector, followed by an attack by Islamic fundamentalists on cultural, economic, and military targets in the United States has presaged the beginning of a new phase in the history of graphic design as it interacts with emerging new histories of the world.

Period: interactive graphics.

Assignment
Continue working on bonus assignment. Study for final exam.

Lesson 11

Final exam:

- Visual analysis of two images.
- Q/A and multiple-choice test.
- Review of contemporary slides with discussion.

Grading

- 30 percent weekly assignments. Nine assignments, graded on image appropriateness, analysis, technical quality, and getting it posted on time.
- 20 percent midterm. Will consist of three parts: slide identification, spot image analysis, and multiple choice.
- 30 percent final. Consists of content from all eleven weeks. Will consist of three parts: slide identification, spot image analysis, and question-answer.
- 20 percent professional behavior. In class and return from breaks on time. Participates in discussions.
- Bonus assignment. If student completes all other assignments, up to an additional 10 percent can be made by doing the bonus assignment.

Weekly Assignments

Each week, beginning the first class and continuing through week nine, students will be required to choose an image and write two articulate and cogent paragraphs analyzing the work's meaning and value. These will be due promptly by the following week, digitally posted on AIP's server.

The image must be from the time period discussed in the slide lecture. The image cannot be one shown already in class.

It should be a work of graphic design, typography, illustration, photography, interactive design, or a work of fine art. (If it is a work of fine art, attention must be given to its social use and context.)

Meaning/Value Analysis

- What is the meaning of the image in question?
- What does it communicate to you?

- What do you think it meant within its own cultural framework? To an individual exposed to it for the first time?
- What is its meaning within the history of graphic design?
- What is the value of the image in question?
- What was its purpose and did it succeed in it?
- Who was the client? What do you think the expectations of the client were?
- What kind of remuneration was involved and how did that impact the result?
- What made it valuable then? What makes it valuable now?

The analysis must be two paragraphs. It is not necessary to do one paragraph for each term, but you must deal with both *meaning* and *value*. The assignment should be well written and cogently argued, and should be corrected for grammar and spelling. Respond to the image—use your imagination, intelligence, and your research skills.

Choose an image from a book in the school's library that inspires you or that you find interesting in some way—something you'd like to "add to your collection." Alternately, choose an image that is problematic for you or that you hate. Use the assignment as a way to discover why you like or dislike the image, by analyzing what it means to you, what you think it meant or means to others, and what value it has or had to you and others.

Specs

- Capture the image digitally.
- Image size should be 8.5" on its longest dimension at 72 dpi.
- Optimize image to a 100k-jpeg maximum size without sacrificing image quality.
- Post image in the specified folder on the school's server.
- Collect and post relevant caption information on forms available on the intranet. This must include: designer (or group), title, date, media, practice, form, historical context, utility, and place, source you found it in, copyright info, your name.
- Post image and caption data no later than the end of the day, one week following the assignment.
- Hand in your analysis in printed form at the beginning of class.

COURSE TITLE _ GRAPHIC DESIGN IN THE TWENTIETH CENTURY
INSTRUCTOR _ Cristina de Almeida
SCHOOL _ Western Washington University
FREQUENCY _ Ten weeks
CREDITS _ Four
LEVEL _ Undergraduate

purpose

To introduce graphic design history as a component of a liberal studies education for undergraduate design majors and nonmajors alike.

To introduce students to a variety of visual examples and design writings and thus expand understanding of graphic design's contribution to the visual culture of the twentieth century.

To promote critical thinking about issues pertinent to the design field and their relationships to cultural, commercial, and technological developments in the twentieth century.

84

description

This course's framework will focus on the process of negotiation designers have engaged to establish their place in the industrialized world during the past century. This will be addressed from the broader perspective of the role visual culture has played in presenting, representing, and transforming society. The materials to be covered will examine the relationships between design, culture, and commerce within the changing social, political, and economic realities of the period. This will entail a look into how the many visual strategies and styles available to designers have been employed in the fulfillment of a variety of agendas ranging from the upholding of the status quo to its total disruption.

The course will be structured around themes that have been manifest since mechanized mass-production processes separated the activities of planning and producing, giving rise to graphic design's professional identity as we know it today. Although the approach to the themes follows a rough chronology, the main goal here is to develop them as issues that still pervade current debates on visual communication.

description of classes

Week 1: Visual Culture and Graphic Design

This class is an introduction to the concept of visual culture and how graphic design history can be studied from this perspective. It will take into consideration the interaction between visual producers and various institutions, markets, and audiences. Various questions will be asked, such as: why is the primary graphic design narrative usually equated with the history of modernism in graphic design? Is it possible that alternative narratives have been left out, and if so why? What value systems lie behind the objects and practices that have reproduced the profession during the past century? As a case study, we will focus on the development of the modern poster as a medium that has consistently inhabited the borderline between fine and commercial art since its inception in the streets of Paris at the turn of the century.

Reading: Malcolm Barnard, "Producers: Artists and Designers" and "Visual Culture and the Social Process," in *Art, Design and Visual Culture* (New York: St. Martin's Press, 1998).

Week 2: Total Design

This segment will examine some of the early-century modern movements from the perspective of Gesamkultur, the utopia of a new universal culture in a totally reformed manmade environment. The aesthetic and philosophical currents initiated in the Arts and Crafts, then later elaborated through the Wiener Werkstatte and the Deutscher Werkbund, advocated the integration of all design elements in a single total artwork (*gesamtkunstwerk*) akin to a cathedral or an opera. This vision of aesthetic homogeneity, reflected also in the first corporate identity systems, prefigured many of the totalitarian tendencies developed later in the century, not only in the arts but also in political and social contexts.

Read: Jonathan M. Woodham, *Twentieth-Century Design* (New York: Oxford University Press, 1997).

Jane Kallir, *Viennese Design and the Wiener Werkstätte* (New York: Galerie St. Etienne/George Braziller, 1986).

Jeremy Aynsley, *Graphic Design in Germany 1890–1945* (Berkeley: University of California Press, 2000).

Week 3: Representing the New

The tension between the old and the new has been a constant theme in twentieth-century art and design. The debate has always been tempered by various degrees of optimism and pessimism toward the future, as well as the pursuit of

85

a definite place for the visual artist in society. This module will examine the formal and ideological agendas of the early avant-garde movements. Their enthusiasm for the "new" engendered visual translations of speed, simultaneity, and mechanical production that later became inextricably associated with the representation of twentieth-century modernity. Among some of the most influential formal developments of the time were the spatial typography proposed by the Futurists and the experiments in photomontage associated with the Dada movement. In spite of their original motivations, the meaning of these formal strategies have evolved throughout time, culminating in their close identification with modern advertising later in the century.

Reading: Dawn Ades, "The Supremacy of the Message," *Photomontage* (London: Thames and Hudson, 1986)

Marinetti, "Destruction of Syntax—Imagination without Strings—Words-in-Freedom," from Michael Bierut et al., eds., *Looking Closer 3* (New York: Allworth Press, 1999).

Week 4: Information and Persuasion

The impasse of either staying as an outsider critic or becoming an active participant in the social process was a crucial shaper of the twentieth-century designer's identity. In times of change and upheaval, many designers have enthusiastically embraced the opportunity of participating in the construction, reform, or maintenance of civic values. This week, we will examine some of the ways in which designers have engaged themselves in political and social agendas. This examination will start with Russian Constructivism and the call for a new type of artist more akin to the engineer than to the nineteenth-century introspective thinker. It will also include how designers lent their talents to the promotion of the war efforts on both sides of the field during the two world wars. Finally, this segment will examine graphic design during the Depression era and the manner in which governments and artists have become partners in the advancement of their mutual interests.

Reading: Harris, "Graphic Art for the Public Welfare," in Mildred Friedman et al., *Graphic Design in America: A Visual Language History* (Minneapolis: Walker Art Center, 1989).

Ellen Lupton, "Design and Production in the Mechanical Age," in Deborah Rothschild et al., *Graphic Design in the Mechanical Age* (Yale University Press, 1998).

Rodchenko and Stepanova, "Program of the First Working Group of the Constructivists," in Michael Bierut, et al., eds., *Looking Closer 3* (New York: Allworth Press, 1999).

Week 5: The Codification of the Modern

After the initial shock of the early avant-garde movements, many individuals and groups took up the task of coordinating the new formal idioms with the technological possibilities available. As part of an overall effort to endorse the aspirations of the industrialized world, these individuals and groups managed to create bodies of work and writings that systematized a new aesthetic based on functional and technical requirements. The works associated with the Bauhaus and the Circle of New Advertising Designers are exemplary of this undertaking. Conversely, the pressures of commerce and profit have also entailed issues of fashion and consumerism that were usually left out of the modernist discourse. These issues often found visual expression in the popular ornamental forms of the Art Deco. In between these two distinct but complementary approaches to the reproduction of modernity in mass communications, we find a number of designers trying to strike a balance between the idealism of the avant garde and the practical demands of the mass market.

Reading: A.M. Cassandre, excerpt from article for *La Revue de l'Union de L'Affiche Française* (1926), in Henri Mouron, *A.M. Cassandre* (New York: Rizzoli, 1985).

Maud Lavin, *Clean New World: Culture, Politics, and Graphic Design* (Cambridge: MIT Press, 2001).

Tschichold, "New Life in Print," in Michael Bierut et al., eds, *Looking Closer 3* (New York: Allworth Press, 1999).

Week 6: The Rise of Consumer Culture

During the thirties and forties, modernist ideas and approaches start to gain momentum in the United States, particularly within fashion, science, and business editorial design. Fueled by young American designers and European émigrés, modernism consolidated into a formal vocabulary particularly suited to the needs of American consumer culture and the then rising corporations. We will examine how this transference took place and compare the attitudes and ideological motivations of designers from both sides of the Atlantic Ocean. One of the main aspects of the introduction of modernist ideas in the United States was their dependency on corporate support for achieving legitimacy with larger audiences. We will look into some of the various relationships between industry and graphic design in the United States, with particular emphasis on the postwar period. As a theoretical framework we will look at three basic types of relationships between producers and consumers of visual culture: namely, patronage, market, and sponsorship.

Reading: Malcom Barnard, *Art Design and Visual Culture* (New York: St. Martin's Press, 1998).

Jobling and Crowley, *Graphic Design: Reproduction and Representation since 1800* (Manchester: Manchester University Press, 1996).

Maud Lavin, *Clean New World: Culture, Politics, and Graphic Design* (Cambridge: MIT Press, 2001).

Week 7: Transnational Identities

A discrediting of totalitarian national regimes and a move toward internationalism marked the end of the World War II. The need for mutual acceptance and cooperation among countries was translated into political initiatives, such as the United Nations, as well as through the expansion of global trade. From now on, multinational companies would espouse the language of the International Style as the epitome of efficiency and forward thinking. Thus designers find a prestigious niche in the task of imparting unified appearances to these large conglomerates. This is a time of enthusiasm for systematic approaches, modulated grids, and sans serif type. It is also a time of the search for universal languages and methods capable of operating in an industrial-technological commonwealth beyond national borders. In literature, the concrete poetry movement seeks a similar cultural communion through a poetry that could be visually understood by all, inspired by contemporary forms such as the slogan and the mathematical formula.

Reading: Müller-Brockmann, "Grid and Design Philosophy," and "The Typographic Grid," in *Grid Systems in Graphic Design* (Niederteufen: Arthru Niggli Publishers, 1981).

Jonathan M. Woodham, "Multinational Corporations and Global Products," in *Twentieth-Century Design* (New York: Oxford University Press, 1997).

Week 8: Rediscovering the Past

This part focuses on the tension between modernism and historicism in graphic design. We see some of this drama unfold during the second half of the century as a number of designers turned back to earlier historical references in reaction against the rigidity of the International Style. Approaches previously dismissed, such as nostalgia, hand illustration, and ornamentation, were revisited and ultimately well received within the context of advanced capitalism. While Pop Art in the sixties celebrated the visual cacophony of mass media, designers in practices such as the Push Pin Studio combined elements of various vernacular idioms into unique visual concoctions that challenged modernist assumptions of objectivity toward content. This taste for the visually eclectic was also used as a means of identification of cultural subgroups, exemplified in the psychedelic posters of the sixties. Later this eclecticism further evolved into the retro movement of the eighties as a general interest in design history was awakened within the graphic design profession. With these events in mind, we will examine the social forces that ensured the success of these design approaches in various mass and niche markets of industrialized countries.

Reading: Ellen Lupton, "Low and High," in Lupton and Miller, *Design Writing Research* (New York: Princeton Architectural Press, 1996).

Woodham, "Pop to Postmodernism: Changing Values," and "Nostalgia, Heritage, and Design," in *Twentieth-Century Design* (New York: Oxford University Press, 1997).

Week 9: Intuition and/or Reason

This part will investigate the place formal experimentation has occupied in graphic design specifically and in visual culture as a whole during the late-twentieth century. As postmodernist theories invited a reconsideration of absolutes such as neutrality and universality, several designers set off to explore the possibilities for incorporating ambiguity and complexity into the communication process. By the early seventies, Wolfgang Weingart's revision of the Swiss typographic style had found large acceptance within American academia. The practices of collage, typographic modulation, and layering of images and texts as ways of revealing hidden semantic relationships found their ultimate facilitating tool during the late eighties in the personal computer. These experiments initially thrived within the insular environments of academic and cultural institutions. Much of these exercises were later codified into surface mannerisms and absorbed by the mainstream, becoming identified with consumer styles such as New Wave in the eighties, and the brand-conscientious youth market of the nineties.

Read: Jobling, "Graphic Design in a Postmodern Context: The beginning and the End?," in Jobling and Crowley, *Graphic Design: Reproduction and Representation Since 1800* (Manchester: Manchester University Press, 1996).

Lupton and Miller, "Deconstruction and Graphic Design," in *Design Writing Research* (New York: Princeton Architectural Press, 1996)

Weingart, "How Can One Make Swiss Typography?," in Michael Bierut et al., eds, *Looking Closer 3* (New York: Allworth Press, 1999).

Week 10: Design Authorship in the Age of Mass Media

As television and other visual/sound-based mediums shave off the supremacy of print in mass communications, the role of designers in visual culture becomes more complex and diffused. Starting in the sixties and running through the close of the century, a surge of publications geared toward specialized interests allowed for a higher level of involvement on the part of designers in the content of their work. Concurrently, the means of mechanical reproduction of image and text became widely available to laymen who avidly embrace these new possibilities for public expression. From photocopy to desktop computers, from zines to Web sites, this is a time of increased voices in the public discourse. Ironically, this is also a time when a small number of large communications conglomerates increasingly monopolizes the channels for the mass distribution of messages. We will examine some of the works of the second half of the century in which graphic designers have played an increased authorial role. Ranging from advocacy campaigns to visual research pieces, we will look at the many attempts on the part of designers to establish a more critical involvement in the content of their work. Along with that, the issues raised by these critical practices pertaining to the designer's relationships with clients and audiences will be addressed.

Read: Malcom Barnard, "Media, Access and Ownership," in *Art Design and Visual Culture* (New York: St. Martin's Press, 1998).

Naomi Klein, "Culture Jamming," *No Logo: Taking Aim at the Brand Bullies* (New York: Picador, 1999).

Rick Poynor, "Design without Boundaries," in *Design without Boundaries: Visual Communication in Transition* (London: Booth-Clibborn editions, 1998).

Assignments

I am giving you five directions that invite you to expand upon the main narrative presented during the lectures. You will select one and develop it into a research paper throughout the quarter.

1. Investigate a twentieth-century visual manifestation that falls outside of the modernist narrative covered by this course. How does it construct and communicate the identity of a specific social or cultural group?

2. Examine the relationships between an example of visual production/consumption and a concurrent event in political, scientific, or economic areas. Here you are encouraged to connect the content of this course with your own major area of studies.

3. Choose an example of contemporary visual communications (a current ad campaign, an identity program, a publication, a movie, a TV series, etc.) and establish connections with the topics approached in class.

4. Select a movement or school covered in class and investigate further the ways its visual and philosophical approach has contributed to reinforce or challenge assumed notions of race, gender, or social class throughout the century.

5. Choose an example of twentieth-century technology of information reproduction or mass distribution and explore how it has contributed to shape people's perceptions of themselves and others. Focus on both the formats allowed by the technology as well as the economic factors that have determined how the technology was to be used.

COURSE TITLE _ DESIGN FOR DIGITAL MEDIA
INSTRUCTOR _ Ric Wilson
SCHOOL _ University of Missouri, Columbia
FREQUENCY _ Eight-week session, two classes per week
CREDITS _ Three
LEVEL _ Undergraduate

purpose

In order to utilize the incredible potential of the computer as a communication medium, designers must attain new practical and conceptual skills. Interactivity requires the participation of the user in order to function properly. Understanding the social and cultural views and biases of the user becomes critical in interactive communication. The purpose of this course is to give the students the opportunity to gain valuable experience in the research, planning, and design of interactive communication, as well as in the production of user interfaces with the industry standard applications. Emphasis will be placed on research and planning to discern useful informational content and usability.

91

description

The class will cover the practice of communications for the Internet and motion graphics. In this course, students will plan, design, and produce user interfaces that incorporate interactive elements with Macromedia Dreamweaver. Instruction begins with planning and designing a Web site, including page content, interactive (intuitive) site navigation, menus, buttons, and graphics. Students will also be introduced to motion graphics with Macromedia Flash, with strong emphasis placed on design principles and typography to create meaningful presentations.

description of classes

Week 1

Monday: Lecture and demonstration of Web site design and interactivity using examples of previously published sites. *Project 1 assigned.*

Wednesday: Research strategies discussed. Class time will be spent doing background research using Internet and library sources. Preliminary critiques on work in progress.

Week 2

Monday: In-class work, individual meetings to discuss work in progress, brainstorm, discuss technical issues, intermediate critiques.

Wednesday: Proposals presented to the class with discussion and Q&A. *Project 2 assigned.*

Week 3

Monday: Preliminary critiques on work in progress on Project 2. Site samples gathered by students will be analyzed and discussed.

Wednesday: Intermediate critiques on screen. Work, work, work . . .

Week 4

Monday: Final critiques on Project 2, with remaining class time available for revisions from class comments.

Wednesday: Project 2 due. *Project 3 assigned.*

Week 5

Monday: Preliminary critiques on work in progress on Project 3.

Wednesday: In-class work, individual meetings to discuss work in progress, brainstorm, discuss technical issues, intermediate critiques.

Week 6

Monday: Final critiques on Project 3, with remaining class time available for revisions from class comments.

Wednesday: Project 3 due. *Project 4 assigned.* Groups formed with discussion of responsibilities for each person in the group. As with all group projects, fellow group members will have an opportunity to grade the performance of each member. Research begins.

Week 7

Monday: Individual group critiques on work in progress on Project 4.

Wednesday: Continued group work on Project 4.

Week 8

Monday: Final critiques on Project 4, with remaining class time available for revisions from class comments.

Wednesday: Project 4 presented to invited guests to gauge reaction and effectiveness of presentations.

Project 1: Web Site Planning and Design Project

Students research and write a proposal outlining the planning and implementation of a Web site, including navigational structure, site map, and design of templates for primary, secondary, and tertiary pages. Research report will include the Web site intent (is the site's main purpose information, advertising, education, entertainment, etc?), a timeline of research-design-production, a site map, and sample front page and secondary page templates.

Project 2: Navigational Structures Project
Students will research an existing site for a museum exhibit and write a critical analysis of the site's navigational structure. Based on this analysis students will design and develop a more effective navigational system that makes the user experience more enjoyable.

Project 3: Environmental Web Site Project
Students will write, design, and produce a Web site that informs/educates the user about an environmental hazard. In the research phase, students will need to organize and prioritize the information and create a site map for the site that will present the material in logical manner.

Project 4: Thirty-Second Television Spot
Students will research, write, and produce a thirty-second public service announcement using Flash. Students will be split into groups of four and assigned roles for research, design, copy, and production. Initial research should include surveys of the intended audience before any work begins. Final projects will be presented to the class, invited faculty, and guests to measure the effectiveness of the spot.

Required Text
Jennifer Niederst, *Web Design in a Nutshell*, Second Edition (O'Reilly & Associates, 2001).
    Robin Williams, *Robin Williams Web Design Workshop*, First Edition (Peachpit Press, 2001).

Additional reading materials will be handed out in class.

conclusion

This class attempts to bridge the gap between the conceptual and technical aspects of interactive media. While there will be an opportunity for the students to become familiar with the software currently used in the industry, their experience will be focused on the concept, design, and planning of the user experience. What concerns me the most is decision making based on strong research skills.

COURSE TITLE _ SERVICE LEARNING: CONNECTING COMMUNITY
    AND DESIGN
INSTRUCTORS _ Elisabeth Charman and Susan Agre-Kippenhan
SCHOOL _ Portland State University
FREQUENCY _ Eleven weeks, two sessions per week
CREDITS _ Three
LEVEL _ Undergraduate

purpose

Since the practice of graphic design is intimately linked to the idea of communicating the message of a specific client to a specific audience, we will be working on assignments that will originate from real community requests and culminate in real products. This will give you an opportunity to participate in the entire process of design, while gaining insight into the client-designer relationship. It is not only a chance to deal with client-related issues such as budget, deadlines, and revisions but also a chance for direct community involvement. This is a community-based learning (or service learning) course where educational objectives will be applied to a community need. Our community partner is in need of a strong visual identity and strategies for getting the word out about its services, mission, and needs. This term, we will be working with a nonprofit service provider in our community.

goals

The primary focus of this course addresses specific goals that build on previous course work:

1. Development of a creative brief and design strategy.
- Define and address specific audiences.
- Apply research methods.
- Organize and structure problems.

2. Development and application of a visual language and an identity system.
- Create materials to reach specific audiences.
- Design graphic mark, logo, or logotype.
- Create original thoughtful conceptual solutions.
- Develop powerful ways to communicate ideas.
- Organize complex material through hierarchical structures.

3. Process.

- Development, demonstration, and documentation of your personal approach to the design process (including a process book).
- Strong craftsmanship and attention to detail.
- Apply computer skills to create digital mechanicals.

4. Critical thinking and presentation skills.

- Demonstrate independent, critical thinking and self-assessment skills.
- Discuss, support, present, and critique ideas.

5. Develop collaborative processes.

- Working with/for a client.
- Working in a group in class to address complex problems.

structure of the class

The structure of this class is based on the professional modes of operation. We will address practical concerns, such as schedules, design rationale, creative briefs, and design strategy. This class will include sessions with our community clients, for presentations, questions, and ultimately feedback, as well as sessions conducted without the client present for class discussion, work periods, and critiques. The class will address two major clusters of activities.

The first cluster of activities will start with each student developing a creative brief and then combining these drafts into one cohesive statement. Once approved by our client the creative brief will serve as a guiding document for every member of the class. Using the brief each student will develop a logo for the client. Through input and a process of elimination through a series of phases we will move from the original large group of logos to increasingly smaller numbers. Each phase will require revision and reworking, and regardless of whether your logo is selected to move forward, each member of the class will continue to revise his own work. At the final phase one logo will emerge and be applied to subsequent collateral pieces. Individually, each student will apply her own logo to a suite of stationery.

For the second cluster of activities we will divide into groups and devote our time to developing collateral materials for specific audience groups that our client needs to address. These groups may include volunteers, corporate sponsors, the general public, etc. To assist in creating continuity amongst the groups, several elected representatives from the class will serve on the "Visual Language Group." This group will meet on Mondays at noon for half an hour (or as needed), and will take the lead in determining the "look and feel," or visual identity, for our client. This group will help to ensure consistency as we move from individual design to a comprehensive program of design applied to multiple pieces. The representatives will report to the class and receive input from the class as to direction. (The representatives will have appropriate modifications made to their course work as compensation for this additional responsibility.)

It is important to note that, as with any real-world project, there will be overlap between the clusters of activities. As simple as that may sound the reality can be frustrating and a bit confusing. We are working with the constraints of the academic schedule and the realities of the nonprofit world, where clients are often over burdened and usually juggling multiple responsibilities for a cause that they fervently believe in. So, it is important to keep the big picture in mind, to remain flexible, and to keep reminding yourself of the progress that is being made.

At the beginning of each week, written responses to assigned readings are due (see specifics under "Readings"). For the first four to five weeks during the second weekly class meeting, the Visual Language Group presents its recommendations to the class for discussion.

description of classes

Week One

Meeting 1: Introduction: Research, Question, and Analyze
Review syllabus and introduce project.

Slide lecture: Trademarks, design programs, visual languages, identity standards, and process books.

Discussion: Prepare for community client's presentation. Prepare, develop, and compile questions for interviewing client.

Homework: Review client's informational materials, research community client, primary audience(s) and like organizations, and prepare questions for client.

Meeting 2: The Client Interview: Collaborating with Our Community Service Client
Community client presentation. Students interview client.

Discussion: Debrief on client presentation. Discuss initial research, audience(s), and creative brief.

Homework: Continue researching community client's organization and like organizations. Start first draft of creative brief. Begin sketching ideas for marks.

Visual Language Group meets to discuss approach to developing a look and feel and to divide up work.

Week Two

Meeting 1: Defining the Problem: The Creative Brief
Lecture/Discussion: Design process, ideation strategies, research, creative brief, and audience(s).

In-class work: Creative brief.

Homework: Finish creative brief. Continue to compile and review research on community client.

Visual Language Group meets and reviews type studies.

Meeting 2: Marks: Conceptual Development

Due: Bring in typed-up briefs. Bring notebook with organized research, concepts, and sketches.

Homework: Twenty-five initial mark sketches. Work only in black and white and organize marks on a grid.

End of the week: Send creative brief to community client. Client to review and send edits back to the class.

Week Three

Meeting 1: Marks: Visual Exploration

Critique: Twenty-five marks. Faculty and students assist each student in determining their strongest three to four marks.

Discussion: Further definition of client's needs, including audiences for informational and collateral materials and means and methods of reaching the audiences. Solidify recommendations on approach and strategy for informational and collateral materials and modes of communication.

Visual Language Group meets and brings color studies. ₉₇

Meeting 2: Modes of Communication:
Reaching an Audience, Addressing Client Input

Discussion: Review and address client's comments on and response to the creative brief.

Discussion and in-class work: Students are divided up into small groups to define and address each specific audience—research specific audiences, how best to reach them.

1. Clearly define and research specific audiences for collateral pieces. Audience profile and creative strategy, including ideas for formats and placement defined for each audience.
2. Each group is to create an audience research notebook (which may include: demographics, travel patterns, lists of care providers, churches, billboard costs and specs, and bus placard specs and costs).
3. How will each group divide up the work? Define group member roles.

Homework: Continue to develop marks, choose strongest four and address comments from critique revision. Black and white only.

Visual Language Group meets and brings ideas for image treatment.

End of the week: Send audiences strategy and initial ideas for formats for reaching audiences to client. Client to provide input.

Week Four

Meeting 1: Marks: Critique and Revision
Critique: Four revised marks. Revise and refine. Choose strongest mark(s) to send to community client.

Homework: Revise marks. Take your strongest mark(s); use given format and prepare for presentation to client. Develop strong written justification of design decisions. Black and white only.

Meeting 2: Marks: Critique and Revision; Campaign and Collateral Material: Concept
Critique: Revised mark(s).

Homework: (1) Marks refined and prepared for presentation (first round) to client. Marks will be edited by faculty and senior TAs.

(2) Meet with your group to develop concepts and formats for reaching your audience. Prepare to present your ideas next class period to instructor/class.

Visual Language Group meets. Organization and creation of identity spec sheet: i.e., typefaces, color palette, and image treatment. Complete spec sheet and distribute to classes.

End of the week: Marks sent to client. Client to select approximately twelve marks to continue to next round of development. Input provided to all students.

Week Five

Meeting 1: Campaign and Collateral Material: Concept and Development
Due: Students present audience and format research, developing concepts for campaign and collateral materials.

Meeting 2: Narrative Structures: Copy Writing
In-class work: Narratives, storytelling, and copy writing. Campaign and collateral material prototypes. Group meetings with instructor.

Discussion: Twelve marks chosen by client. Review and address client comments on marks. Analyze the feedback and decide on direction.

Homework: Revise marks, apply two colors from the VL color palette to mark and work on letterhead.

Week Six

Meeting 1: Marks: Critique and Revision
Critique: Refined, two-color marks and letterhead, envelope, and business card.

Homework: Revise campaign and collateral material prototypes based on feedback from class. Continue to work on marks and letterhead system.

Midweek: Twelve revised marks sent to client. Client to provide input and select three marks to move to next round of development.

Meeting 2: Campaign and Collateral Material: Further Development
Critique: Campaign and collateral material prototypes: each group presents collateral material sketches.

Homework: Revise campaign and collateral material prototypes based on feedback from class. Continue to work on marks and letterhead system.

Week Seven

Meeting 1: Campaign and Collateral Material: Critique and Revision
Work in class: on campaign and collateral material prototypes.

Meeting 2: Campaign and Collateral Material: Critique
and Revision. Addressing Client Input
Critique: Campaign and collateral material prototypes.

Discussion: Three marks chosen by client. Review, analyze, and address client comments on marks. Finalist students to present their marks to client.

Homework: Complete campaign and collateral material prototypes based on input from class. Continue to work on marks and letterhead system.

End of the week: Send three revised marks and the campaign and collateral material prototypes to client. Client to provide input, select final logo, and give input on prototypes.

Week Eight

Meeting 1: No Class

Meeting 2: Addressing Client Input: Execution
and Production of Campaign Pieces
Discussion: Announce the final mark. Review, analyze, and address client comments on campaign materials. Pre-flight and digital mechanicals.

Work in class: Groups work on campaign materials. Distribute and apply final mark to all materials.

Homework: Refine campaign and collateral materials, marks, and letterhead.

Week Nine

Meeting 1: Execution and Production of Campaign Pieces
Critique: Campaign and collateral materials, marks, letterheads, process books, etc. Tie up any loose ends.

Work in class: on refining campaign materials and digital mechanicals. Support team members.

Homework: Work on digital mechanicals. Refine as needed: campaign and collateral materials, marks, and letterhead.

Midweek: Send revised campaign and collateral material prototypes to client. Client to provide input.

Meeting 2: No Class
Thanksgiving. University Closed.

Week Ten

Meeting 1: Execution and Production of All Work
Critique: Campaign and collateral material prototypes, marks, etc. Tie up any loose ends.
    Homework: Work on digital mechanicals. Refine as needed: campaign and collateral materials, marks, and letterhead.

Meeting 2: Evaluation, Debrief, Post Mortum
Discussion: Analyze and evaluate group members, self, course.
    Homework: Work on digital mechanicals. Prepare files for the printer.

Week Eleven

Final Meeting: Celebrate
Client throws a thank you celebration for the students.
    Due: All term deliverables are turned in.

Assignments

1. Write a creative brief, define/determine audiences.
2. Each student will design and revise a visual mark for our community social service organization.
3. Each student will prepare a written justification of her logo design that connects points in the creative brief with her design decisions.
4. Each student will apply her logo to letterhead, etc.
5. Each student will create a process notebook of research, marks, sketches, etc.
6. In groups students will create an audience research notebook and then design, create, and produce two or more prototypes applying the visual identity to a specified audience.
7. In groups students will create digital mechanicals for their prototypes for printing/production.
8. Each student will have reading responses for assigned reading.

Logo Design

1. Marks must have a strong strategic concept based on clients needs/creative brief.
2. The mark must communicate the essence of the organization. It must be memorable and engaging.

3. The weights of the graphic mark must be designed with proportion and scale in mind. Marks are applied to materials at a variety of sizes and are displayed in both color and black and white. Consider that the mark will be used very small and how it will read once it is photocopied or faxed.

Group Work

Working in teams, students will define and address specific audiences and create a campaign and collateral material. Designers often work in teams, and in collaboration with the client, illustrator, photographer, writer, etc. Students are asked to research, define, and reach the audiences.

Creating a Process Notebook or Book

Designers must be able to have a strategic process in place for developing strong ideas. Prospective employers may want to review your sketches and your design process. A process book will illustrate your approach to problem solving and the scope of your research and your conceptual and visual exploration. A process book can reveal much to a prospective employer. A weak process book does not demonstrate creative thinking and will not have multiple solutions and explorations. The way you refine, edit, and finish the mark or marks will illustrate your critical and formal abilities. Refining a mark requires precise craftsmanship and great care concerning form, counterform, weight, proportion, etc.

Creating Mechanicals/Preparing the Work
for Production and Printing

Students will create digital mechanicals for their audience collateral pieces. The process for prepping a file for production is referred to as "pre-flight" and/or can be called "pre-press." A pre-flight reading for Quark and Illustrator files will be required reading. Much of this you learned in Computer Graphics; this reading will serve as a refresher.

critiques

Students are required to be in attendance, and to participate and contribute to the critical dialogue and class discussion of work. Critiques are conducted in small groups, one-on-one with faculty and with the entire class.

Constructive criticism is the process by which you learn about your design process and theory and how you may improve your work. The critique process helps design solutions to mature and improve. Critiques also serve as preparation for client presentations, job interviews, and creative direction.

The ability to present and critique work is integral in professional studio environments. Students are graded on their ability to articulate and support their ideas thoughtfully and clearly.

This space, our class, is a dynamic one: every person contributes to creating our community. Creating an exciting, energetic, respectful, creatively open, and productive space is a collective effort that requires engagement. Each student should be an active participant and feel confident in offering comments and thoughts regarding critique, work, readings, and course objectives.

I welcome any discussion regarding strategies for pushing work and maximizing the critique process. As a career in graphic design means receiving input from clients and creative directors, considering how you respond to constructive criticism and how you analyze and apply those comments is an important part of maturing as a designer. When critiquing your classmates' work, be aware of the manner in which you prefer to receive constructive comments regarding your own work.

4th year

COURSE TITLE _ INTRODUCTION TO COMMUNICATIONS DESIGN
INSTRUCTOR _ Katherine McCoy
SCHOOL _ Institute of Design, Illinois Institute of Technology
FREQUENCY _ Sixteen weeks
CREDITS _ Four
LEVEL _ Undergraduate; preliminary year before graduate study

103

purpose

This sixteen-week, seven-hour-a-week workshop project sequence provides an incoming group of pregraduate students from nondesign backgrounds (young to midcareer professionals from other fields preparing for a master's degree in design) with their first experience in visual communications design. It provides an intense introduction to communications design theory, process, form giving, aesthetics, history, and culture. Within this pregraduate year, these students also take a second communications workshop, as well as workshops in product design, photography, multimedia, and design history.

Each week's seven-hour session includes a group critique of the previous week's assignment, a class discussion of the reading assignment and course handouts, a slide lecture on design theory, and a discussion of the new project assignment. Graphic arts methods, including hand skills, software, and output processes, are discussed briefly in the context of project critiques, but not taught; students are responsible for acquiring these skills independently.

This student group is quite mature—typically between age twenty-five and thirty-five—and comes from a wide range of professional and educational backgrounds. Most have technical, scientific, and business backgrounds and strong undergraduate educations; some have previous master's degrees.

Because all students can read and write, regardless of their varying inexperience with visual aesthetics, the project sequence begins with words. Also, page-design software is the easiest to master quickly. The initial projects convert texts into typography with structure, composition, and hierarchy, and move incrementally into abstract form, diagramming, imagery, and symbolism.

One of the project sequence's assumptions is that basic formal principles—point, line, plane, figure/ground, contrast, gesture, etc.—can be taught within the context of typographic page structure and applied communications problems. In this course, there is not enough time to teach these on their own, as in the Bauhaus/Swiss tradition, and it seems increasingly questionable whether these ever should be taught outside of an applied context.

The essential communications theories are always introduced within the context of a design exercise as well. Lecture examples are drawn from the history of twentieth-century visual communications design and fine art.

A central premise is that hand skills are relatively unimportant for this student group, whose graduate work and future professional roles in design management and strategy will involve minimal handcraft. Visual acuity and aesthetics can be taught while using software design processes—after all, mousing *is* a hand-eye skill and the computer allows rapid multiple iterations, allowing students to visualize far more variations than previously possible.

goals

1. To acquire basic problem-solving processes
2. To assimilate the basic principles of composition in two-dimensional media space
3. To acquire a basic typographic grammar to structure verbal messages in visual terms
4. To feel comfortable with imagery and understand its communicative role
5. To understand basic communications theories concerning audiences' interpretation of text and image, including semiotics, rhetoric, and narrative, and their applications to communications problems and the evaluation of design solutions
6. To acquire a basic knowledge of the history of typefaces and graphic design since the early Renaissance, and an appreciation of the historical context surrounding contemporary design
7. To acquire the requisite hand skills and software skills to execute Institute of Design graduate projects and to function effectively in future professional environments
8. To develop a comfort with and criteria for evaluating design solutions

9. To acquire a verbal vocabulary of design terms to articulate ideas about design
10. To assimilate and appreciate design culture
11. To discover an excitement about making design and planning design
12. To understand the range of professional practice contexts, i.e., media, scale, client types, organization style, lifestyle, location, etc., to inform realistic goals and graduate-course choices

description of classes

Weeks 1–2

All examples are from a project sequence by Jun Lee, Fall 2000: "Spying for love," based on a Yellow Pages *ad for a private investigator.*

Project 1: An 8″ × 8″ grid composition of a basic Yellow Pages ad text using one typeface family of limited variables.

Project 2: Photo documentation of the business site.

Visual skill: Message analysis, grid structure, and basic typographic page composition of a Yellow Pages ad text.

Theory: Grid syntax, typographic anatomy, introduction to classic typeface families, typographic history.

Lecture: Historical type structures and syntax.

lawrence investigations   38 years experience   24 hour service   domestic cases
free consultation   worldwide   criminal
civil
confidential   312 641 2121   illinois license
reasonable rates   117 000 597

spying for love

larry mayer featured in   sandy martin in
wall street journal   newsweek
chicago magazine   chicago tribune
channel 2 news

electronic bugs   surveillance   child custody
uncovered

missing persons   pre-marital

video and still
photography   background   undercover

106

Project 3's final typographic composition of a sketch sequence applies a judicious choice of typographic variables—two sizes and two weights of Bembo—to a four-column grid.

Project 3: A final 8" × 8" grid composition refined from several variations in which new typefaces are substituted in the previous week's composition.

Visual skill: Basic typographic page composition, an awareness of serif/sans serif distinctions and typographic variables.

Theory: Grid syntax, typographic anatomy, introduction to classic typeface families, typographic history.

Lecture: See/read discourse.

Week 4

Project 4: An 8" × 8" graphic diagram notating eye movement and composition.

Visual skill: Diagrammatic composition, invention of an abstract set of forms, color coding; user observation of five audience members' reading sequence of Project 3's typographic composition.

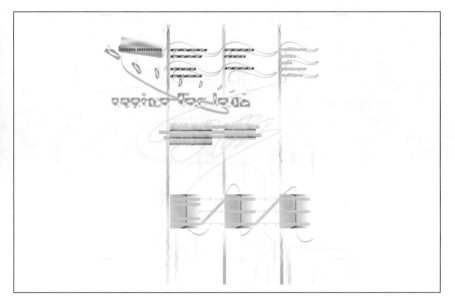

Project 4 notates the typographic composition's massing, structure, and hierarchy, and the readers' eye movement paths, using abstracted imagery taken in the student's concurrent photo class.

Theory: Semiotics classification of syntax, semantics, pragmatics. 107
Lecture: Charles Morris's three semiotic divisions: syntax, semantics, pragmatics.

Week 5

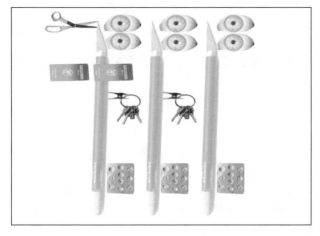

Project 5 notates the same elements of the typographic composition as Project 4, but replaces the abstract forms with images associated with marital conflict.

Project 5: Image substitution for the 8" × 8" eye movement notation's abstract elements.

Visual skill: Imagery as compositional form and gesture, color-coding.

Theory: Semantics and Charles S. Pierce's three "Classes of Signs": icon, index, symbol.

Lecture: Semantics: icon, index, symbol.

Week 6

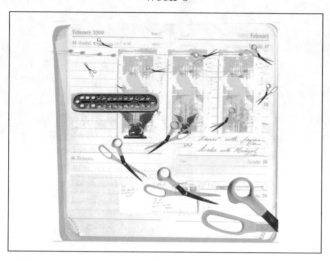

Step 6 continues the typographic composition notation, now using a narrative sequence of images that tell a story about an attractive woman involved with two men: she finds herself in a difficult situation that might involve pregnancy or the risk of it.

Project 6: Narrative image substitution for the 8" × 8" eye movement notation's first images.

Visual skill: Using semantic meaning to tell a story; imagery as indexical signs and symbols.

Theory: Narrative and visual storytelling.

Lecture: Narrative.

Week 7

Project 7: Typeset and proof by hand a selected text phrase from a *Yellow Pages* ad in lead type at the Galvin Library Special Collections Workshop.

Visual skill: Assimilate a physical sensibility of the significance of letter-spacing, leading, and point size.

Theory: Evolution of classical book tradition, typeface design, and reproduction technology.

m_ss_ng

The "i" letters are missing from the word "missing".

Project 8:
Semantic typography. Design a word from the *Yellow Pages* text that expresses its meaning through visual semantics.

Visual skill: Making typography visually expressive.

Theory: Typographic expression of meaning through visual coding as well as verbal coding.

Lecture: Semantic typography.

Week 9

Project 9 uses by, a bi-associational matrix system to generate identity symbols. A bat, a black cat, a cat's eye, and an officer's shield evolved into the final design in which a cat's eye emerges from the officer's shield/bat's wing.

Project 9: Identity symbol for the *Yellow Pages* business using indexical and symbolic imagery without letterforms.

Visual skill: Identity symbol design, reductive form development.

Theory: Identity symbol typology, corporate identity, branding; hybrid symbology, biassociation.

Method: Bedno's symbol-conceptualizing matrix.

Lecture: Identity symbols.

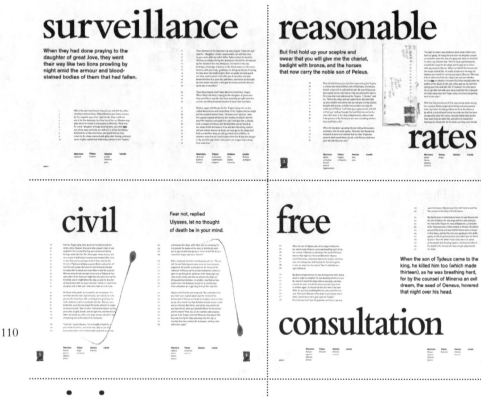

In Project 10, a section of the Iliad parallels and inter-relates with the Yellow Pages ad's text in brochure spreads.

Project 10: 8½" × 11" brochure with a second text juxtaposed to the *Yellow Pages* ad's text.

Visual skill: The design of a multiple-page document; organizational sequencing, compositional pacing; development and application of a consistent graphic language on a grid in theme and variation.

Theory: Grid system, sequential formatting, typographic theme, and variations.

Lecture: Katherine McCoy portfolio retrospective of grid systems in a multiple-page document design.

reasonable

But first hold up your sceptre and
swear that you will give me the chariot,
bedight with bronze, and the horses
that now carry the noble son of Peleus.

rates

civil

Fear not, replied
Ulysses, let no thought
of death be in your mind.

criminal

Diomed struck him in the middle of his neck with his sword and cut through both sinews
so that his head fell rolling in the dust while he was yet speaking.

free

When the son of Tydeus came to the
king, he killed him too (which made
thirteen), as he was breathing hard, for
the counsel of Minerva on an evil dream,
the seed of Oeneus, hovered that night
over his head.

consultation

111

domestic

When the sea-water had taken all the
sweat from off them, and had refreshed
them, they went into the baths and
washed themselves.

cases

*The images from the story about an
attractive woman involved with two
men are sequenced through the
brochure's page spreads, paralleling
the Iliad narrative and the* Yellow
Pages *ad's text.*

Project 11: 8½" × 11" brochure with two texts and narrative imagery from
Project 6.

Visual skill: The design of a multiple-page document; organizational
sequencing, compositional pacing; development and application of a consistent
graphic language on a grid in theme and variation; the creation of meaning
through juxtaposition; the placement and cropping of photographic imagery.

Theory: Relationship of imagery to typographic structure.

Narrative sequence: Writing systems and alphabets.

Lecture: Graphic language and writing systems.

Week 12

To advertise the private detective's investigative service to people experiencing marital difficulties, plaster wedding cake bride and groom figurines are encased in a plastic food storage bag, in an effort to preserve a marriage.

Project 12: A billboard or bus sign using rhetorical text and imagery for the *Yellow Pages* ad's business.

Visual skill: Writing a rhetorical text, designing a rhetorical hybrid image, and combining the two conceptually.

Theory: Rhetoric, persuasion, and seduction as communication design methods; text/image conceptual interaction.

Lecture: Rhetorical figures and strategies.

Week 13

To advertise the private detective's investigative service to young women experiencing marital difficulties, the student photographed a couple holding hands while the wife crosses her fingers behind her back.

Project 13: A billboard or bus sign using rhetorical text and imagery tailored for an interpretive community or subculture.

Visual skill: Writing a rhetorical text, designing a rhetorical hybrid image, and combining the two conceptually; using visual/verbal codes and rhetorical appeals appropriate to a targeted interpretive community.

Theory: Audience-centered communications strategies; rhetoric, persuasion, and seduction as communication design methods; text-image conceptual interaction.

Lecture: Audience-centered communications design.

Weeks 14–15

Refine projects and assemble portfolio binder.

Week 16

Final review: Final critique of projects and portfolio binder of mounted projects; individual reviews.

Notes on Images

Fall 2000 student project examples by Jun Lee.

Jun came to the Institute of Design at IIT with an undergraduate degree in neurobiology from Columbia University and two years as a research assistant at the Rockefeller University.

113

After completing the Institute of Design's one-year pregraduate program, he is now pursuing a Masters of Design in Communications Planning and Human-Centered Communications Design.

COURSE TITLE _ DESIGN REALITIES AND PROFESSIONAL
   PRACTICES
INSTRUCTOR _ Jan Conradi
SCHOOL _ SUNY, Fredonia
FREQUENCY _ One semester, fifteen weeks
CREDITS _ Three
LEVEL _ Undergraduate seminar for final semester, senior year

purpose

This course is intended as a transition course, shifting those enrolled from the mindset of student to that of design professional. Rather than working on visual problem solving and development of creative skills, the course instead focuses on other issues that can make or break a design career. While the instructor acts as facilitator in setting up a schedule, the students take responsibility for organizing discussions, researching to find answers and sources of information, and documenting and sharing information.

114

programmatic goal

Through this course we have an organized, logical place to discuss critical issues and ideas that may only have been touched upon in other coursework. It allows us to keep a tighter focus on creative development in other studios without being sidetracked, knowing that business and production information will be addressed here in a comprehensive fashion with adequate time to discuss and develop ideas and viewpoints. The faculty's goal is that students will gain a healthy respect for how little they do know, but through this overview they will also have erased some of the fears about asking questions and will have a basic understanding to guide them into knowing what sorts of questions to ask.

student goal

Students will use the information and contacts gathered during this course as resources to help them as they begin their design careers. Upon completion of the course, they will be more aware of and more confident about diverse aspects of working professionally. They will have a familiarity with terminology and issues and will have become accustomed to seeking answers to their questions. They will also have had an opportunity to polish written and spoken communication skills.

description of course

The course meets twice weekly for one and a half hours each time. The first meeting of the week generally focuses on student-led discussions; the second is consumed with a visiting professional who shares information, viewpoints, and dialogue with the students. Research and readings are independently conducted prior to each meeting. At each meeting, students are responsible for establishing a dialogue, sharing information, and documenting discussion content. The results of this are compiled by each student into an individual reference/resource notebook.

The course content falls predominantly into four categories: understanding how work is actually prepared, printed, and distributed; awareness of the network of people involved in the profession; realization of the impact of business practices; and concern for ethical and legal issues. The professor acts as a facilitator but is not the primary source for information. A regular influx of working professionals and shared information from classmates provides the majority of the content in this course.

A more detailed overview of content is this:

1. Printing and pre-press; media and technology
   - Press capabilities and limitations: offset, Web, flexography, etc.
   - Scanning and electronic file management for output preparation
   - Issues in pre-press planning, costing, and job coordination
   - Paper selection and specification
   - The importance of press checks
   - Supplier and service-bureau relationships
   - Press runs and price breaks

2. Legal affairs
   - Copyright and fair use
   - Influences and plagiarism
   - Business ethics
   - Business contracts for clients and job proposals
   - Contract preparation for freelance suppliers: photographers, illustrators, production artists, etc.

3. A productive workplace
   - Owning and managing a studio business
   - Successful freelancing
   - Marketing your strengths and building a client base
   - Time management: balancing work with the rest of your life
   - AIGA standards for professional practice
   - Record keeping and accurate cost estimating for creative professionals

4. Peripheral vision

- The relationship between copywriters and visual creatives
- Working with illustrators and photographers
- Health and safety in the professional studio
- Priming the creative pump
- Breaking into the global marketplace

assignments and projects

Assignment 1: Speaker Presentation Summary

Each student will be assigned as "reporter" for a speaker or a field-trip meeting. The reporter will be responsible for writing two things: a meeting summary and a thank you. The summary of the meeting includes a brief biography of the speaker, a synopsis of the material that was presented, and an overview of the follow-up questions and comments that were made. Inclusion of visual materials can be a part of the summary as appropriate. This will be typed and presented to the class during the following class period, with copies distributed to all members of the class and the professor.

The reporter is responsible for sending a thank-you to the speaker for generously sharing time and expertise with the class. A photocopy of the thank-you will be given to the professor. The thank-you must be mailed to the speaker within a week of the presentation.

Assignment 2: Project Cost Estimate

Working in teams and in consultation with the professor, students will select a completed design or typography project from another course and will be responsible for writing a thorough project specification sheet, contacting a printer, and getting estimates for printing the project. After getting the estimates, each team will write a summary report about the process they completed and what they learned from it. The summary report will include comparisons of pricing and a discussion of price differences between seemingly similar projects. Again, each team should write a thank-you to the printer who provided cost estimates.

Assignment 3: Topic Research Paper and Presentation

Imagine that *Print* has contacted you to write an article, so your audience is other professional designers. In consultation with the professor, select a specific topic to research. If the topic is an editorial opinion, it must be backed up with researched examples. Document all sources that were consulted. Visuals are recommended as appropriate, but are not required. Students will also give a presentation about their topic to the class; five to ten minutes in length. Be prepared to lead a discussion about the topic after your presentation.

Possible topics include:

- Work for hire. How has this affected others (look up Condé Nast)? How could this affect you?
- Type legalities. Font licenses, downloading, sharing with printer— what is legal?
- Design competitions. Do they have value?
- Starting your own firm. The pros and cons.
- Spec work. What is it, why is it not recommended, and what if a client wants it?
- Global design. What do you need to consider when translating work into other languages?
- Design with an agenda. The designer as an agent of social change.
- Market research. What role can/should this play in a designer's work?
- Packaging. Are people buying the product or the package? Does it matter?
- Imitation versus inspiration. Where is the line?
- How can you ignite the creativity spark?

Assignment 4: Assembled Reference Notebook

Each of you will create a notebook documenting all materials read, researched, and discussed during the semester. The intent of this notebook is to provide you with a relatively current and comprehensive source for referral when you begin working professionally. Copies of articles beyond those discussed in class should be included. Remember, I do not want to see plain photocopies: I want to see highlighting and side notes and other signs that you have actually read and thought about these materials.

When the final notebook is submitted, include a two- to three-page paper. This is a summary of the course and its content from your viewpoint. Analyze what was done, what you learned, and how this impacts your decisions as you begin looking for a professional position. It should be titled and any quoted materials should be documented.

description of classes

NOTE: There are specific speakers scheduled on speaker nights; for the purpose of this text, I have just given topics as a guideline.

Week 1

Introduction; brainstorm on topics and content; select research topic.
Speaker: Visit printing firm and talk to the senior press operator.

Week 2

Open discussion.
Speaker: Paper selection and specification.

Week 3

Discuss printing and paper terminology.
Speaker: Issues in digital pre-press technology (trapping, color correx, etc.).

Week 4

Discuss impact of design history; what makes a design timeless?
Speaker: Press checks and working with printers.

Week 5

Research paper due; open discussion.
Speaker: Copyrights, contracts, and permissions.

Week 6

Two presentations and discussion
Speaker: Small design studio (emphasis on two-dimensional and advertising)

Week 7

Two presentations and discussion
Speaker: Large multifaceted design studio (exhibition, retail, and packaging)

Week 8

Two presentations and discussion
Speaker: Accountant (the financial business of design)

Week 9

Two presentations and discussion
Speaker: Operating a studio (managing people and time)

Week 10

Cost estimate due. Discussion of cost-estimate findings.
Speaker: Freelance designer.

Week 11

Two presentations and discussion.
Speaker: Illustrator.

Week 12

Two presentations and discussion
Speaker: Photographer

Week 13

Two presentations and discussion
Speaker: Copywriter

Week 14

Speaker: Web design and new media.
Discuss: New media issues.
Course notebooks are due by the end of the week.

Week 15

Final meeting; summary discussion

evaluation comments from students
who have taken this course

"I learned that to make it in this industry you need to be proactive. All of the knowledge I gained in this course is an asset to all of us. We need to start living and breathing design and get our heads out of the classroom. This class showed me this."

"This class has definitely impacted my decisions as I am beginning my professional career. I have dreamed about starting my own design studio. I have learned that it takes a lot more than a dream."

"I feel that this course was a huge benefit to me. It gave an enormous understanding of the bigger picture and how the concept is carried through to reality."

"One of the most beneficial parts of this class was the Cost Estimate Project. Discussing different paper stocks, size formats, quantities, and even varnishes within our group was a great way to learn. Understanding what the printer requires is the most critical part of producing our work."

"The goal of the class was to have an understanding of the complexities of a graphic designer's daily career. The objective of the class was to create a living, working, useful binder. The process of the class was teamwork. I liked the class. The speakers were wonderful and I learned so much from them. They added so much to my life. I don't think I'll ever get an opportunity to experience learning like that again."

COURSE TITLE _ GRAPHIC DESIGN V, PROFESSIONAL POSITIONING
INSTRUCTOR _ Deborah Huelsbergen
SCHOOL _ University of Missouri, Columbia
FREQUENCY _ Sixteen weeks, fall semester
CREDITS _ Three
LEVEL _ Undergraduate

purpose

The goal of this course is to allow advanced students to choose between projects so that they can fill in gaps in their portfolios. They are given limited direction so that they can write their own project briefs, thus tailoring them to their individual needs.

description

This course is about choice and making the right decisions for your future. You will choose the projects that are right for your particular needs. The projects here will often be given to you with few limitations, thus forcing you to make decisions and budget your time appropriately. It is important to remember that the high expectations of this course are specifically structured to give you the best possible preparation for the profession of graphic design.

You will start with a menu of options in four categories. After selecting an option you will write a brief to clarify all details of the project. These are both required and graded parts of the project and they must be typed and formally written. The brief should include your objectives for the project; why you selected this particular project and what you hope to achieve by doing it; how you plan to solve the problem, i.e., your methodology; and what the finished piece(s) will entail.

description of classes

The course is essentially broken down into four, four-week chunks. Projects are introduced and students turn in their briefs the following class meeting. Students meet with other individuals who select the same project and devise a schedule for the four weeks. Lectures and demonstrations are scattered throughout the semester. The dates for these depend on the schedules that the students devise. There are lectures and demonstrations on days where a major critique is not planned. Lecture topics are as follows: readability and legibility, printing, navigational structures for Web sites, and self-promotion and portfolio structures. Demonstrations range from bookbinding to digital photography to Flash.

Assignment Menu

Appetizers

Calendar Design

(A delicious little project—just the thing to start a semester off right!)

This will need to be a unique and individual way to present the months and days; it can be text and image, or just text. The calendar should have a theme or concept behind it to unify the design, and you will need to present all months and a cover.

For/Against Posters

(Looking for something with a little more spice? Try this two-part project.)

Pick a controversial topic and produce one poster for the topic and one poster against the topic. Both posters need to be equally convincing and powerful no matter which side of the argument you agree with most.

Abstract Symbology

(An assortment of tasty designs really hits the spot if your portfolio is light in the logo department.)

Devise a series of symbols that encompass all aspects of each of the following three abstract terms: *education, religion,* and *agriculture.* The symbols will need to be black and white and work at a variety of sizes.

121

Trip Down Memory Lane

(An old-time favorite: choose from one of the fabulous projects from Graphic Design One or Two and see what happens.)

Choose a project from Graphic Design One or Two and rework from the beginning of the project. This is not meant to fix up an old project, but rather to see how you would solve it now with your added experience.

First Course

Annual Report

(Hungry for type? Try this beefy project—a real challenge for designers!)

You will be redesigning the 2000 annual report from the Clearly Canadian Beverage Company. If photos are to be included, they will need to be your own.

Newsletter

(Perhaps a little lighter than the annual report, but still a great display of text-heavy design.)

For this you will need to use an existing newsletter from a campus organization. Using their text and images, rework the design and format of the newsletter. You should approach this as a very limited-budget project.

Chair Book

(This all-time favorite will have your creative juices flowing and allow the kid in you to help with your design.)

Design and produce an interactive book for a fourth-grade audience that explains a chair design. Please have your chair and designer approved with me before beginning.

Book Design
(A perfect project for the reader, this classy portfolio piece has been a real hit.)
You will begin by selecting and reading one of the books on my reading list. You will be required to redesign the inside and outside of the book and produce a full-size, bound mock-up. In addition to the dust jacket, you will be required to design all front material in the book as well as three chapters.

Cookbook Design
(This mouthwatering project will have all of your friends begging you for samples.)
Design a unique cookbook for a unique audience. You may pull recipes from an existing cookbook but the concept will be your own. A full-size, bound mock-up will be required. In addition to the cover, you will need to include a minimum of twelve recipes.

Second Course

Packaging System
(A refreshing change from two-dimensional pieces, this one will leave you satisfied.)
For this selection you may choose between two of the projects that we do in packaging design. The first problem is to develop a system of packages for a beverage company. This could be for juice, soda, water, beer, wine, etc. There needs to be a minimum of three packages in this system. The second choice is a highly conceptual problem. You will need to package something intangible, for example fear, love, hate, sadness, tranquility, confidence, etc. This is all about concept and form and how this thing will look, feel, taste, sound, or whatever it takes to get the idea across.

Game Design
(A flavorful choice for the gutsy designer, this project has been a portfolio favorite around here.)
The problem here is to research, plan, design, and present rough sketches of a game through a full-color, working comprehensive, including packaging and logo. The games must be complete, including all rules and pieces, as the class will need to be able to play them. This game should be of your own making, not a reworking of an existing game.

Typeface Design
(This typographic project will have your fingers flying and your friends in awe of your talent.)
Here you will need to design and produce a working typeface. You will begin with sketches and then produce the face in the program Fontographer.

To present the typeface you will design a poster advertising the typeface. You will need to include all twenty-six letters, upper- and lowercase, numbers, and limited punctuation (. , ? ! : ; ").

Branding

(An exquisite assortment of pieces that show off your talent to create identity.)

For this choice you will need to design an identity system for an imaginary company. You will need to decide on the name of the company and all relevant information before starting. You will need to show, in as many ways as possible, the versatility and completeness of your identity system.

Dessert

Promotional Web Site and Résumé

(This delectable project is the perfect way to end your undergraduate career.)

Design and produce a Web site that showcases your work and résumé. This should be something that you can send (such as the URL) to a prospective employer. I expect this to be unique and well thought out in terms of navigation—just spend a little time on the Web and you can see loads of examples of bad personal Web sites.

Creative Portfolio and Résumé

(A yummy choice for those of you who are feeling like something more tangible.)

When I was a student, I really wanted my résumé to be able to fold up into a fun party hat. My teacher said that was dumb; I still think it isn't.

Sorry . . . O.K., back to the point. Design an original presentation of your portfolio and résumé: is it a key chain, a stick of gum, a sandwich, a book? Think not only creatively but also about where these might be sent and who will be looking at them.

Personal Campaign and Résumé

(This unique choice is just the thing for the maverick in the crowd who just has to be different.)

When a new product is introduced onto the market, an entire campaign is set in motion. Here, you are the new product that is going to be introduced when you graduate. If you pick this option, you are thinking about your portfolio, résumé, follow-up cards, etc.

purpose

Graphic Design Thesis is designed to define the complex intersection between personal voice, conceptual understanding, and the ability to conduct and use research effectively in the service of creating a compelling, finely crafted public communication.

description of classes

With the exception of the initial class meeting (presentation of topic), midterm critique and the final critique, each student meets with two faculty members individually every week. Faculty rotate, so that if, for example, four faculty are teaching, the student will always be reviewed by one faculty member from the prior week and one faculty member who has not seen the student for two weeks (addressing the needs for continuity and fresh perspective). Student progress in research and form development is assessed and redirected as necessary. Faculty do not always agree with each other, but at this level of development, the disagreements often serve to inform.

Introduction

Thesis (Graphic Design 5) is the culmination of your design education at CCAC. It was created by Michael Vanderbyl to challenge and ultimately broaden our understanding of what it means to be a designer. The class is largely self-directed and presents you with an extraordinary opportunity to identify an area of interest and investigate it, using design as the vehicle through which you present your findings.

Students are graded on the creation and presentation of four components: a thesis proposal, research, a thesis project, and a process book.

The Thesis Proposal

The thesis proposal is a proposition or argument—usually based on an original observation—which you intend to support through research. The proposal might detail your anticipated investigation or address the potential implications of your proposition.

Successful Thesis Proposals

Your thesis proposal is your map for the semester. A clear, well-written proposal will direct your research, the form of your thesis project, and its design. A muddy, illogical proposal will lead you into the design wilderness, where animals, faculty, and other nasties will nip at your heels.

Let's consider the following proposal (reproduced in its entirety) from Toshie Hayakawa:

> I will examine how national identity is reflected and defined by the idea of size in the United States and Japan.

You will find that brevity is a blessing for both inaugural speeches and thesis proposals. That aside, what argument is the student making? What is her thesis? Namely, that national identity is reflected and defined by the idea of size in the U.S. and Japan. Simple.

Here is a more complex proposal written by Ellen Gould:

> **Text as Memory**
> Visual organization plays a crucial role in any effort to receive or recover written information. I intend to show that the visual form of a text can serve as an aid to memory, by developing new mnemonic systems for the page. Drawing on medieval practices known as the "Art of Memory," I want to introduce the architectural mnemonic—the room as a unit of memory—into the world of print, where the page becomes a unit of memory. Of particular importance is the idea that typographic space provides an additional level of meaning and is essential to the visual memory of text.

Longer, yes, but equally compelling. (If this were a steak, it would be large but lean—all the fat has been trimmed off.) The observation? Reread the first sentence. The proposition? Reread the second sentence. The anticipated investigation? Look at the third sentence. The map is neatly in place, for both the student and the faculty.

Unsuccessful Thesis Proposals

Consider the following proposal:

Functional objects for the home are aesthetically enhanced as a method of enticing and delighting the user. I intend to examine the relationship of the aesthetic enhancement to the object and whether it enables, overpowers, destroys, or eclipses its function. In addition, I will examine the cases in which functional objects of business have been introduced and popularized in the home office through aesthetic enhancement.

What is the student's thesis? Reread the proposal.

There is no thesis because there is no argument. That functional objects for the home are aesthetically enhanced to entice and delight the user (i.e., the consumer) is well known and not surprising. What are objects for the home supposed to do, anyway? Frustrate and torment the user? This is not an argument because no one would argue the point. It is an observation only, and an obvious one at that.

Unsuccessful proposals tend to rely on sloppy writing, which stems from sloppy thinking. Consider the following statement excerpted from a proposal:

Technology has led to the death of interaction among people.

Really? The death? Don't we use technology to interact when we make a telephone call? When we hand a store clerk a credit card? There may be a decline in meaningful interaction in America in 2002, but is this due to technology? If so, which technology? And what is meant by "technology" anyway?

Don't disregard logic (or what we know) to try to prove your point. A proposal that raises questions because it is illogical or confusing is unhelpful to both you and your audience. Recall that design is a communication art, not an obfuscation art.

Tips:

1. Start with what interests you. What are you obsessed with? What are you passionate about? What do you like reading and thinking about? What topic will sustain your interest for fifteen weeks?
2. Make sure you *have a point*. What are you arguing?
3. Do not base your proposal on the obvious. For example, noting that "gardens have become a pseudo-version of nature" is not a new or original observation, and few would argue this point.
4. Shorter is usually better. Pretend your proposal is a logo: if it ain't necessary, take it out.
5. Think through your claims. Are they true? Logical? Do you believe them? Will others believe them? If they are true, what are the ramifications? (Exploring the ramifications may be the bulk of your project!)
6. Do not make sweeping statements for dramatic effect or without supporting them with documentation.
7. Define your terms. What do you mean by "aesthetics" or "utopia"? And use the most common definitions of these terms! A proposal that depends on the least-used definitions of key words is doomed.

8. Do not claim that you will prove anything—we are designers, not cold-fusion scientists.

9. Please be aware that you will revise your proposal as your research dictates and your process evolves. (Sometimes it will change completely—including your topic!) The fortunate aspect of this is that all of your writing and rewriting will become content for your process book.

Research

Readings, visual audits, interviews, and bibliography. Generally speaking, research will form the backbone of your project: it is the structural support on which your design flesh will hang. Done properly, research will help you generate ideas and hone your concept. The following notes on research were adapted from a text written by Karen Fiss.

Research for this class involves developing a thesis (a proposition or argument) that you will support with primary and secondary sources. The purposes of your research are many: to understand how to evaluate what you see and read; to develop your own opinions and critical frameworks based on informed judgments—not simply on what you like and don't like; to acquire the critical skills to discern reliable/useful sources from the junk; to evaluate your own work in light of what you learn through research; to develop your own understanding of the relationship of history/theory to practice; and, ultimately, to have the chance to explore a topic that interests you in a more in-depth fashion.

You can use materials from your everyday life as research, but you should also be reading texts of intellectual merit. Generally speaking, a source has "intellectual merit" if that source has been "juried." (All university press books and journals are juried.) This means that each manuscript is first sent out to a series of "experts" in the field of inquiry and then rewritten and edited according to their recommendations. Realize that you cannot overly depend on one source, but that you will need to find multiple sources offering different perspectives on your subject. You will then need to evaluate these different opinions in order to forge your own argument.

You should develop a bibliography first. Make sure you can get your hands on the materials and determine the usefulness and merit of each source. When you find a good text, you should mine its footnotes and bibliography for additional sources. You should also use catalogue databases. There are dozens of specialized databases devoted to different disciplines. This "book and article" research should become an organic component of your working process. You need to learn how to delimit your topic, when to stop reading, when to make things, and when to return to reading to refine your ideas.

The Web can be a useful research tool. A word of caution, however: you need to learn how to evaluate Web sites just as you need to learn how to evaluate the scholarly merit of printed texts. In the humanities, printed texts still tend to be more reliable than Web sources.

Tips:

1. Let your topic dictate the type of research you do, and have an idea of what you are looking for.
2. Maintain a level of cynicism. Be critical of your sources, and do not merely adopt a point of view without reading competing sources/opinions.
3. Consult with an expert mentor in your chosen field of study. His input will be invaluable.
4. Develop a system for note-taking as you read. Transcribe salient thoughts and quotes as you encounter them so you don't waste time looking for them later.
5. Footnote your sources.
6. Avoid reading pseudo-science. Remember *Chariots of the Gods*? (It held that extraterrestrials built the pyramids at Giza. It was a best-seller.)
7. Interviewing all of your friends about your topic is not research of intellectual merit.

The Thesis Project

The thesis project is a proposition or argument explicated by design and supported by research.

Your thesis project is the physical manifestation of, and the conclusion to, your thesis proposal. The form that it takes should be determined by the nature of your proposal and its content: "Form-making in the service of an idea," as Michael Vanderbyl has put it. Some proposals will best be explored in a time-based medium like video; other ideas will communicate more effectively as installations or as books. The goal is to wed your proposal with the most appropriate form for your message. (You may not know the exact form your thesis will take until midterm, or shortly thereafter.) Successful thesis projects have taken a variety of forms over the years, and have included book design, furniture design, installations, multimedia design, painting, performance, sound design, type design, and video.

Interestingly, Maya Lin, designer of the Vietnam Veterans Memorial, works in a similar way to thesis students. Louis Menand describes her creative process: "The response is where Lin starts her work as a designer. . . . There is no image in her head, only an imagined feeling. Often, she writes an essay explaining what the piece is supposed to do to the people who encounter it." The form of the project only comes to Lin after she has articulated the purpose/intended effect of the project.

Regardless of the form your thesis project takes, you should be aware that you are creating a narrative—that you are in fact engaged in the process of making an argument. What is your core message? (What is the one thought your audience will walk away with after experiencing the piece?) What are your secondary messages, and what is their relationship to the core message? What are the ramifications of this message? (What is its meaning to you, to me, to society, to design?) How are you supporting this core message? What evidence—visual and otherwise—are you supplying to argue your point? The novelist Anna Quindlen offers a piece of advice for writers that is applicable to thesis students: learn to distinguish between those details that simply exist and those that reveal. Do not merely compile information, in other words, but choose, edit, and present your content to inform, surprise, entertain, challenge, and argue.

Think about the sequence and pacing of this narrative. What is your introduction? (A well-written thesis proposal usually functions as a de facto introduction.) What is your conclusion? Consider the tone of your narrative. Is it authoritative? Reverential? Tongue-in-cheek?

If your thesis project explores a personal theme, it is incumbent upon you to make the personal universal. As Vanderbyl has noted, "Communication is the crux of thesis and the crux of the profession." If your project is so personal that it fails to communicate, it fails.

Tips:

1. Do not have preconceived ideas about what form your project will take. Let the form be determined by your proposal and content.
2. Create a written outline of your narrative/argument diagramming your core and secondary messages. This outline, when paired with visuals and select research, will serve as a guide to the realization of your thesis project.
3. Give your audience "multiple access points" to your content. Deliver your information on several levels: the "quick read," or overview, as well as the elaborations. The overview will allow you to hook them and then lead them deeper into your content.
4. The visual language of your thesis should be appropriate to your subject/content. (Bauhaus Modernism might create a cognitive dissonance if your subject is poodles, for instance.)
5. If you are unfamiliar with your chosen medium—video, for instance—don't assume you will successfully accomplish your project in ten (or seven or five or three) weeks. Make realistic time allowances for the inevitable learning curve.
6. Approach the idea of creating an installation with some trepidation. It is extremely difficult to do well!

The Process Book

A bound record of your thinking and design process.

Your process book should include your writing, research, design investigations, successes, and failures—in short, it should document how you got from point A to point Z in fifteen weeks. (Include all of your steps, including

129

abandoned topics!) It should also include annotated footnotes and a bibliography. For those who create something temporal as their thesis project (like a performance piece or installation), the process book is quite likely the only artifact from the thesis you will be able to show a prospective employer in an interview.

Tips:

1. Work on your process book in tandem with your thesis project. Sometimes at midterm it becomes clear that the process book is actually a better model for the thesis project than your proposed prototype. (If you haven't worked on your process book you lose the opportunity to make this observation.)

2. Consider hiring a bindery to bind your book. It'll look swell . . .

Strategies

The gulf between an interesting topic and a workable proposal can be vast. The goal here is to elucidate an original observation about your topic—to make us (your audience) reconsider the topic or see it in a new light.

A perfect example of this can be found in Michael Pollan's book *The Botany of Desire*. In it, Pollan proposes a refreshing thesis: namely, that plants have evolved to gratify certain human desires so that humans will grow these plants and further their species. In short, plants are using us. (If you are interested in how he arrived at this observation you should read the first few pages of Pollan's introduction.) Pollan's thesis was (unconsciously) arrived at by adopting a conceptual strategy. He took the prevailing opinion—humans use plants—and proposed the opposite: plants use humans. This is a strategy of opposition, and is the basis for a student arguing that "suburbia is utopia," or that "driving an automobile is an illusion of freedom."

Other strategies include using the personal to communicate the universal; examining societal taboos (the public/private space of the public bathroom); proposing new avenues for design (designing a typeface for dyslexics); or elevating the little-noticed to a place of prominence in the world ("the mechanical click is an essential intermediary between humans and machines").

Tips:

1. Your topic is separate from your thesis proposal. It is possible to have a promising topic and a problematic thesis proposal. Learn when to jettison your topic and when to merely rework your proposal.

Sequence/Schedule

Jennifer Morla recommends adhering to the following sequence of work:
Research > Analysis > Design Intent > Methodology > Fabrication > Documentation

Research: From readings, visual audits, interviews, observations, etc.

Analysis: What have I learned from this research? What does it mean? (Diagrams are organized research.)

Design Intent: What could I do with this research? What point am I trying to make? (What is my thesis?)

Methodology: How could I do it? What would be the best form to convey my ideas? (Is it a book, film, etc.?)

Fabrication: How will I make it? Do I need to collaborate with anyone to make it?

Documentation: Your process book.

Your own experience will no doubt be more fluid than the sequence outlined above, but this should help you create a schedule so you know you are making progress at the correct pace. In a perfect world you will have determined your methodology by midterm.

Midterm

Generally speaking, your midterm crit will be more challenging than your final crit. There are two reasons for this: you will be reviewed by the full thesis committee for the first time, and they will be unfamiliar with your thesis; moreover, at midterm there is still time to address fundamental deficiencies in your thesis proposal. At midterm you will present a refined thesis proposal and a detailed prototype (or layouts, storyboards, scale drawings, etc.) of your thesis project. Your process book—truly "in process" and not bound—and a schedule detailing how you will execute your thesis project in the remaining weeks are due as well.

Tips:

1. Tape record your midterm crit so you can review the committee's comments at a later date. Some of the criticism may not make sense to you until later and you risk forgetting valuable insights.
2. Take responsibility for your critiques. What is it you want to know? What feedback are you looking for? Ask questions. If your critique is generating unhelpful information, change the direction of the critique.
3. If your thesis proposal and project are insupportable at the midterm, you should seriously consider withdrawing from the course. You have until the tenth week of the semester to do so.

conclusion

This class may be the only time in your life when you will be encouraged to research an area of personal interest, author an original viewpoint, and then design a piece of your choosing to showcase this research and viewpoint. It is a tremendous opportunity that should be both challenging and fun. Make the most of it! As your faculty, we are committed to helping you do so.

Bob Aufuldish, Leslie Becker, Karen Fiss, Terry Irwin, Jim Kenney, Jennifer Morla, and Michael Vanderbyl contributed to the ideas and text of this guide.

addendum one: further examples of successful thesis proposals

A Proposal by Ellen Malinowski: Context Yields Definition

A word's meaning consists of its inherent definition and the interpretation implied by the context in which it is used. Context is the tool we use to grasp meaning, and in some cases it dictates meaning when the definition of a word is unintelligible. I intend to show that a word does not have meaning without context regardless of its established definition. I will undermine the process by which language is understood in order to subvert the idea of definition.

A Proposal by Wendy Li

We live in a world of globalization, an age of fast information exchange and mobility. With the blurring of boundaries, what in the world is authentic? I intend to question the existence of authenticity. In my exploration, I will examine the notion of authenticity by juxtaposing the old to the new, the primitive to the modern, and the natural to the artificial.

addendum two: advice and observations from fellow students

Three Tips

1. Don't believe *anything* you've heard about the instructors; none of it is true. Those preconceived notions might cause you to be on the defensive during crits rather than receptive to helpful advice and criticism. They know what they are talking about, and they know a lot.

2. The more original the topic, the more fun you will have, and the better response you will get. The more cliché the topic, the more struggle you will have finding an interesting angle that hasn't already been done.

3. Stating a thesis means you have to *make a point*. (Ellen Malinowski)

Make a Schedule

I made a very rough schedule for my project right after the first class. I divided the semester into six phases according to the steps Jennifer mentioned (research, analysis, design intent, methodology, fabrication), so that my project could be produced properly. I think it was very helpful for me to maximize the limited number of crit sessions. I needed to do a lot of work everyday to meet the schedule, but I found that the more I investigated during the week, the more I could show at the crit. The more I showed at the crit, the more feedback I received. A schedule enabled me to work steadily to complete the project, and spared me from doing everything at the last moment. (Aya Akazana)

Make Connections

Imagine Thesis as a cross between a research paper and a design project. Once I realized the connection between assembling a research paper and assembling a design project, things started to happen for me. I had to learn how to connect seemingly disparate ideas together, and not to be afraid to look outside the cultural theory realm to find some answers. (Amy Lam)

Research

Address students to do research in *support* of their project. Some people were just doing research randomly and wasting their time because they were simply told to do so. (Helena Seo)

133

Trust Yourself

It's impossible to please all four instructors, so ultimately you must make decisions based on your own intuition and design sense. (Amelia Leclaire)

This class was set up in such a way that each week we were looking for approval. There came a point at which waiting for approval was counterproductive and I just had to have faith that I could run with the concept. (Rosana Mojica)

Last Thoughts

Words cannot justly describe how profound an effect Thesis had on me. In addition to the self-discipline, Thesis pushed me to really see things as a designer and artist in a whole new realm. The vigor and intensity have given me a whole new approach to my work. (Rachel Pearson)

This class really helped me to learn how to *think*, how to *plan*, and how to *convey*. And not only the aspects of improving my visual skill; it gave me a great opportunity to understand myself better. I found out what I'm good at, and more importantly what I'm *not* good at. (Helena Seo)

I appreciated the Thesis faculty's interest in my project. Up to this point most of my work was seen as "weird" by instructors and students alike. It still is, but I see it as a strength now. Weird is good. Weird is me. The class had the level of thoughtfulness and intensity I looked forward to when I enrolled at level three. (Eugene Young)

COURSE TITLE _ BORDERLAND
INSTRUCTOR _ Cheryl Brzezinski-Beckett
SCHOOL _ University of Houston, Graphic Communications
CREDITS _ Three
FREQUENCY _ Semester (fifteen weeks)
LEVEL _ Undergraduate, seniors

purpose

Cross borders, cross boundaries to encourage an examination of self and the surrounding environment. Remove barriers: go beyond the familiar and the comfortable to activate the senses. Designers should continually reach into the unknown, discover, and be surprised. For the student, a broader worldview, receptivity to new ideas, questions of accepted norms, and exploration of possibilities evolve by venturing beyond the classroom.

Houston's close proximity to Mexico, with its powerful social and political influence on everyday life, offers a unique opportunity to develop a semester on the topic of borders. A four-day bus journey through the Rio Grande valley from Laredo to Brownsville, daily traversing the river, is a fitting site for exploration and research of the "borderland." Projects for the semester investigate connections between cultures, land, customs, people, and the built environment. The journey is expanded through the knowledge of local experts, activists, and writers. On one such journey, the first expert, an architectural historian, narrated walking tours of the border towns. These tours drew comparisons between the urban planning of towns and cities on each side of the border and its effect on the local community. Vernacular architecture links history, the land, and the people. The Laredo Planning Commission, the second group of contributors, introduced the history and relationships between Laredo and Nuevo Laredo. As sponsors for the international architectural competition to redesign the Bridge of the Americas connecting the two cities, the commission described the meaning and rationalization behind the submissions. The final individual, a poet and long-term resident of both sides of the border, presented language as a voice of expression altered by place. Ideas and attitude change with the transition from Spanish to English and back again.

course introductory handout: borderline

A border, by definition, is an edge. When speaking in geographic or political terms, this edge demarcates a place, distinguishing it from other places. Countries, nations, states, counties—the world is segmented into units of definition and separation—one place from another, us from them. Identities are determined by your position in relation to this borderline at the time of your birth. The border may become a boundary, with its implication of limitation, a barrier or prison wall that may be mental, physical, emotional, cultural, or constructed. Knowledge or ignorance, sanity or insanity, are borders of our mind. Cultural expectations, rituals, mores, and taboos establish social boundaries. Our own physical body defines a boundary that may be broken through the virtual world of cyberspace or through spiritual journeys.

This semester, we will visit a specific border. The U.S./Mexico border stretches two thousand miles, from San Diego, California to Brownsville, Texas. Sometimes defined geographically by prominent features such as the Rio Grande (*Rio Bravo del Norte* if you were born south of the river), often as not, this border is represented by "the wild places of the desert, stark canyon, and semi-tropics where the border is nothing more than a line on a map that you carry in your back pocket."[1]

Although a border demarcates an edge, this edge is not impervious. The U.S./Mexico border has been labeled "MexAmerica," with cultural distinctions spilling over both sides of the Rio Grande. The region has been described as porous,[2] a sponge, and an osmotic membrane.[3] It "supercedes the more abstract state boundaries on either side and . . . is considered by the powers that be . . . as irrelevant except as a place of passage for goods and people. [The people of the border] are living in a 'deconstitutionalized' zone."[4] Despite the cultural leak, an ever vigilante border patrol (*la migra*) attempts to maintain solidity and definition to this edge.

With globalization through the media and the constant transaction of people, services, and goods, political staking may be the only border of any major consequence. Questions about cultural identity are raised as we move toward more shared experiences through television and the Internet. Does the border help protect a cultural heritage defined by history and tradition? Or is cultural heritage passé, destined to oblivion in our contemporary society? By showcasing traditional crafts, language, music, dance, and ritual, are we commodifying heritage (the "Disneyfication" of the culture), branding the border, enhancing a myth, or preserving cultural distinctions?

As we explore the border, we move away from the lenses of others—books, research, television, newspapers—and actually experience what the border reveals to us. We become "cultural nomads," better understanding the world and learning more about ourselves through the eyes of others.

Design by Kandy Lloyd

description of classes

Projects

Project 1: From the Edge: Postcards

As "cultural nomads," we will explore our southern neighbors for insight into their history and culture. Past and present weave together, forming a visual, cultural, political, and social fabric that portrays similarities and differences from our own personal experiences. As observers from a distance, we rely on the research of others to capture a world revealed through imagery, symbolism, and language.

137

The postcard is often a format that represents "place." They are cards that say "we are here," at a place unique from our familiar territory. Postcard imagery tends to mythologize through super-saturated colors and idealized imagery. These cards allow sentiments to cross over borders and boundaries, linking locations—a correspondence between places as well as people.

Objectives: Create a series of four postcards that analyze and stylize imagery from Mexico's culture. Research your assigned topic, collect imagery, and organize information to present in class. The collective data will form a foundation for understanding a sample of influences that have shaped Mexico's culture. This increased knowledge acquired before the border journey will add meaning and context. When designing the postcards, view them as correspondence from one language to another, from one location to another, from one time period to another. Provide imagery and text to imply place, time, history, and meaning.

List of Topics: Since the topics are broad, conduct initial research to focus the content. Many regions and towns specialize in a craft, food, dance, music, and/or architecture.

- Day of the Dead
- Religion
- Cuisine
- Dance
- Music
- Aztecs
- Mayans
- Traditional clothing (select a region)
- The Spanish Conquistadors

- Zapatistas
- Vaquero
- Hacienda
- Crafts (select a specific town/region that excels in the selected craft)
  —Carved and painted animals (Oaxaca)
  —Pottery/tile (Talevera)
  —Weaving

—Jewelry/silver (Taxco)
—Copper (Santa Clara de Cobre)
- Architecture
- The land
- Toys
- War
- Frida Kahlo, Diego Rivera
- Mexico City history

System: Design the front and back of each 6" × 8.5" card. Concentrate on image-making, stylization, and media. Present the four cards as a series, with systematic similarities developed through: color palette, imagery, icons, mood, media, structure, typography, and language (Spanish/English).

Project 2: Defining Boundaries: Posters

The upcoming border trip provides an opportunity for experiential observation and sensory insight. The people, the land, the river, the built environment, history, language, customs, war, politics, and economics have made their mark. Though unable to witness all that has shaped this region, we should be conscious of its significance as we travel the border.

Objectives: Create a 24" × 36" poster that presents one or more definitions of the border using the Rio Grande river symbolically as the boundary between Mexico and the United States.

Concept: The poster must make a statement about the border—political, social, cultural, architectural, historical, personal, mythical, etc. Consider using photos taken during the trip. Combine the experience of the trip with researched information, ideas, and commentary. The poster must demarcate the river at parallel entrance and exit points defining a 9-inch strip. This represents the river symbolically. This poster will be part of a series of twenty-three posters, one by each student. All posters must use black as the linking color. Additional colors may be incorporated as long as black remains dominant. The posters may be horizontal or vertical.

Documentation: Reduce the poster series to approximately 6" × 9" color copies to be distributed among the class. Design a box or folio.

Project 3: Journal (Optional)

Create a more personal statement documenting the journey. Collect photos, text, ephemera, and information while traveling. Be prepared to take notes based on personal observation and the information of Stephen Fox, the Laredo Planning Commission, and Rachel Senties. Format possibilities include: an accordion fold (with the river delineated), boxes, bags, scroll, envelopes, letters, or other options that enhance the concept. Upon returning to Houston, combine information and images about the border, the idea of borders and boundaries, being a cultural nomad, and the spirit of Mexico. Create a refined version.

Project 4: El Portal: A City Embraced by Two Countries—*the Catalogue*
Organize and design a catalogue showcasing the entries for the international architectural competition to redesign the Bridge of the Americas linking Laredo to Nuevo Laredo. The international bridge is currently nondescript and disregards the connectivity between Mexico and the United States. The new bridge design will celebrate this gateway between cultures and urban centers. The catalogue documenting the competition will encourage a continued dialogue on the meaning and significance of this bridge to the Texas-Mexico border community. The catalogue will be used to compete for continuing projects that preserve and promote Laredo's cultural heritage.

Catalogue contents:
1. Cover
2. Fly sheet
   • Title (front)
   • Jurors and credits (back)
3. Table of contents
4. Introduction
   • Intro to Laredo
   • History
   • Timeline
5. Winning entries (full-color, double-page spread per entry)
6. Remaining entries (black and white, four entries per spread)

139

Process: Think about the history of Laredo/Nuevo Laredo and the significance of the Bridge of the Americas. How does the juxtaposition of cultures, cities, the river, and the connecting bridge affect the conceptual aspect of your book? What do you view as the meaning of the bridge: for cultural exchange, trade, symbolic representation of the relationship between the two countries, beauty, politics, etc.? What ideas did the architects consider in their proposal for the bridge and the surrounding land? Develop an appropriate concept for the catalogue.

Set up a Quark document with all pages. Make the grid and establish general style sheets for margins, page numbers, text, headings, etc. Place all of the text in the layout on appropriate pages. Establish a clear and consistent hierarchy of information. Select four spreads to refine layout details (select the widest range of entries by the architects: longest, shortest, poetic text, unusual presentation, winner, etc.). What is necessary to unify the spreads and what creates variety within these style-setting layouts? Do five sets of the four spreads for a total of twenty sketches. Print out at full size.

Session 2:

1. Place images into entire catalogue on the correct spreads.
2. Begin to refine Laredo introductory layouts and timeline.
3. Bring in any refinements from previous layouts.

Session 3:

1. Design cover, table of contents, and fly sheet using your finalized grid, style, and format.
2. Create three sets of variations using the stylistic and conceptual direction defined in previous studies.

Session 4:

1. Refine the four contestant spreads, Laredo section, cover, and table of contents.

Session 5:

1. Apply design to the entire book.

Session 6:

1. Refine design of the entire book.

Session 7.

1. Invite Laredo Cultural Arts Commission to review book.
2. Print and bind a dummy of the entire book.
3. Have paper swatches and ink swatches mounted. Print and mount on blackboard a cover and two interior spreads.

140

Notes

1. Bobby Byrd, *The Late Great Mexican Border: Reports from a Disappearing Line* (El Paso, Texas: Cinco Puntos Press, 1996), p. vii.

2. Ibid., p. viii.

3. Dwayne G. Bohuslav, Trans-Border, "Three Houses by Lake/Flato Architects," *Cite* 30 (spring/summer 1993), p. 24.

4. Bobby Byrd, *The Late Great Mexican Border,* p. viii.

COURSE TITLE _ CORPORATE CULTURE AND
   ALTERNATIVE VISIONS
INSTRUCTORS _ Maud Lavin, Sol Sender
SCHOOL _ The School of the Art Institute of Chicago, Department
   of Visual and Critical Studies
FREQUENCY _ Fourteen weeks
CREDITS _ Three
LEVEL _ Undergraduate

purpose

In the design field, corporations are the most common client. Defined legally as economic individuals in our society and informally simply as businesses, the corporations hire designers to create their visual faces, their corporate identities, and often to contribute to their marketing strategies and brand cultures. Taken cumulatively, the look of corporations, their products, and their self-promotions are dominant aspects of our broader visual culture in the United States. This course aims to ask questions about the visualization of corporate culture and the designer's role. Is there an outside to corporate culture? Are there variations of expressions within it?

What about the designer's power to express self, politics, and other issues and complexities not foregrounded in corporate culture? What about the designer's power to choose clients and influence content in corporate work—while still paying the bills? What about the designer's power in general to intervene in mass visual communication and participate in the democratic exchange of images? What about possibilities on the Internet? What about multitasking and examples of design practices that combine work for love and work for money?

The course combines reading, discussion, writing, and studio work. No previous studio work in the design field is required. We encourage students from any field to take the course. A mixture of disciplines and the asking of broad, imaginative questions are welcome. The readings draw from both contemporary and historical material and focus on twentieth-century U.S. culture; the emphasis is on contemporary issues.

Studio projects will primarily involve photography and typography (the visual language, after all, of corporations), but other media may be integrated as a means of developing a particular idea. Students will be asked to participate in a process which mixes documentary, stages documentary/expression, and "purely expressive" modes. This source material will ultimately be used as a means of questioning the nature of representation and expression within a culture saturated with the thoroughly branded visual and verbal messages of international corporate capitalism.

This is an upper-level undergraduate course, also open to graduate students. It is a Visual and Critical Studies course cross-listed in the departments of Art History, Theory and Criticism, and Visual Communications.

course requirements

Students will be required to do weekly readings and participate fully in discussions, as well as to prepare one final project, which will take the form of either a ten- to fifteen-page, well-researched, and opinionated seminar paper or a predominantly visual design project. In addition, once during the semester each student will prepare comments on the weekly reading.

The emphasis in this course is on participation: credit (and grades for those who are getting them) will be based as much on regular participation in class discussions of readings as on student reports and papers. It is expected that students will have no more than one absence per semester. When, due to a pressing reason, a student is absent, he or she must hand in to the instructors a one- to two-page opinionated paper on the readings for the missed session. If a student is going to be absent, the student should e-mail the instructors to let them know or leave a note in their departmental mailboxes. If there are two absences, this should be discussed with the instructors. A student with three or more absences risks receiving a no-credit for the course.

description of classes

Week 1

Discussion: Introduction.

Reading for next week:

The chapters on "Design for Commerce and Alternative," "Introduction," and "Portfolio: Women and Design," in Maud Lavin, *Clean New World, Culture, Politics, and Graphic Design* (Cambridge: MIT Press, 2001).

Week 2

Discussion: Design, contemporary corporate culture, and some case studies of alternatives (including the work of Rebeca Mendez, Sylvia Harris, Bethany Johns, Marlene McCarty, Lorraine Wild, etc.).

Reading for next week:

Ellen Lupton, *Mechanical Brides: Women and Machines from Home to Office* (Cooper-Hewitt exhibition catalog). (New York: Princeton Architectural Press, 1996). Read the section on the telephone (also in a photocopied packet and on reserve).

Week 3

Discussion: The permeation of U.S. visual culture by corporate culture
   Studio preparation: Documentary and creative imagery development based
on parameters in handout
   Reading: Chapter on "For Love, Modernism, or Money: Kurt Schwitters
and the neue ring werbegestalter," in Lavin, *Clean New World.*

Week 4

Studio: Brand culture
   Studio preparation: Written language documentation and creative written
language development based on parameters in handout
   Readings: Various corporate identity guidelines, selections from:
   Claude C. Hopkins, *My Life in Advertising and Scientific Advertising: Two
Works* (New York: McGraw-Hill/Contemporary Books, 1986), pp. 53–75.
   David Ogilvy, *Ogilvy on Advertising* (New York: Vintage Books, 1987), pp.
7–30, 70–101.

Week 5

Studio: Brand culture. Discussion of written language, in conjunction with
imagery from Week 4
   Readings for next week: Neil Harris, in *Cultural Excursions: Marketing
Appetites and Cultural Tastes in Modern America* (Chicago: University of Chicago
Press, 1990). Read the essay, "Designs on Demand: Art and the Modern
Corporation," pp. 349–78.
   Roland Marchand, *Advertising the American Dream: Making Way for Modernity,
1920–1940* (Berkeley: University of California Press, 1986). Read chapter 6,
"Advertisements as Social Tableaux," pp. 164–205.

143

Week 6

Discussion: The growth of U.S. corporate culture between the wars
   Readings for next week: Roland Marchand, *Creating the Corporate Soul: The
Rise of Public Relations and Corporate Imagery in American Big Business* (Berkeley:
University of California, 2001). Read chapter 4, "A 'Corporate Consciousness':
General Motors, General Electric, and the Bruce Barton Formula," pp. 130–63,
and the conclusion, "Like a Good Neighbor," pp. 357–63.
   Thomas Frank, *The Conquest of Cool: Business Culture, Counterculture, and the
Rise of Hip Consumerism* (Chicago: University of Chicago Press, 1998). Read
chapter 4, "Three Rebels: Advertising Narratives of the Sixties," pp. 74–87.

Week 7

Discussion: Recent history, U.S. corporate culture, and social issues.
   Readings for next week:

Chapter on John Heartfield in Lavin, *Clean New World*. Students should hand in a sentence or two about the topic of their final project next week.

Week 8
Field trip: American Girl Place and Niketown, corporate culture as urban center and entertainment
Readings for next week:
Tibor Kalman, "First Things First Manifesto," in *Tibor Kalman, Perverse Optimist*, Peter Hall et al., eds. (New York: Princeton Architectural Press, 2000).
Ellen Lupton et al., *Design Culture Now* (New York: Princeton Architectural Press, 2000). Read the sections on Art Chantry, B. J. Krivanek, and Sheila Levrant de Bretteville.

Week 8
No class, crit week

Week 9
Studio: Alternative design; the design of dissent, change from the outside—is it possible?
Readings for next week:
Section on David Small in Lupton et al., *Design Culture Now*. Skim entire catalog and look at recent issues of Abbott Miller, ed., *Twice*, and Patricia Williams, "The Death of the Profane," on wheatpasting and Benetton, in *The Alchemy of Race and Rights*, pp. 44–51.

Week 10
Studio: Alternative design—the art of creative consent, change from the inside. Is it possible?
No readings for the rest of the course; students are working on their final projects.

Week 11
Discussion: Authorship and collaboration; guest speaker, Cheryl Towler Weese, principal, Studio Blue

Week 12
Field trip to Design Kitchen

Week 13
Discussion: The economics of possibility

Week 14

Final projects due, no extensions, in-class discussion of projects

assignments

Studio Project 1: "Target Audience"

Part A

1. Determine your most successful creative project of the past year.
2. Now determine who your target audiences were for that piece. At whom was your piece directed? To whom did it speak? How did it speak to audiences at whom it was not consciously directed? How did it speak differently to different audiences? How do you define the differences of your target audiences? (i.e., race, gender, age, sexuality, nationality, etc.)
3. Now develop five images that describe your target audience(s). These images should be unique enough to function as a foundation for a future project of yours. These images should most likely be photographs. They can be as simple as snapshots or, for those of you who are photographers, more finished. Images can be historical, found, documentary, or staged. Please limit found imagery (i.e., magazine, newspaper, etc.) to two images and re-photograph them. Presentation can be simple. I will probably just ask you to pin the images to the wall. Alternatives include video, slides, film, performance. If you choose any of these alternatives, please come to class prepared to present (arrange to bring a video player and monitor, etc.).

145

Part B

1. Choose a corporate subject (i.e., McDonald's, Citibank, IBM, The Art Institute of Chicago, etc.) that is accessible to you.
2. Now determine who the target audiences are for that corporation. To whom do they sell? To whom do they speak? How do they speak to audiences to whom they do not consciously speak? How do they speak differently to different audiences? How do they define those differences in their audiences? (i.e. race, gender, age, sexuality, nationality, etc.).
3. Now develop five images that describe your corporate subject's target audience(s) (same as above). These images should be unique enough to function as a foundation for a future project of yours (assuming "uniqueness" is something that you seek in your work). These images should most likely be photographs. They can be as simple as snapshots or, for those of you who are photographers,

more finished. Images can be historical, found, documentary, or staged. Please limit found imagery (i.e., magazine, newspaper, etc.) to two images and re-photograph them. Presentation can be simple. I will probably just ask you to pin the images to the wall. Alternatives include video, slides, film, performance. If you choose any of these alternatives, please come to class prepared to present (arrange to bring a video player and monitor, etc.).

Questions to ponder: (Please come up with your own as you develop your solutions.) Successful corporate design work is often determined by a creative understanding of the corporation's or brand's target audience. At least, that's what designers and corporations like to think. On the other hand, we might consider the potential separation of "the intention of the designers from the reception of the audience and grant that advertising is not necessarily received in the spirit it is pitched . . . " (Lavin, *Clean New World*, 73). How do we, as creative people, negotiate this difficult terrain between author/artist/designer and target audience? How do we manage those ambiguities? How do we manage the demand for a clear message? How have/do corporations place limits on that interaction and what are the results?

Consider Ellen Lupton's essays from *Mechanical Brides* and her description of the ways in which the corporate history of the telephone and the typewriter are intertwined with the politics of gender. Surely this is but one example of how a particular target audience (women) become associated with particular professions and those professions' limitations and opportunities. Think about how we've spoken of the complexities of our own interactions with those same consumer products. What of the complexities of our experiences of consumer objects that have been sold to us?

Consider Lavin's comments in her essay "For Love, Modernism, or Money," regarding the modernists' propensity to concentrate on the means of communication and the technologies of communication, rather than the content of the communication or the implications of those communications. Doesn't a love of form and a love for the exploration of form continue to exist today? In design, in art? How do we understand the problem of the target audience in instances when form and beauty are privileged? How do we balance aesthetic exploration and accomplishment with successful communications? Who was the target audience for those modernists? For that group of avant-garde artists/designers?

Studio Project 2: "Target Audience," Part 2

Part A1

1. You should now have five images that describe your target audience(s) for a given creative piece of your making.

2. Now, for each of these images, answer the following question: what does the target audience want from your piece?
3. You should respond with a word or short phrase for each of your images. This word, or short phrase, can be presented in the following formats: spoken, typeset, written, recorded, photographed. Whatever format you choose to present your word or short phrase— it should be purposeful: that is, choose your format for a reason.

Part A2

1. Now, for each of these images, answer another question: what is it that you want/wanted your target audience to get from your piece?
2. Again, you should respond with a word or short phrase for each of your images. This word, or short phrase, can be presented in the following formats: spoken, typeset, written, recorded. Whatever format you choose to present your word or short phrase—it should be purposeful: that is, choose your format for a reason.

Part B1

1. You should now have five images that describe your corporate subject's target audience(s).
2. Now, for each of these images, answer the following question: what does the target audience want from the corporation?
3. Again, you should respond with a word or short phrase for each of your images. This word, or short phrase, can be presented in the following formats: spoken, typeset, written, recorded, photographed. Whatever format you choose to present your word or short phrase—it should be purposeful: that is, choose your format for a reason.

Part B2

1. Now, for each of these images, answer the following question: what does the corporation want the target audience to have/do/buy?
2. Again respond with a word or short phrase for each of your images. This word, or short phrase, can be presented in the following formats: spoken, typeset, written, recorded, photographed. Whatever format you choose to present your word or short phrase—it should be purposeful: that is, choose your format for a reason. Result: Twenty words or phrases, purposefully formatted.

selected reading

Ewen, Stuart, and Elizabeth Ewen. *Channels of Desire: Mass Images and the Shaping of the American Consciousness.* New York: McGraw Hill, 1982.

Frank, Thomas. *The Conquest of Cool: Business Culture, Counterculture, and the Rise of Hip Consumerism*. Chicago: University of Chicago Press, 1997.

Frank, Thomas. "Brand you," *Harper's* (July 1999): 74–79.

Frank, Thomas. *One Market Under God: Extreme Capitalism, Market Populism, and the End of Economic Democracy*. New York: Doubleday, 2000.

Freud, Sigmund. *Civilization and Its Discontents* (1930). New York: W. W. Norton, 1989.

Hall, Peter et al., eds. *Tibor Kalman, Perverse Optimist*. New York: Princeton Architectural Press, 2000. (Especially Tibor Kalman, "First Thing First Manifesto.")

Harris, Neil. *Cultural Excursions: Marketing Appetites and Cultural Tastes in Modern America*. Chicago: University of Chicago Press, 1990. "Designs on demand: Art and the modern corporation," pp. 349–78.

Hopkins, Claude. *My Life in Advertising and Scientific Advertising: Two Works*. National Textbook Company Trade, 1986.

Lasky, Julie. "Restless Photography," *Print* (May/June 1990): 53–65, 144–146.

Lavin, Maud, *Clean New World: Culture, Politics, and Graphic Design*. Cambridge: MIT Press, 2001.

Lupton, Ellen. *Mechanical Brides: Women and Machine from Home to Office*. New York: Cooper-Hewitt National Design Museum and Princeton Architectural Press, 1993.

Lupton, Ellen, and J. Abbott Miller. *Design Writing Research*. New York: Princeton Architectural Press, 1996 (paperback ed., Phaidon).

Lupton, Ellen et al. *Design Culture Now* (Triennial exhibition catalog). New York: Cooper-Hewitt National Design Museum, 2000.

Marchand, Roland. *Advertising the American Dream: Making Way for Modernity, 1920–1940*. Berkeley: University of California Press, 1985.

Marchand, Roland. *Creating the Corporate Soul: The Rise of Public Relations and Corporate Imagery in American Big Business*. Berkeley: University of California Press, 1998.

Ogilvy, David. *Ogilvy on Advertising*. New York: Random House, 1987.

Williams, Patricia. *The Alchemy of Race and Rights*. Cambridge: Harvard UP, 1991.

Williams, Raymond. "The Magic System," in *Problems in Materialism and Culture*. London: Verso, 1980, 170–195.

Williamson, Judith. *Consuming Passions: The Dynamics of Popular Culture*. London: Marion Boyars, 1986.

COURSE TITLE _ NEW INFORMATION ENVIRONMENT/
EXPERIENCE DESIGN
INSTRUCTOR _ Rob Wittig
SCHOOL _ North Carolina State University, College of Design
FREQUENCY _ Four sessions
CREDITS _ Three
LEVEL _ Undergraduate

purpose

Examine and explore the *mediaverse* through the lens of literary history, literary experience design, and recent literary projects in electronic media. This class is a synthesis and analysis of relevant aspects of meaningful human interactions in a networked and mediated environment, including physical, cognitive/emotional, social, political, economic, and cultural dimensions of these interactions, and the relationships of such interactions to commerce, learning, work, play, community, and gaining access to the privileges of democracy. In an exploration of language structures (storytelling) that enhance understanding and support users' objectives in a variety of contexts, students will explore the construction of verbal messages and the roles they play in defining experiences.

149

class project

Create and display a systematic log of one of your own major cultural usages for the period of the course.
    This log will include:

- Time, date, duration, and location of each instance
- Content description/cultural description
- Affect report (how you feel during the experience)
- Concurrent activities (multitasking)

Each week you will write a brief summary of the week's experiences (one-half to one page), commenting on patterns, describing special events that affect that week's data, noting what you are learning about your own habits from the logging process, etc.

information display sketches and midterm

Find a way to display the information from your log in a scannable and meaningful way in html/Web format, one week at a time, in such a way that each week can be printed on a single piece of paper. The weekly summary may be a separate page from the display page.

- February 23–24: Show sketches and ideas for the information display of your log, posted on Web and printed.
- March 5, midterm: Post refined information display for your log so far, posted on the Web.

final

1. Complete the display of each week of your cultural usage log, along with the accompanying weekly summaries.
2. Create a project pitch in Web form (equivalent to three printed pages) for a new information or entertainment project that uses the same usage pattern described in your log.

description of classes

Session 1

- Introduction and skill sharing
- Lecture/discussion: One path into the new environment—"the word guy in design"
- In-class activity(s)
- Lecture/discussion: Literature for designers
- Getting started with the class project, individual and ensemble

Session 1 Readings

Antonio Damasio, *The Feeling of What Happens: Body and Emotion in the Making of Consciousness* (Harcourt/Brace, 1999). Read chapter 1, "Stepping into the Light," pp. 3–31; chapter 2, "Emotion and Feeling," pp. 35–81.

Umberto Eco. *Travels in Hyperreality* (HBJ, 1986). Read "Casablanca: Cult Movies and Intertextual Collage," pp. 197–211. (See the film *Casablanca*, if you can, and if you haven't ever seen it.)

Session 2

- Discussion of readings
- Presentation of midterm projects
- In-class activity(s)
- Lecture/discussion: Character creation with copy and image

Session 2 Readings

"Patchwork Girl" by Shelley Jackson (hypertext from Eastgate Systems).
Spend several hours with this piece.
Umberto Eco, *Travels in Hyperreality*, pp. 3–58.

Session 3

- Discussion of readings
- Update presentation on projects
- In-class activity(s)
- Lecture/discussion: Design for writers

Session 3 Readings

Roland Barthes, *The Eiffel Tower and other Mythologies* (University of California Press, 1997; Farrar Straus & Giroux, 1979), pp. 3–17.
Scott McCloud, *Understanding Comics* (Kitchen Sink Press; reprint edition, 1994).
A comic book/graphic novel of your choice.

Session 4

- Discussion of readings
- Presentation of semester projects
- Combined analysis of all projects together; identification of disruptions and synergies

conclusion

This course grew out of my abiding interest in multitasking and mixing in culture, specifically the actual behaviors of reading, which my literary background has taught are often shrouded in mystery, assumption, and denial. Some accounting must be made for the fact that many readers mix input—listening to music, watching television, eating, riding, and even walking as they read.

The course also was prompted by the utility I have found in having a powerful, graphic way to represent complex user behaviors. Most excitingly, these representations can be used not only to describe existing experiences, but also to project and plan new kinds of cultural experiences based on hybrid models. Example: "Let's design a work of online literature that people will use the same way they use 'morning zoo' radio shows."

The work in this course falls into three distinct, and ambitious, phases: data gathering, information design, and data interpretation. I knew from the start that there would be a trade-off between depth and breadth. I decided in favor of breadth—having students plan, research, display, and interpret—so that they had at least walked through the entire process, beginning to end. What was being modeled was qualitative research, not quantitative; the goal was insight, not proof.

For most students the data-gathering process is demanding, sometimes arduous, and usually enlightening in itself. One student who tracked e-mail was astonished to see in her records how often she checked her inbox in a day. Another was surprised at how many minutes of reading a day she could actually squeeze in at bus stops, on buses, and while eating. The student who chose to log his interactions with music was overwhelmed by the sheer amount of overheard music there is in the everyday American environment. For future classes, I might be tempted to narrow the data-gathering focus a bit (just evening hours, for example, or just music of one's own choice), but I don't regret casting the net wide with this group of students.

The information-design phase proceeded in a presentation/critique/discussion format and required a definite change of gears from the early sharing of raw data (which was more personal and autobiographical). I used a three-level criteria approach, asking that each of the 11" × 17" representations of a week of each student's activity be designed so that: (1) it communicated a title and a visceral summary of the week when viewed from across the room; (2) it told a more detailed story in outline form when held in the hand and skimmed for a few seconds, and (3) it supported use as a complex data display.

The student work was quite successful over all, including some outstanding displays. One showed data about the frequency and nature of daily conversations arrayed over photographic self-portraits, which summed up the week with mournful or happy eyes. Another logged a student's Internet chatroom communication with friends half a world (and half a day) away in a right-side-up/upside-down format that required turning and showed how noon in one world was midnight in the other.

COURSE TITLE _ THE THINKING EYE: SIGHT, INSIGHT,
    AND GRAPHIC DESIGN
INSTRUCTOR _ Roy R. Behrens
SCHOOL _ University of Wisconsin-Milwaukee, Art Academy of
    Cincinnati, and University of Northern Iowa
FREQUENCY _ One semester
CREDITS _ Three
LEVEL _ Undergraduate

purpose

To acquaint college-level undergraduate students with generic, cross-disciplinary aspects of graphic design, especially visual perception, improvisation, and problem solving. While fundamental to design practice, these subjects are often taken for granted or discounted as peripheral, in part because they focus on issues more commonly thought to belong to psychology, biology, anthropology, literature, and so on.

153

description

This course is half lecture, half participatory lab or studio. Its participants are a mixture of design and nondesign students (many of whom are studio artists), and those from the sciences, humanities, and other non-art disciplines. The full group meets once or twice weekly to witness a lecture, performance, or video; to discuss an assigned reading; or to critique the results of a studio assignment, completed independently during allotted lab periods and at other times outside of class.

description of classes

Week 1

Lecture: Visual perception, including (but not limited to) gestalt perceptual psychology, and historic, ubiquitous uses in art, architecture, typography, page layout, etc., of perceptual organizing principles (or unit-forming factors), such as similarity and proximity grouping, continuity (edge alignment), closure, and so on. Definition of style as an array of visual attributes that reflect the concerns and beliefs of an age—e.g., Gothic Revival versus Prairie Style, or late modern versus postmodern. How form functions. Aesthetics versus anesthetics. Monotony versus mayhem. The importance of being implicit.

Studio problem: Using cameras that allow exact viewfinding; use unit-forming factors to create "visual bloopers"—found or constructed arrangements in which two or more separate things appear connected, or parts of one thing look disconnected. Search magazines, books, and photographs for examples of inadvertent visual confusion.

Reading(s): Roy R. Behrens, "Art, Design and Gestalt Theory," in *Leonardo* 31, no. 4 (1998), pp. 299–303; selections from R. L. Gregory, *The Intelligent Eye* (New York: McGraw-Hill, 1971), H. G. Barnett, *Innovation: The Basis of Cultural Change* (New York: McGraw-Hill, 1953), and/or L. L. Whyte, ed., *Aspects of Form* (Bloomington: Indiana University Press, 1951), pp. 196–208.

Week 2

Lecture: The perceptual basis of biological and military camouflage, e.g., figure-ground blending, figure disruption, mimicry, and displacement of attention (distraction or deflection). Review of Abbott H. Thayer's work on the subject, and his subsequent influence on World War I French, British, German, and American military camouflage, including the "dazzle painting" of ships. Comparison of his "laws of disguise" with gestalt psychologists, unit-forming factors.

Studio problem: Apply a known camouflage strategy in a surprising way, or invent and demonstrate a new method of visual deception, using unit-forming factors. Search magazines, books, and other material for examples of purposeful visual deceit.

Reading(s): Eric Sloane, *Camouflage Simplified* (New York: Devin-Adair, 1943); Hugh B. Cott, "Animal Form in Relation to Appearance," in L. L. Whyte, op. cit., pp. 121–156; Roy R. Behrens, "On Max Wertheimer and Pablo Picasso: Gestalt Theory, Cubism and Camouflage" in *Gestalt Theory* 20, no. 2 (June 1998), pp. 111–118; and/or selections from Roy R. Behrens, *False Colors: Art, Design and Modern Camouflage* (Dysart, IA: Bobolink Books, 2002).

Week 3

Lecture: The perceptual tendencies that underlie sleight of hand and other kinds of magic tricks, beginning with a performance by a magician. This is followed by a slide-illustrated overview of the history of magic, stage and close-up, its accoutrements, and printed ephemera, with a discussion of standard magic ploys (especially misdirection) in relation to unit-forming factors and camouflage strategies. Compare with the diversionary tactics of pickpockets.

Studio problem: Invent a new magic trick (if only by reapplying the tactics of an old one), or a magic-based children's toy, and introduce it to the group.

Reading(s): Warren Steinkraus, "The Art of Conjuring," in *Journal of Aesthetic Education* (1979); Jehangir Bhownagary, "Creativity and the Magician," in *Leonardo* 5 (1972), pp. 31–35; and/or selections from Nicholas Schiffman, *Abracadabra!: Secret Methods Magicians and Others Use to Deceive Their Audience* (Amherst, NY: Prometheus Books, 1997).

Week 4

Lecture: The principles of typographic design. Demonstrate how the connected-ness of letters, words, and other language components is typically adjusted by letterspacing, word spacing, line spacing (or leading), tracking, kerning, and so on. Serifs, weight, slant, and other shape characteristics as stylistic attributes that facilitate grouping. Discussion of legibility versus readability. Typographic unit-forming and unit-breaking compared to parallel strategies in camouflage and magic. Examples of typographic grouping in the design of complex page spreads.

Studio problem: Using only letterforms, devise a series of innovative human portraits ("type faces") or figures.

Reading(s): Selections from Robert Bringhurst, *The Elements of Typographic Style* (Vancouver, BC: Hartley and Marks, 1996); Erik Spiekermann and E. M. Ginger, *Stop Stealing Sheep and Find Out How Type Works* (Mountain View, CA: Adobe Press, 1993); and/or Steven Heller and Gail Anderson, eds., *American Typeplay* (Glen Cove, NY: PBC International, 1994).

Week 5

Lecture: Compositional analysis. Projection and discussion of a wide range of examples of visual art, design, and architecture, including book covers, interior page layouts, magazine advertisements, corporate logos, paintings, illustrations, photographs, and so on. Lecture explicitly focuses on the use of underlying visual rhymes, proportional harmonies, edge alignment (or grid lines), closure, and other unit-forming factors in design-based compositions.

Studio problem: Search magazines, books, and other sources for examples of the expert use of the strategies covered in the lecture. Scan the best single example, analyze it, and construct an annotated diagram of its functions.

Reading(s): Selections from Suzanne West, *Working with Style: Traditional and Modern Approaches to Layout and Typography* (New York: Watson Guptill, 1990); Willi Kunz, *Typography: Macro + Micro Aesthetics* (Switzerland: Verlag Niggli, 1998); Gyorgy Doczi, *The Power of Limits: Proportional Harmonies in Nature, Art and Architecture* (Boulder, CO: Shambhala, 1981); and/or Kimberly Elam, *Geometry of Design: Studies in Proportion and Composition* (New York: Princeton Architectural Press, 2001).

Week 6

Lecture: Edge alignment (referred to by gestaltists as "continuity" or "good continuity"). Slide-illustrated overview of the application of aligned edges to flat compositions, such as page layouts, more commonly called "grid lines." When used as indicators of illusory depth, they function as perspective grids, e.g., Renaissance-era checkerboard floor patterns, or the alignment of fallen soldiers in Paolo Ucello's "The Battle of San Romano." Brief consideration of isometric perspective (as in Ukiyo-i prints), stage illusions, and other derivatives, including anamorphic art. The use of perspective anomalies by artists, graphic designers, scientists, and stage-set designers (e.g., Hans Holbein, Adelbert Ames, Jr., A. M. Cassandre, Ladislav Sutnar, John Pfahl, Patrick Hughes, and special-effects film-set designers).

Studio problem: Reconstruct and experiment with Ames, distorted rooms, rotating trapezoid windows, etc., and/or develop new applications of "forced perspective" and other distortion strategies.

Reading(s): Roy R. Behrens, "Adelbert Ames and the Cockeyed Room," in *Print* (March/April 1994), pp. 92–97; and/or selections from Fred Leeman, et al., *Hidden Images: Games of Perception, Anamorphic Art, Illusion from the Renaissance to the Present* (New York: Harry Abrams, 1976).

Week 7

Lecture: Gestaltists' contention that "the whole is greater than the sum of its parts," that the appearance of a thing is determined in part by its context or surrounding. In the Ames room, for example, normal objects look distorted when placed in a physically skewed but normal-looking environment. In Jonathan Hoefler's Gestalt typeface, some individual letters are recognizable only in higher-level contexts, such as words or sentences. Overview of nineteenth-century scientific research of French chemist M. E. Chevreul of the function of "simultaneous contrast" (of color, value, shape, etc.), and the later application of these principles by Josef Albers to his "Homage to the Square" paintings. One consequence is the synergistic effects of accents (small amounts of high difference). John Donne: No man is an island. Alan Watts: All things are like the rainbow.

Studio problem: Look closely at Albers, demonstrations of the simultaneous contrast of color, as discussed and illustrated in his *Interaction of Color*. Using his method of side-by-side comparisons, invent new, surprising demonstrations of the simultaneous contrast of any visual attributes other than color, such as size, light/dark value, texture, slant, proportion, perspective, and so on. For example, one might experiment only with the occurrence of simultaneous contrast in typographic examples, in page layouts, or in documentary photography.

Reading(s): Selections from John F. A. Taylor, *Design and Expression in the Visual Arts* (Mineola, NY: Dover Publications, 1964); and/or W. I. Homer, *Seurat and the Science of Painting* (Cambridge: MIT Press, 1964). See also video titled *Light, Darkness and Colors* (First Run/Icarus Films).

Week 8

Lecture: "Less is more," implicitness, leaving out, suggesting—thereby eliciting closure—and other aspects of what art historian E. H. Gombrich called "the beholder's share." Discussion of Walter Gropius, Fagus factory, and Dessau Bauhaus, in which load-bearing corner supports are replaced by glass and steel facades. Compare to various modern chairs, in which the rear legs are omitted, and examples of cantilever architectural construction by Frank Lloyd Wright (Fallingwater), Gerrit Rietveld (Zigzag chair), and others. Relate to implicitness in historic and current illustrations (e.g., Coles Phillips, J. C. Leyendecker, Ludwig Hohlwein, Robert Gibbings, et al.), constellations, connect the dots, crossword puzzles, embedded figures, and other picture puzzles. Review of Bluma Ziegarnik's research of memory and incompleteness.

Studio Problem: Adopt the format and method of the Tangram, an ancient Chinese puzzle game, but instead of using a black domino shape, begin with one that has on its surface a complex typographic shape or a detail from a photograph. Divide it into seven parts (as is customary with tangrams) and experiment with their recombination. Or, explore the possibilities of cognitive contours, whether typographic or pictorial, in which meaningful forms can be found in the background areas of explicit figures.

Reading(s): Roy R. Behrens, "Revisiting Gottschaldt: Embedded Figures in Art, Architecture and Design," in *Gestalt Theory* 22, no. 2 (June 2000), pp. 97–106; selections from Kevin Nute, *Frank Lloyd Wright and Japan* (New York: Van Nostrand Reinhold, 1993), Florian Rodari, et al., *Shadows of a Hand: The Drawings of Victor Hugo* (New York: Merrell Holbertson, 1998), and/or James Elkins, *Why Are Our Pictures Puzzles?: On the Modern Origins of Pictorial Complexity* (New York: Routledge, 1998).

157

Week 9

Lecture: Apparent movement (the illusion of motion produced by a sequence of still pictures). Max Wertheimer's use of a motion-picture toy (zoetrope) in his research of perceptual organizing principles. The early motion photographs of Eadweard Muybridge and E. J. Marey, and subsequent experiments in stroboscopic photography by Harold Edgerton. Attempts to capture movement in the artwork of Frans Hals, John Singer Sargent, Robert Henri, George Bellows, Alexander Calder, Jean Tinguely, George Rickey, and others. Portrayal of motion compared in the work of Cubists, Futurists, and others. Marcel Duchamp's *Nude Descending a Staircase*. The history of animation. Gyorgy Kepes, *The New Landscape in Art and Science*. Norman McLaren film, *Pas de Deux*.

Studio problem: Using a camera, experiment with moving subjects, resulting in blurred or disrupted images; or with moving the camera while photographing a static subject. Conduct similar motion experiments with photocopying machines, scanners, novelty cameras, and other devices.

Reading(s): James Sheldon, *Exploring the Art and Science of Stopping Time: The Life and Work of Harold E. Edgerton*, CD-ROM (Cambridge: MIT Press, 1999); and/or selections from Laszlo Moholy-Nagy, *Vision in Motion* (Chicago: Paul Theobald, 1947), and Gyorgy Kepes, ed., *The Nature and Art of Motion* (New York: George Braziller, 1965).

Week 10

Lecture: Metamorphosis, Darwinian evolution theory, and computer-based morphing. The transformation of one thing into something else within a span of space or time. Use slides or preferably living examples of the metamorphosis of insects (e.g., from egg to caterpillar to cocoon to butterfly). Images of human growth from infancy to old age. Chalk talk sequences. Grandville's metamorphic drawings. D'Arcy Wentworth Thompson's book *On Growth and Form*. Verbal metamorphoses. The evolution of style. Sequence and series in graphic design, e.g., A. M. Cassandre's Dubonnet advertisement; Paul Rand's Westinghouse logo animation; cinematic page sequences in books designed by Merle Armitage or Richard Eckersley; or Thomas Ockerse's A–Z Book. Charles and Ray Eames film, *Powers of Ten*.

Studio problem: Each person is arbitrarily given any two items. These might be printed images or three-dimensional objects. Through any method of construction, in any combination of media, create a sequence of five missing stages that might exist if Item A were to evolve (or metamorphose) into Item B. Or, conduct experiments with sequential copying: within the time of a few minutes, make a moderately complex drawing. Give that and a blank sheet of paper to another person, and ask him or her to copy it within the same time limit. Then give that second drawing and another blank sheet of paper to a third person, and ask him or her to copy that (without having seen the first drawing), and so on. Do this with about twenty or twenty-five people, then compare the first and last drawings, and study the sequence of changes.

Reading(s): Selections from Carl Zimmer, *Evolution: The Triumph of an Idea* (New York: HarperCollins, 2001).

Week 11

Lecture: Chance and improvisation, a lecture delivered by chance. Assemble slides having to do with chance-related subjects, such as Dada, John Cage, exquisite corpse, serendipity, I Ching, dice, radical juxtaposition, etc. But toss the slides into a pile, and arrange them in the carousel in a haphazard sequence. Or, better yet, have others collaborate in assembling a tray of unrelated slides, with no intended relevance to the lecture topic. Improvise the lecture as each slide is shown for the first time.

Studio problem: Choose a set of books in which the typesetting and page layout are standard throughout, such as, for example, the Harvard Classics. Photocopy a dozen or so unrelated text pages, randomly chosen. Cut the text into strips of entire, single lines, and rearrange them to make new, continuous but nonsensical paragraphs. Or, use the exquisite corpse and other adaptations by Dadaists of Victorian parlor games to arrive at bizarre combinations.

Reading(s): Selections from Alastair Brotchie, *A Book of Surrealist Games* (Boston: Shambhala Publications, 1995); James Adams, *Conceptual Blockbusting*

(San Francisco: San Francisco Book Company, 1976); Charles Jencks and Nathan Silver, *Adhocism: The Case for Improvisation* (New York: Doubleday, 1972); and/or Susan Stewart, *Nonsense: Aspects of Intertextuality in Folklore and Literature* (Baltimore, MD: Johns Hopkins University Press, 1990).

Week 12

Lecture: Spurious resemblance. Present and discuss visual, verbal, and auditory examples of any and all kinds of mimicry, simulacra, counterfeiting, trompe l'oeil, ventriloquism, parody, etc.

Studio problem: Construct illustrations from extraneous, unrelated components, as can be seen, for example, in Pontus Hulten, et al., *The Arcimboldo Effect* (New York: Abbeville Press, 1987).

Reading(s): Selections from Hillel Schwartz, *The Culture of the Copy: Striking Likenesses, Unreasonable Facsimiles* (New York: Zone Books, 1996); John Michel, *Natural Likeness: Faces and Figures in Nature* (New York: E. P. Dutton, 1979); and/or Wolfgang Wickler, *Mimicry in Plants and Animals* (New York: McGraw-Hill, 1968).

Week 13

Lecture: Visual metaphors and puns. Discussion of the function of analogies, similes, metaphors, and other figures of speech (or "sort-crossing") in prose, poetry, jokes, and dreams. Review of contention by Koestler and others that all forms of human invention (whether art, science, or humor) are produced by translogical thinking (A is A and Not-A) and unexpected shifts of attention.

Studio problem: Participants are divided into groups of two or three, and given two randomly chosen lists of common, unrelated objects. Arbitrarily link any two items, one from each list, then brainstorm to create inventions, unusual uses, visual and verbal puns that make combined use of those two items. Or, develop a play or a story in which a random selection of the items listed is critical to the narrative.

Reading(s): Warren Shibles, "The Metaphorical Method," in *Journal of Aesthetic Education* (April 1974), pp. 25–36; Paul Hammond and Patrick Hughes, *Upon the Pun: Dual Meanings in Words and Pictures* (London: W. H. Allen, 1978); Beryl McAlhone and David Stuart, *A Smile in the Mind: Witty Thinking in Graphic Design* (London: Phaidon, 1996); Steven Heller and Gail Anderson, *Graphic Wit: The Art of Humor in Design* (New York: Watson-Guptill, 1991); and/or selections from Arthur Koestler, *The Act of Creation* (New York: Macmillan, 1964).

Week 14

Lecture: On ethological consequences of form, e.g., cuteness, sexual response. For visual examples and background, see Wolfgang Wickler, *The Sexual Code: The Social Behavior of Animals and Men* (Garden City, NJ: Anchor Books, 1973).

Studio problem: Search magazines, books, artwork, and other sources for examples of explicit and implicit uses of sexual and other biologically based imagery.

Readings: R. G. Cott, "The Ethological Command in Art," in *Leonardo 1* (1968), pp. 273–287; Samuel Jay Keyser, "There Is Method in Their Adness: The Formal Structure of Advertisement," in *New Literary History* 14, no. 2 (1983), pp. 305–334; and/or selections from Steven Heller, ed., *Graphic Design and Sex Appeal* (New York: Allworth Press, 2000).

conclusion

The course concludes with an extended gathering of all participants, in part to arrive at an overview of the major findings of the class, but also as a way to learn about individual discoveries and insights. As a concluding event, the group looks at projected examples of current graphic design, and discusses how these are examples of the methods and topics addressed in the course.

COURSE TITLE _ COMMUNICATION DESIGN INTERNSHIP
INSTRUCTOR _ Susan Agre-Kippenhan
SCHOOL _ Portland State University, Art Department/
   Communication Design
FREQUENCY _ Ten weeks
CREDITS _ Four
LEVEL _ Undergraduate

purpose

This internship course is intended to help you make your way into the professional design world. The class serves as a bridge providing both a professional and academic experience. It also serves to promote a community of designers and learners who can share experiences, opinions, and resources.

description

An advanced course with a required one-hundred-hour placement (minimum) in a professional design setting. In-class sessions will center on discussions of professional topics and issues. This is a one-term course for design majors focused on client-oriented projects with exposure to multiple aspects of the professional design process: client meetings, cost estimates, presentation, design/production. Portfolio required.

objectives

• Provide a mode of transitioning into the professional design community.
• Examine issues related to a profession in design.
• Create a meaningful, self-reflective, and critical dialogue around design issues.

activities

There will be four types of activity in this class.

1. Professional placement: working in a professional setting
2. Work/life themes: reading, discussion, guest presentations
3. Roundtables/show and tell: Forums for sharing your professional experiences and work
4. Individual faculty/student meetings

Professional Placement: Individual and Outside of Class

This will require collecting your work, interviewing (and landing) a work placement. You will be logging your activity, first in the interviewing mode and after placement in a work log. You will be responsible for designing these logs and keeping them up to date. First steps include filling out the survey sheet (included here), collecting your work, making contact, procuring interviews, and finding placement (I will assist throughout). Success at an internship is not solely determined by the quality of the work you do or the prestige of the firm you work for; other key factors that contribute: the way in which you handle yourself, your attitude, your initiative, your ability to take input and give it, and your ability to become an integral participate. General requirements are for one hundred hours of placement in the term (ten per week).

Required to pass this class:

- Placement.
- Interview logs will be reviewed and collected at time of placement.
- Work logs will be collected at midterm and finals.

Work/Life themes: In Class on Wednesdays

There will be three areas investigated.

1. First impressions: you and your work
2. Professional expertise: making presentations, how to estimate and plan jobs
3. Design career: office smarts, future plans

Required: participation in three per term (additional for extra credit)

Roundtables/Show and Tell: In class on Wednesdays

These are sessions to discuss work issues and to show work (and get feedback). Their purpose is to spread your individual experiences out to your peers and solicit advice, to give you a forum for feedback and critique. They will be topical and related to the work/life themes.

Required: participation in two per term (additional for extra credit)

Individual Meetings: By Arrangement on Mondays

I will be available to meet with you on Mondays during the regular class time. I will have a sign-up sheet for these meetings. You are required to meet with me at midterm and at the end of class, and you are free (but not required) to meet with me more often.

Required: two meetings per term—midterm and finals

Mandatory: one final group meeting (celebration!) to be scheduled together by the class

description of classes

Class meets Monday and Wednesday. Monday class time will be reserved for one-on-one meetings.

Session 1: Work/Life Theme
Session 1, "Work/Life Theme," will be a session devoted to making a first impression. How do you present yourself? In-class role-playing interview.

Session 2: Work/Life Theme: First Impressions, Your Work
Bring in two of your best pieces. Be prepared to address objectives, personal approach, and results. We will be looking at work through the lens of process, content, form, and craft. In-class guest speaker (creative placement firm director) discusses placement and interviewing. In-class individual presentations with written critique by class.

Session 3: Round Table/Show and Tell
Come prepared with two observations about first impressions. (How were those initial phone calls, discussions, first days at work, etc.?) Bring in one piece of work from the firm where you are placed. In-class guest designer discusses work. In class, each class member frames one question and leads an informal discussion.

163

Session 4: Work/Life Theme:
Professional Expertise; Making Presentations
In class, working in teams to tailor presentations to address key concerns of clients.

Session 5: Round Table/Show and Tell
Come prepared with two observations about presenting ideas (how have you done it? how have you seen it done?) Bring in one piece from your internship or work outside of class to discuss workflow. In class, individuals lead the class through the working process at their placement firm.

Session 6: Work/Life Theme: Professional Expertise
Estimating and planning jobs. In class, guest designer discusses estimating strategies. In class, review various approaches, estimate a sample job.

Session 7: Work/Life Theme:
Office Smarts, Politics, and Professionalism
In class, individuals submit case studies of situations and the class provides input on solutions.

Session 8: Work/Life Theme:
Office Smarts; How to Plot a Design Career

In class, guest designer discusses moving up in the design world. In-class written exercise on setting goals.

Session 9: Round Table/Show and Tell

Come prepared with two observations on "what's next." Bring in your best piece for show and tell. In class, individuals use their learnings from the class to present their work.

assessment and evaluation

As with all classes in your major you must receive a letter grade for this class (A–F). A portion of your grade will be related to each of the types of activities for the class.

Professional Placement

You will be evaluated on the steps that you take in order to procure your placement. Your direct report at your professional placement will be asked to fill out an evaluation form for you at midterm and at finals, which will assist in the portion of your grade related to your internship. The reviewer will be asked to comment and rate you on the following: comparison to other interns, quality of the work, the way in which you handle yourself, your attitude, your initiative, your ability to take input and give it, and your ability to become an integral participate. (Note: I will be using these evaluations in an important, but advisory capacity.) The design for your logs and your consistent reporting of activity will also contribute.

Work/Life Themes

Work/life themes may have brief preparatory readings, and may include in-class exercises, group work, and role-playing. These are not passive sessions.

Round Table/Show and Tell

Round tables require you to come prepared with individual contributions and to participate in the informal give and take.

Individual Meetings

Follow through is key here. Make and keep appointments with me, be prompt and prepared with orderly logs and work samples. For meetings outside of midterm and finals come ready to take the lead with questions and concerns, etc.

Participation/Attitude Statement

In each evaluation area there is a component of participation and attitude. Regular class participation is a crucial element in the learning process. Obviously, it is not possible to participate if one is absent; however, it is possible to attend class and not participate. Therefore, attendance alone does not adequately describe the expectations in this class. Consistent and meaningful participation will help both your understanding and aid in my evaluation of that understanding.

Attitude is also important. Do you take and give criticism well? Are you open to suggestions? Are you working consistently and hard?

grade breakdown

Professional placement (logs, evaluations)	40%
Work/life themes (preparation/attendance/participation, number attended; three required)	20%
Round tables/show and tell (preparation/attendance/ participation, number attended; two required)	20%
Individual meetings (midterm and final)	20%

internship survey

(to be filled out on the first day of class)

Name ——————————————————————————

E-mail ——————————————————————————

Address ——————————————————————————

Phone (day/evening) Any restrictions on phone calls? ——————————

(1) Do you have a professional placement? Yes—continue No—skip to question 2.

Have you reviewed it with me? Yes—continue No—see me.

Firm: ——————————————————————————

Contact information/contact person: ————————————————

Description of any arrangements you have made (number of hours— times/days, responsibilities).

(2) Why did you decide to pursue graphic design?

(3) Describe your skills and expertise (be thorough and thoughtful). What are you particularly good at? _____

(4) What personal skills and interests outside of your major do you have? (Do you have a previous degree, a minor, fluency in a language, do you write well . . . ?)
_____

(5) What is your work style? (i.e., collaborative, independent) _____
_____

(6) What areas in design are you curious about? _____
_____

(7) If you could describe the perfect placement, what would it be? (print, digital, both, small, large . . .) _____
_____

(8) What type of placement do you want to avoid? _____
_____

(9) Are there any critical restrictions on your time, or are there geographic considerations that will affect your placement? _____
_____

(10) What else should I know about you? _____
_____

COURSE TITLE _ INQUIRIES INTO THE DESIGN OF NARRATIVES
INSTRUCTORS _ Hans Allemann, Inge Druckrey, Chris Myers
COLLABORATING CRITICS _ Joel Katz, Sherry Lefevre, Nancy Mayer,
   Martha Nichols
SCHOOL _ The University of the Arts (Philadelphia, Pennsylvania)
FREQUENCY _ Two semesters, sequential course
CREDITS _ Six credits total, three credits per semester
(Enrollment in the second semester is dependent upon successful
   completion of the first semester.)
LEVEL _ Undergraduate
(Restricted to graphic design majors or enrollment with permission of
   the instructor.)

purpose

The primary focus of this course is on storytelling, both in words and images.
The aim of the course is to train students to choose the appropriate media, format, and structure to present a story.

description

The course begins with an introductory assignment—a short, autobiographical
story—to analyze different narrative structures and alternate ways of interpreting narratives visually:

- continuous text
- listing
- diagram
- various text/image combinations

The choice of narrative might be a factual account or an expressive interpretation. This series of exercises will serve as the introduction and testing ground
for the independent degree project.

   The second assignment of this course is an independent degree project, a
narrative that most likely will be an existing text, chosen by the student. Text
authored by the student will be considered by the instructors of the course on a
case-by-case basis.

In support of the two assignments, special presentations will be scheduled by the instructors to review, analyze, and explore various formats of narrative communications such as: textbooks, illustrated books, guidebooks, how-to books, children's books, newspapers, newsletters, magazines, manuals, brochures, documentaries, videos, and interactive designs.

course overview

The investigation of the narrative is a year-long course. In the fall semester, the student develops a personal narrative or vignette and develops several visual approaches to the presentation of that narrative. The fall semester begins with a one-day writing workshop to jump-start the creation of the personal narratives. The personal narratives are finalized in the third or fourth week of the semester. Students will be devising speculative visual strategies for the presentation of that text prior to the finalization of the text. Simultaneously, the student undertakes a process to develop proposals for a Degree Project that are reviewed by outside critics to judge their viability for execution in the spring.

The spring semester is wholly dedicated to the execution of the Degree Projects that were approved in proposal form in the fall semester. Although many students decide to use existing text, those who choose authorship must arrive with their rough draft on the first day of the spring semester and have completed their writing revisions by the end of the first month of the spring semester.

The following is a breakdown of these processes.

fall semester: the autobiographical narrative

A narrative exists when we are witness to change. This change might happen over time or all at once. It is usually a change in both space and time. In traditional storytelling, a narrative has a beginning, a middle, and an end. In modern times, however, the concept of simultaneous narrative has been explored. In such a case, everything or many things happen at once. In most cases, narratives are bound to a sequential structure: the succession of incidents in a novel, poem, drama, the recounting of events in a person's life, or the changes of scenery in a travel description. A narrative might be written, pictorial, diagrammatic, or any combination of these.

Since you are the authority on your life history, this will be your text to experiment with different narrative structures. Any life history is multilayered, rich and meaningful. You might see it as a succession of events in chronological order, as parallel tracks of the inner and outer self, or show your life in relationship to outside influences, events, or people. You might track change through various names you were given and what they meant, or show photographs of different stages in your life, symbols, or images that were meaningful at different times.

Use selected material from your autobiographical sketch and explore different narrative structures.

1. A writing workshop (detailed description follows) and experiments in developing visually continuous text structures.
2. Verbal listing, text-based:
   a. Could also include another viewpoint or character.
   b. Could involve a secondary text that enriches the context of the original text.
3. Diagram, overview of events ordered by time, location, or any other ordering principle.
4. Text/image interaction in a linear account featuring the following potential approaches, among them:
   a. Visual metaphor
   b. Historical reference or parallel
   c. Documentary imagery
   d. Iconography
   e. Archetype

Format

Two 8½" × 11" sheets, either vertically or horizontally attached to form a bi-folio, or three sheets attached to form a tri-fold.

Process

1. Manuscript preparation and typesetting, image research
2. Series of studies investigating typographic layout
3. Series of studies investigating diagrammatic representations
4. Series of studies investigating interactions of type and image

In these exercises you should focus on the generation of many interesting ideas. Only meaningful ideas merit later refinement. Sketches should be produced quickly by drawing, cutting, and pasting. In the early sketch phases, the computer should only be used to generate raw material for collage or as a source for drawn sketches. This is also a good time to test your research skills and your ability to organize research material.

Week-to-Week Description

Fall semester: The Autobiographical Narrative

Week 1

Project introduction and writing workshop
[Editor's Note: For writing workshop, see description below.]

Week 2
Typographic layout studies with dummy copy. Written autobiography submitted for critique.

Week 3
Class critique to review initial typographic studies. Further explorations and refinement. Suggested corrections of the autobiographical writing submitted to students. Selected students may be required to schedule individual sessions to discuss the revisions with the Liberal Arts critic.

Week 4
Individual reviews to discuss typographic layouts and the beginning of the diagrammatic and timeline studies. Autobiographical text should be finalized.

Week 5
Class critique to review timeline studies. Further explorations and refinement.

Week 6
Individual reviews to discuss timeline studies and the beginning of text/image compositions.

Week 7
Class critique to review text/image compositions. Further explorations and refinement.

Week 8
Individual reviews to discuss text/image compositions. Further explorations and refinement.

Week 9
Individual review and final selection of studies for refinement.

Weeks 10–15
Refinement of selected studies. Final review. Presentation of the project to a jury of section faculty.

Description of the Critique(s)
The critique in the first semester is by informal jury of the section faculty. The student is evaluated individually by the following criteria:

- Research
- Personal initiative
- Use of time
- Communication with faculty
- Participation in class critiques
- Inventiveness

- Quality of design process
- Craftsmanship
- Overall quality of the final result

fall and spring semester: the degree project

The Degree Project begins in the fall semester and is simultaneous with the autobiographical narrative.

Introduction

As graphic designers we often have to deal with visual, written, or spoken narratives, so it is of interest to us to observe how different forms of a narrative affect the reader's experience. How for example does a diagram, a comic book, a narrative painting, a novel, a travel description, a play, a diary, a route map, a log book, a guide, book, a how-to book, a timetable, or a dance notation system symbolize time and space? The study of such different forms of narrative might help you in your own project.

Narrative Subjects

Select a text from any realm of narrative and in any area of interest—art, design, history, science, cultural studies, environmental studies, sports, music— and reinterpret it using visual, verbal, typography, and/or sonic means. Your reinterpretation might strengthen and clarify an existing point of view or it might add a new perspective to the story. You might annotate your text with another narrative, with visual elements, or your narrative might be mainly visual, annotated by typography. Your choice of media or venue might also enable you to address motion, sound, and physical dimension.

The form you choose to present the narrative text will influence the interpretation of the text: the interactive qualities of a book, the directed motion of digital video, or an interactive program with a digital interface will have profound effects on the reader. Choose your format and media carefully.

Thesis

A thesis is an analytical, conceptual position. It is important that you establish a viewpoint or a perspective on the text or subject matter that you intend to reinterpret. Without a thesis, you are merely rearranging your material to make a better visual presentation. That is not the object of this course. Your thesis is the criteria by which your overall success will be measured. It will direct your visual choices. In this way, your project is like an argument. Your thesis is your assertion and your design and presentation become part of the evidence that supports your thesis. To test your thesis, imagine saying, "This is so," and then state your assertion. Does it make sense?

Working Title

It is important to develop a working title. A working title is an important test to find out if you have a thesis. A working title does not simply announce your subject matter. It reflects that point of view and often the scope of your project.

Project Guidelines

The text selection need not be lengthy but should provide a rich opportunity for interpretation.

The complexity of the topic should be appropriate to the time available and each student's demonstrated ability of skills related to different media.

Since most students will be working with an appropriated text, the source must be properly cited as part of your final presentation. In addition, the final presentation should include a traditional colophon, which should also credit any other consultants to your project as well as any outside critics.

Project Format and Scope

The format for the project must be appropriate to the subject matter chosen, the intended audience, and the student's expertise within that format or medium. A suggested maximum guideline for the project length, if in book form, is thirty-two pages plus cover, front matter, and back matter. The scope for media outside of traditionally printed matter will be determined by the section faculty and the student.

Other Faculty Resources

Other faculty, both within the graphic design department and the university community may be consultants to the project at the discretion of those faculty members and the faculty project advisors. Other advisors outside the university may be consulted at the discretion of those experts and with the permission of the faculty project advisors.

Description of the Critique(s)

This is a formal review of written proposals that is conducted by an invited outside critic in concert with the section faculty of the course. The proposals have been forwarded to the critic previous to the review. The proposals are judged for viability both conceptually and in regards to the proposed scope of the project.

The critique in the second semester is two-fold. The first evaluation is to determine the awards for distinction in the execution of the projects. This critique takes the form of a public presentation of all sections of the course, which is juried by the section faculty, collaborating critics, and invited jurors from both the university faculty and from professional practice. The jury is approximately ten to twelve in number. The awards are determined by ballot in which all candidates are scored in the following categories:

1. Interpretation of the content
2. Visual resolution
3. Craftsmanship
4. Overall presentation

The second evaluation is conducted individually by the section faculty, which results in the grade for the course and the awarding of academic credit. Criteria for evaluation is as follows:

1. The clarity and relevance of the project proposal, its structure and content, as reflected in the proposal statement.
2. The degree of difficulty of the project.
3. The quality of the design process, especially the usefulness of sketches to define intentions, the independence in decision making, and the ability to self-criticize and evaluate progress critiques.
4. The quality of physical format decisions, in both its external and internal structures.
5. The quality of the visual resolution of the project, the text/image interaction, the range of appropriate expression.
6. The clarity of communication.
7. The originality of expression.
8. The quality of the typographic craftsmanship of the text: spelling, punctuation, and grammar.
9. The physical craftsmanship and all material aspects of the final presentation.
10. Completion according to the announced schedule.

description of classes

Week-to-Week Description Fall Semester: the Degree Project

Weeks 1–5
Introduce project. Begin the planning stage. Decide on subject matters about which you are interested. This is a very important stage, you have to find something you truly care about.

Week 6
Proposals for three subjects/theses are submitted in duplicate.

Week 7
Feedback from section faculty.

Week 8
Refined outline/proposals and text selections (if appropriate) of two of the three previous proposals.
    Formal proposal presentation to outside critic and section faculty.

Week 9
No class.

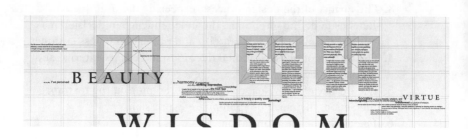

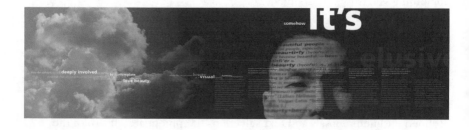

Keith Wantanabe

Week 10
Individual reviews with the instructor and final degree project selection. Begin work on concept development phase.

Final Review
Progress report on the degree project with amended project proposal.

Winter Break
If you have determined to write your own text and have been authorized by the section faculty to do so, you must complete the first draft by the beginning of the spring semester.

If your project is location specific, for imagery, documentation, and/or access to research archives or particular outside resources or people, you must have completed your preliminary research by the beginning of the spring semester. You must also be able to return to these people or sites at least once during the spring semester to augment or verify information as your project develops.

If your project is particularly hinged upon a reference bibliography, your reading must be completed by the beginning of the spring semester.

Week-to-Week Description Spring Semester: The Degree Project

Week 1–5
Investigation and development of informational structures. Preparation of prototypes that address all salient aspects of the project.

For those students authoring text or synthesizing and editing text from several sources, text should be revised and refined toward a final draft that is due on Week 5.

Week 6
Formal review of prototypes with an outside critic and the section faculty. Prototypes should be developed to the level that they might answer as many of the unique characteristics of the information as possible.

Week 7–12
Synthesis and realization of the project.

Week 13
Public presentation and jury review of the degree projects.

the writing workshop

(Sherry Lefevre, Liberal Arts Critic)
[Editor's note: The writing workshop runs through the fall semester.]

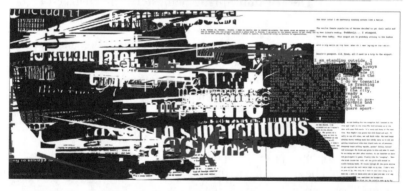

Agnes Sekreta

We have chosen several children's books to provide examples and inspiration for this assignment (see reading list.) Moreover, we have selected books that attempt to communicate layers of information in ways that might be instructive to you as you make your way through your exploration of various ways of visually framing your story.

It's important to begin thinking about this project by considering the specifications:

1. Four hundred words is not a long narrative. For example, it is less than half the length of the *Red Canoe* narrative, even subtracting the pieces of the text that one might call contextual information (recipes, knot-typing, maps).

2. A spread or tri-fold does not offer the experience of time passing in quite as tactile a way as page turning in a book like *Red Canoe*. There are spatial limitations to how much the text can be broken up in the interest of separating out the various episodes in your sequence.

3. The various assignments that follow the composition of the narrative might influence your selection process, especially Assignment 2, which calls for some sort of diagram, timeline, map, etc.

Section 1: Beginning

You will probably begin this assignment by thinking cosmically of the whole spectrum of your life. You might look for broad themes that help define what your life has been about so far. This is the impulse of many writers: find an organizing idea, or principle, or theme that helps one make sense out of life. (Finding a theme for a graphic designer is just as important. For this project, you'll help yourself immensely if you keep thematic coherence in mind as you compose your narrative.) You may see your life as a sequence of revelations that helped you define yourself as an individual, apart from your surroundings. You may see your life's narrative as a movement from innocence, through a sequence of harsh awakenings, to an understanding of how the world really is. Or you may see it as a series of mistakes (drugs, friends, work) to a gradual enlightenment.

While it is possible for you to devote your narrative assignment to a thematic sequencing of your entire life, there are certain dangers that you want to keep in mind, given the fact that you only have four hundred words and a two- or three-page spread to do it in.

The challenge is to abbreviate the narrative without making it so abstract, or so much a summation, that it has no experiential value—i.e., no impact on the reader.

See how differently you experience each of the following variations on the same narrative sequence. This is the most abstract summary:

When my father died, it changed my life. Our economic circumstances were more difficult and I had to assume more responsibilities both for myself and my family.

This is only slightly less abstracted:

My father died when I was seven and that began a series of changes in my life that affect who I am today. First, my mother went to work. She was no longer around when I came home from school. Then it became clear that we could no longer afford private school, so I had to go to the local public school. Just when my social life began to take off, so did my mother's and that meant I had to baby-sit my younger siblings on weekend nights. By the time I was fifteen and began thinking about college, I realized that if I wanted to go to college, I had better start working in order to save up money. . . .

Neither of these narratives have much emotional or dramatic punch. On the other hand, they are concise, which is one of your objectives. So how can you have your cake and eat it too?

One choice is to develop a microcosm: take a single episode in the sequence as emblematic of all of the other shifts and evolution. What happened when your mother started working after your father died may, in some ways, stand for all the other changes that were to occur. The beginning of a microcosmic sequence might read:

The day my mother went back to work after my father's death, it was already 103 degrees outside by 8:00 in the morning. We were no longer turning on the air-conditioning, since my father had had no life insurance. I went downstairs to find there was no lunch-box waiting for me on the kitchen counter. I started to look for things . . . in the refrigerator, but then my brother came in, asking where mom was and where his red Phillies t-shirt was. When I told him to wear something else, he started to cry because dad had given it to him and that was the only thing he ever wanted to wear. . . .

The virtue of taking a microcosm of experience, a single episode, is that you can develop detail. Detail gives the reader empirical evidence that allows the reader to share in the experience. Hopefully, you have felt this happen as you moved through these examples.

Another way to go is to use the poet's trick of finding a key image that works metaphorically and therefore accomplishes generalization and detail at the same time. A friend of mine used the detail of slats falling out of the shutters on her house to express the gradual dissolution of her life after her husband left. In a sequence of scenes, the common thread was her casually taking note of the new losses in the shutters.

What key image might tie together the autobiographic narrative of the kid's life after his father's death? If you were writing for television, it would be a pocket watch given to you by your dad. Initially, it sat in its cotton-padded box in your top bureau drawer. One morning you needed it to tell you when to wake up to get your younger brother on the school bus; it is stolen from you at your new public school; but, is returned, mysteriously to the lost and found; it sits in your brown uniform pocket when you work for UPS, but finally attaches proudly to your outside pocket when your mother gives you a gold chain as a graduation present. This is not brilliantly conceived (a five-minute exercise) but it gets the point across. Your focus on the concrete life of the pocket watch allows you to tell the whole broad story, without it sounding so broad.

You may be thinking that this image-based thread is something you will leave to the design stage of your project. But I am warning you. Make your life easier by planning ahead. If it's not in the story, you may not be able to work it into the design.

Brainstorming: Exercise A
Imagine as many sequences in your life as you can. Let your imagination run the gamut from the sublime to the ridiculous. Think concretely: a sequence of houses; schools; girlfriends; boyfriends; parents (step-mothers/fathers); pets; clothing styles . . . now you take over.

Brainstorming: Exercise B
Attach as many clichés to your life as you can arguably make a story for:
"If you want something done right, do it yourself."
"Love means never having to say you're sorry."
"The road to hell is paved with good intentions."
"Use it or lose it."
"No pain, no gain."
Now you take over.

Section II: Narrative Genres
After you have scanned the broad expanse of your life for a meaningful sequence, you may realize that you might do just as well choosing neither micro- nor macrocosm. Your narrative doesn't have to represent your whole life or your true self. It can be a small piece of your experience, like a trip or something incredibly frightening, amusing, touching, mortifying, etc., etc., that happened within a short span of time.

I'm using superlatives, because the story should carry enough emotional weight to interest both you and your readers over a long portion of the semester (and you may want to treasure it in the autumn of your years).

The following are several categories of stories you might consider.

On-the-Road Narratives
Many people use travel experiences as a resource for an autobiographical narrative. You have an example of a picture book that features a three-day journey in a canoe. We have other examples of travel narratives. As in all narratives, an important place to start is to ask yourself, "Why is the reader interested in this travel episode?" Clearly the author of the canoe narrative decided to make the book quasi-practical—to engage the reader with the possibility that he/she too might make a journey like this. At least the book offers the possibility of *imagining* a practical application, which may be all a reader wants anyway. So it combines travel with "how-to"—recipes, tent-pitching diagrams, etc. Often on-the-road stories do become a little like guidebooks. In this case, the book isn't specific about its location so it's only generically a guidebook to river canoeing.

If you choose to write a travel story, consider the following issues:

1. What is the predominant feature of your narrative: plot, characterization, or setting? Setting is most often the focus of travel stories but it may not be in yours.
2. What is the theme, or what gives the trip continuity? This usually depends on the answer to number one. An attribute of character or a predominant quality of the setting may give a travel story continuity. Plot may provide continuity if, for instance, your focus is on change, suspense, risk, surprise, etc.
3. What is the shape of the journey? Does it move like an arrow to a determined goal? Does it go straight for a while and then take a sharp detour? Does it wander gracefully? Does it resolve itself by coming full circle or is closure reached some other way?

The Dramatic Narrative

If you want to write a dramatic narrative, remember that drama largely arises out of conflict, so you need to see clearly where the conflict in your narrative lies.

What's conflict? Conflict is really just various forms of disagreement. You may have disagreed with your parents about something you wanted to do, done it anyway, and suffered repercussions; you may have disagreed with your school and taken a stand; you may have disagreed with your government, and left your country, etc., etc.

Conflict can also be within a person. Sometimes your "will" is in conflict with an instinct like fear. Internal conflicts are often difficult to externalize on a page, but it can be done.

Conflict can also be between a person and forces of nature. Many travel journals derive their drama, their suspense, from this conflict. (Think *The Perfect Storm.*)

The introduction of a conflict immediately develops the expectation that it will ultimately be resolved, as, for some reason we do not assume chaos to be the natural state of things; instead, we believe equanimity to be the norm. Thus, conflict breeds suspense—suspense about how it will be resolved. Usually dramatic narrative develops toward greater risk-taking as the hero confronts the conflicting force.

The Comic Narrative

We are probably most grateful when someone chooses to tell a comic story about him/herself. But we also know how difficult it is to really pull it off. Comedy is not easy to define. We know it when we laugh. In all good drama, what happens is not what we or the hero expected, but in comedy, it's off-the-wall opposite of what we expected. The trick is to keep undermining expectation without hint or comment. Comedy is diffused by analysis.

We recognize this in ourselves as we are acting out the role. Otherwise, we would probably not be comic. Comedy depends on our not recognizing our blind obsessions, our not realizing the gap between who we think we are and who we are. If we recognize it and can turn to someone and say, "My problem is, I think I'm really suave and sophisticated but I'm not," then we're just another pathetic person—we're not funny.

So, if you want to write about a funny thing that happened to you, don't superimpose too much of your analysis and self-awareness—just tell it. I think of the time I was robbed.

I'd finally gotten the house to where it was looking pretty good, and with not much expenditure, too. I'd bought these chiffon scarves that passed for curtain swags when I nailed them up right. I'd even managed to put together a still life of shells and driftwood on the big dresser top in my master bedroom. Then I come home one day and just as I'm turning the key in the front door, I hear the back door crash to the floor with a terrible boom and I see this tall guy in shadow leap over the mess and then, just as quick as water in hot oil, leap back 'cause he sees me and bolts out the door.

So I call the police, of course, my hand shaking, and since I'm two doors down from the biggest mobster in South Philly, they're here in fifteen seconds. One guy starts to ask me questions, but I'm still shaking so he stops and tells me to sit down and take it easy. He goes back to examine the broken door while the two others head up to the bedroom, where the jewels would be, I guess. I hear one of them whistle, "Whooeee!" he says and then pokes his head around the stairs, half-way down. "Listen, lady," he's wagging his head from side to side, "I wouldn't come up here if I was you. The place has been ransacked. Your stuff's all over the place and I mean it, drawers out . . . closets. He's gone through everything. I've never seen anything like it." For a second, I don't know what he's talking about. "But he . . ." and then I stuff that right back down my throat and say, "My goodness, and just when I had it looking so nice."

181

The Educational Narrative

I'm only partly joking. You have an example of the children's book about a kid who learns about etching in his grandfather's workshop. Couching "how-to" information in a narrative sequence is a neat way of making education "fun." You've certainly had education experiences in the past few years that might be constructed as a narrative and allow for all the layering of information that the assignment requires.

readings

References on Writing and Editing

Grossman, John. Preface, *The Chicago Manual of Style: The Essential Guide for Writers, Editors and Publishers*, Fourteenth Edition. Chicago: The University of Chicago Press, 1993. An American standard for typesetting styles, punctuation, grammar, and writing construction.

Hacker, Diane. *A Writer's Reference*, Fourth Edition. New York: Bedford Books, 2001. The Modern Languages Association standard reference book used for writing style, grammar, and punctuation.

Strunk, William Jr., E.B. White, Charles Osgood, and Roger Angell. *The Elements of Style*, Fourth Edition. Needham Heights, MA: Allyn and Bacon, 2000. A classic author's guide.

Zinsser, William Knowlton. *On Writing Well: The Classic Guide to Writing Non-Fiction*, Sixth Edition. New York: Harper Reference, 1998. An especially good reference guide for writing nonfiction travel narratives and interviews.

Narrative Examples in Children's Literature

Aragon, Jane Chelsea. Illustrated by Leslie Baker. *Winter Harvest*. Boston: Little, Brown and Company, 1988.

Bunting, Eve. Illustrated by Ted Rand. *Night Tree*. New York: Harcourt Brace Jovanovich, Publishers, 1991.

Geisert, Arthur. *The Etcher's Studio*. Boston: Houghton Mifflin Company, 1997.

Holling, Holling Clancy. *Paddle to the Sea*. Boston: Houghton Mifflin Company, 1941.

Williams, Vera B. *Three Days on a River in a Red Canoe*. New York: Mulberry Books, 1981.

Yolen, Jane. Illustrated by John Schoenherr. *Owl Moon*. London: Liber Press, 1992.

References on Visual Information Analysis

Tufte, Edward. *Envisioning Information*. Cheshire, CT: Graphics Press, 1990.

Tufte, Edward. *The Visual Display of Quantitative Information*. Cheshire, CT: Graphics Press, 2001.

Tufte, Edward. *Visual Explanation: Images and Quantities, Evidence and Narratives*. Cheshire, CT: Graphics Press, 1997.

part 2

undergraduate/
graduate

COURSE TITLE _ WEB DESIGN FOR E-COMMERCE/GRAPHIC
   APPLICATIONS
INSTRUCTOR _ Sunghyun Kang   185
SCHOOL _ Iowa State University
FREQUENCY _ One sixteen-week semester, four hours per week
CREDITS _ Two
LEVEL _ Undergraduate and graduate level (cross-listed for
   graduate students)

purpose

The purpose of this course is for students to understand e-commerce and the
Web, and to learn how graphic design can improve its usability, enhance the
branding and identity of a Web site, and organize the information. In order to
achieve this, students should understand:

- The characteristics of the Web and e-commerce
- Design elements and principles on Web design
- How to integrate and communicate information according to visual
  hierarchy and information hierarchy
- Usability issues such as icon/menu usage and navigation methods

description

The course is designed to help students develop advanced and experimental Web design for applications to e-commerce, education, and the communication of visual information.

This course is based on lectures, research, and projects. Students are expected to complete two major projects and two assignments. Graduate students are required to conduct one additional research project.

description of classes

Week 1
Lecture: Characteristics of the Web; understanding the differences between traditional media and the Web

Week 2
Lecture: Understanding e-business
Assignment 1: Experience report of usability

Week 3
Lecture: Web usability
Group discussion of Assignment 1

Week 4
Lecture: Design elements for Web design
Group discussion of Assignment 2

Week 5
Lecture: Color on the Web: Web-safe color, the meanings of specific colors; color palette, and color combinations on the Web

Week 6
Assign Project 1: Web catalog redesign
In-class analysis of an existing e-commerce site (Web site will be given to each student to analyze the problems)

Week 7
Finding problems. Ideation for problem-solving

Week 8
Work session: development of design

Week 9
Assign project 2: E-commerce/educational Web sites
Presentation and critique of Project 1

Week 10
Research on the product/company/organization: purpose, audience, and product

Week 11
Design considerations: developing the communication concepts, managing branding and identity, the effect of content on design style

Week 12
Lecture: architectural design of Web sites: sitemap, navigation flow, navigation methods

Week 13
Work session: layout on the Web and development of the final design

Week 14
Work session: refining the design

Week 15
Work session: cording

Week 16
Presentation and critique of final designs

assignments

Assignment 1: Experience Report of Usability
The purpose of this assignment is to understand usability. Students will report their experiences with Web sites, ATM machines, copy machines, etc., and discuss how easy they are use and the obstacles to usability.

Assignment 2: Research the Elements of the Web
The purpose of this assignment is to learn the elements of the Web and its usage.

Students are required to research icons, buttons, hypertexts, color, image, layout, etc. Students will evaluate the elements according to an evaluation matrix.

Project 1: Web-Catalog Design

The purpose of this project is to understand the layout on the Web and learn how layout on the Web differs from traditional print media. This project will include layout and typographic considerations, navigation method, and color usage.

Project 2: E-commerce/Educational Web Site Design

The purpose of this project is to create an actual working Web site. From this project students will learn how to plan and develop a large-scale Web site, organize the information, and build a user-friendly interface design using their graphic design knowledge.

Students will apply their knowledge of conceptual and analytical thinking skills as well as advanced technology skills to accomplish this project.

required text

Ray Kristof and Amy Satran, *Interactivity by Design* (Adobe Press, 1995).

recommended texts

Marcia Robinson et al., *E-Business: Roadmap for Success* (Addison Wesley, 2000).

Jae K. Shim, et al., *The International Handbook of Electronic Commerce* (AMACOM, 2000).

Steffano Korper and Juanita Ellis, *The E-Commerce Book: Building the E-Empire* (Academic Press, 2000).

Steve Krug, *Don't Make Me Think! A Common Sense Approach to Web Usability* (Que, 2000).

Jacob Nielsen, *Designing Web Usability* (New Riders, 1999).

www.useit.com. Biweekly articles by Jacob Nelson.

COURSE TITLE _ FLASH INTENSIVE

INSTRUCTORS _ Natalie Zee, Susan Harris, Anna McMillan,
   Josh Ulm, Taylor

SCHOOL _ San Francisco State University, Oakland Multimedia Center

FREQUENCY _ Five days per week for three weeks

CREDITS _ None

LEVEL _ Undergraduate, graduate

purpose

The curriculum is structured into morning lectures, with afternoon labs to support the integration of information from each morning. Five design-veteran instructors alternate teaching roles, according to their specialties and special passions. All are present at the beginning and the end, to celebrate the students' accomplishments.

description

Find your flow . . . from intermediate to beyond advanced. If you've been learning Flash and want to take it to the limit, this is the place for you. You already know that Flash is the ultimate tool for the art geek—part design, part programming, and all inspiration. Our faculty of renowned designers will take you from the solid grounding you have to creating some truly amazing portfolio work, including professional fundamentals you won't find in any other program, like pitching Flash successfully to clients, storyboarding, and prototyping. The final stage of the Flash Intensive is a portfolio 'zine showcasing your perspective in visuals, movement, and direct expression of ideas.

Who should take this course? Flash designers who want to go from intermediate to the outer limits.

Prerequisites: Flash I or solid initial experience in Flash.

description of classes

Week 1

Morning lecture topics:
Monday: Introduction/orientation

Tuesday: Principles of graphic design
Wednesday: Storyboarding/presenting
Thursday: Drawing tools (within Flash)
Friday: Initial animation (within Flash)

Week 2

Morning lecture topics:
Monday: Sound
Tuesday: Usability/interface design
Wednesday: Begin final project planning
Thursday: ActionScripting—button activity
Friday: ActionScripting—functions and objects

Week 3

Morning lecture topics:
Monday: ActionScripting—external applications, XML, databases
Tuesday: Putting it all together
Wednesday: Final project workshop, Q/A
Thursday: Final project workshop, Q/A
Friday: Final project show and celebration

purpose

The purpose of this class is to teach strategies and processes for developing and utilizing original images. Whether digital or analog, students learn to seek the full potential of an image and exploit the possibilities within it. Students also examine the relationships between images and text and how meaning changes depending on the context used. Narrative, hierarchy, scale, metaphor and sequence are also explored. Whether the student is an illustrator or designer, the class will help expand image generation/exploration skills. Sketching is a must, in any form. Whether writing, taking pictures, or drawing in a sketchbook, students should be willing to take risks and try something they haven't done before.

description

Three projects will be assigned, each with a different emphasis. In addition, students will be required to keep an image journal over the semester. At least five original images should be added each week. Journals will be collected at various times during the semester. Students should collect anything and everything they find interesting. Receipts, trash, shoe prints, photographs, packaging—whatever sparks interest. Various reading and writing exercises will be given throughout the semester. Class time is divided between ongoing projects, critiques, exercises for the day, demonstrations, and videos.

description of classes

Assignments

Project 1

Create a series of five sheets of wrapping paper based on one of the seven deadly sins: pride, envy, gluttony, lust, anger, greed, or sloth. Each sheet should be different but together they should form a series.

Think about:

- Wrapping paper is usually considered disposable. How can you make paper that people will want to keep and not tear apart? How can the paper be the "gift" rather than what it contains?
- What makes something a series? Can each sheet be unique but still form a cohesive series?
- Does your message change once the flat wrapping paper becomes three-dimensional on a package?

Project Requirements

- You must use original images.
- You must include text, hand generated imagery (illustrations, painting, etc.), an object you have found, and an original photograph. They can be on separate sheets or together on each one.
- Each sheet size is 20" × 20".
- Final consists of two sets of the five different sheets. One set is flat; use the other set to wrap five different packages. These packages should be various sizes and shapes of your choice.

Project Schedule

Week 1: Project 1 assigned; begin research and ideation
Week 2: Concept sketches, visuals, imagery due; class discussion
Week 3: Continue sketching and refining; work in class; individual discussions with instructor
Week 4: Project due

Project 2

Create a visual essay based on your interpretation of a story (or stories) from Einstein's *Dreams*. The final format of your piece will be a photocopied, stapled sixteen-page booklet, 10" × 16" (folded to 8" × 10").

Think about:

- What is your essay from the book about? How can you explain it to others? Through text, your own words, and images?
- This project is about examining form and sequence. Think about scale and pacing from page to page. How can you keep the viewer interested?
- How does black and white affect your decisions on images and text?
- How can you build up to the message of your essay rather than give it away at the beginning?

Requirements

- Everyone must use text and *at least one* original illustration, original photograph, and found object (receipt, video still, etc).

- Follow the format! Remember to give yourself time for your piece to progress; this is just as much about the process as it is about the final product.
- Final booklet must be black and white. No other colors please.

Project Schedule
Week 1: Project assigned; begin research and ideation
Week 2: Working in class, at least ten sketches/concepts due. Individual discussions with instructor. Be prepared to talk about your ideas. Take lots of photos, collect lots of stuff!
Week 3: 8" × 10" sketches due, group discussion about the work. *Everyone* should be putting work in progress on the walls. At this point you should be past pencil sketching and into combining real images and text.
Week 4: Individual discussions with instructor. You should be working at 100 percent size with several pages. Think about sequence and pacing as you are designing. Be prepared to work in class.
Week 5: Project 2 due; class critique

Project 3
Create a poster about urban legends. Final size is 24" × 36". You can take any approach you want.
    Think about:

- Research and collect everything you can about urban legends.
- Look on the Internet, go to the bookstore, and interview other people about urban legends.
- Find as many examples of urban legends as you can. What are they? How did they get that name?
- Can your poster be about a particular urban legend that you have heard?
- What about propaganda: Can you make your urban legend seem real to the viewer?
- Can it be a documentary-style poster about urban legends?
- What about humor?

Project Requirements

- Your poster must include text.
- You must include a definition of an urban legend somewhere on the poster.
- Use at least one urban legend on your poster (you can use more if you want). You can use the actual text or images to tell your story.
- Some of your text should be created outside the computer (photos, hand-drawn, etc).
- You must use at least two different media on your poster: video stills, photos, sketches, photocopy, ink, wax, etc. Your elements can be composed on the computer.

193

Project Schedule
Week 1: Project 3 begins with research and ideation.
Week 2: Working in class, individual discussions. Bring all your research and
materials to class. Photos, quotes, books, sketches, etc.
Week 3: Group discussion on your half-size sketches.
Week 4: Individual discussions with instructor; be prepared to work
in class.
Week 5: Project due, class critique.

critiques

Dialogue amongst the students is required. Critiques range from the students presenting their work, to the student not being able to speak until the end of the critique. Students are encouraged to be concise and direct when speaking about their work. If they cannot articulate their idea verbally then it will never work visually.

conclusion

I approach this class as a chance for illustration and design majors to learn from each other. For the most part when they begin the class, the illustrators don't use photography or typography, while the designers go straight to the computer and never draw or sketch. In my experience, all of the students rely too heavily on the computer and found images rather than making their own. This class encourages experimentation, image making, and process-oriented work. The designers and illustrators learn from each other, and usually by the end of the semester it is difficult to tell which department each student is from.

COURSE TITLE _ EXHIBITION DESIGN
INSTRUCTOR _ Lisa Fontaine
SCHOOL _ Iowa State University
FREQUENCY _ One semester
CREDITS _ Two
LEVEL _ Undergraduate or graduate (dual listed)

purpose

This course is a unique opportunity to apply your graphic design expertise in a three-dimensional environment. While studying theories of museum exhibition design, you will apply your knowledge to the development and design of interactive exhibition spaces.

description

In this course you will be exposed to the multitude of considerations typical in museum design. These include learning theory, communication theory (as applied to both visual and verbal communication), architectural space, ergonomics, visual hierarchy, design principles, and process. Your focus will be on interactive, conceptually driven visual communication. This will enable you to make use of your previous experience in two-dimensional graphic design.

It is not expected that you master all areas of exhibit design and planning, rather that you increase your interdisciplinary proficiency and understanding, thus enabling you to function well in a three-dimensional design environment.

Exhibition design is an area of sub-specialization within design, which is often accomplished through interdisciplinary collaboration. We will attempt, therefore, to involve our design colleagues in architecture and interior design in our critiques whenever possible.

In addition to the studio projects, course activities include the following:

- Interpretative exercises
- Basic instruction in architectural drawing conventions
- Field trips to science and history museums
- Interdisciplinary critiques with students and faculty from architecture and interior design

assignments and projects

Exercise A: Interpretation of Three-dimensional Environments

Objectives: This assignment will encourage you to consider the *hidden dimension** of places—to explore the emotional messages communicated by each environment we experience. It will also allow you to study the functional needs of different spaces.

Procedure: Museum design requires a sensitivity to space, both emotionally and functionally.

Each person's emotional interpretation of a space may differ depending on his or her background, personality, and experiences. A space that seems overwhelming to some may be exhilarating to another. Your emotional interpretation of a space may be influenced by such tangible factors as the lighting level, the colors used, textures, smell, sound level, scale, and activity level; less tangible factors may also play a part: sense of history, privacy/intimacy, grandeur, and your own familiarity with the space. For example, does Beardshear Hall seem beautiful and stately to a campus visitor, while seeming oppressive and cold to a student with business to accomplish there?

We will compile a list of local public spaces to be visited, with each student providing a suggestion. Visit at least three of the spaces on the compiled list, recording brief notations about their differing functions and activity levels as well as your observations of their emotional aspects.

In studying spaces, it is also important to determine whether or not their functional needs are being met. See what you can find out about each of the following for the spaces you visit:

- Dimensions of the space
- Height of the ceiling
- Lighting (natural or artificial; bright or dim)
- Floor surface
- Sound level
- Function of space
- Is the space designed for the traffic it currently receives? For the activity level?
- How difficult would this space be to maneuver if you were in a wheelchair?
- Do people easily understand how to navigate the space?
- Is the lighting adequate and appropriate for the activity?
- What makes this space feel unique from others?
- What are the two most significant adjectives you could use to describe this space?

Exercise B: Plans and Elevations

Objectives: This assignment will introduce you to some of the architectural drawings standards that are used for two-dimensional translation of three-dimensional spaces. You will also gain experience with the use of an architectural scale ruler.

Procedure: When designing three-dimensionally, it is important to be able to articulate your ideas in two-dimensional form. This will allow you to save time and money in the ideation phase, and will also enable you to be able to "read" architectural drawings done by others.

Draw a floor plan and elevations (each of the four walls) of the studio classroom at 3/4" scale that include all permanent elements (doors, windows, and built-in cabinetry) and show all relevant measurements. Repeat the exercise with a room in your apartment/dorm.

Submission format: Create the drawings on tracing paper (these should not be rendered on the computer).

Tape the drawings to bristol board or another opaque white paper surface. *Do not* submit as rolled-up drawings.

Exercise C: Field Trip Reports

Objective: This assignment will document the insights and observations made on our museum field trips.

Procedure: Since we are focusing on interactivity in museum design, it is essential to experience exhibits ourselves, to more fully understand the interactive learning environment. While at museums, we will also be able to witness other visitors of differing ages, and considering their varying responses to the exhibitions.

Select *one* exhibition gallery from the museums visited. Record your specific observations about the exhibition's functional, formal, and conceptual issues below:

Functional considerations:

- Has traffic flow been planned for? Any bottlenecks?
- Do exhibit materials seem durable? What are the materials used?
- Are reading heights comfortable? If not, why not?
- Are there any dangerous aspects within the exhibit? If so, what are they?
- Could a handicapped person experience most of the exhibit? If not, why not?
- Is typography easy to read? If so, why? If not, why not?

Formal considerations:

- Describe color palette; evaluate its effectiveness.
- Describe typographic aesthetics; evaluate its effectiveness.
- Is there visual unity of elements/components within the exhibit?
- Is there a clear information hierarchy throughout? If so, how is it achieved?
- Does the exhibit seem to have a visual style? If so, describe it. Is it appropriate?

Conceptual considerations:

- Describe the overall message of the exhibit (as you understand it) in one sentence.
- What is the narrative tone? Is it presented in different ways to appeal to several different ages?
- How do the interactive experiences help to communicate the content? Use examples.
- Which of the interaction types is being used here?
- Which of the multiple intelligences is being encouraged in these interactions? Use examples.
- How are metaphors used in the exhibits? What is being compared to what?
- Does the content have a linear sequence (a starting and ending point), or is it a fluid sequence (the visitor can start at any point in the exhibit and move to any other point)?
- Is the type of sequence effective and obvious to the visitors?

Visitor observations:

- What are the most and least popular aspects with visitors under the age of ten?
- What are the most and least popular aspects with visitors over the age of ten?
- How are exhibit components mistreated or misused? Why does it happen?
- Can visitors share the experiences with others, or are they designed to be individual experiences?
- If you could change one thing in this museum, what would it be? Why?

Project 1: Modular Exhibit Components

Objectives: This assignment will allow you to translate your two-dimensional design skills to a 3-D environment. It will introduce you to the basic formal and functional considerations that occur in this format.

Procedure: The success of your two-dimensional design work has continually relied on your understanding of basic design principles and concerns for the functional needs of the work. Yet these skills do not automatically translate when graphic designers move from 2-D to 3-D; in fact, often they are temporarily forgotten in the early sketches and models. It is important to focus on these existing skills immediately to accelerate the 3-D learning process. The same formal principles apply in two- and three-dimensional work, although now you will be considering *volumes* more than *planes*. The functional issues differ from print media, but your experience in problem solving will translate easily.

Using the simple plans and elevations provided, elaborate and articulate this modular structure to be both functional and visually appealing. Your structure will serve as an activity or experimentation station. The nature of the activity is your choice.

Phase 1: Functional Emphasis
Based on the enclosed drawings, create new elevation and plan drawings (one-inch scale) of the structure with three-dimensional enhancements and alterations as you deem necessary. The specific functional needs of the structure must be resolved. After working on paper, experiment with foam core, clay, or florist foam to build a scale model of your drawn ideas. To concentrate on the functional issues, do not apply colors, graphics, or typography at this phase. Build two of the modules to show how they might be used together. Include scale model figures, sitting and standing, with your model.

Phase 2: Sculptural Emphasis
Revise your existing design: this time your emphasis should be on the manipulation of the volume, rather than surface treatment (think of yourself as carving it rather than painting it). How do you apply principles of composition (contrast, repetition, etc.) to a volumetric form? How do you bring visual impact and uniqueness to the basic requirements of the structure? Build a second model (keep your phase 1 model intact). To concentrate on the three-dimensional issues, do not apply colors, graphics, or typography at this phase. For this phase, you only need to build one module. Include scale model figures, sitting and standing, with your model.

199

Phase 3: Graphic Communication and Color
Revise your existing design: this time your emphasis should be on the graphic presentation of type, images, and color. Build a third model (keep your phase 1 and 2 models intact). Create a visual identity for the exhibit; build two of the modules to show how your graphic approach provides visual unity and variety. Each of the modules should now include headers, a color scheme, secondary text as needed, and supplementary graphic elements or images as appropriate for your design. Color and type should be applied through color printouts adhered to the foam core structure. Include scale model figures, sitting and standing, with your model.

Submission format: Produce each of your three models in either foam core, board, and/or florist foam. Identify the design principles that are effectively employed, as well as the functional issues resolved, in a written statement.

Project 2: Historical Exhibition in Shallow Space
Objectives: In this assignment you will continue translating your graphic design skills to a large-scale format. By conforming to the exhibit's shallow dimensions, you will be able to focus your attention on the graphic application of type and image on a large scale.

Procedure: Design an interpretive historical exhibit that effectively displays the text, artifacts, and images supplied.

The same formal principles apply in print and environmental graphics, yet often they are temporarily forgotten when we move to large-scale format. Underlying grid structure, visual hierarchy, color, contrast, and compositional balance are all essential to the effective organization of exhibit panels.

The gallery space is twenty feet wide, ten feet high, and two feet deep. Your exhibit elements will include the following:

- Headers
- Interpretive text
- Artifacts (three-dimensional)
- Artifacts (two-dimensional)
- Supportive images

All artifacts are considered valuable originals and must be protected from visitor handling. You cannot resize artifacts; they must be shown in their original form. Supportive images, however, can be reproduced at any size, and can be manipulated by cropping, screening back, etc. You are free to add other supportive images or visual patterns.

Headers and interpretive text can be any font or size. You must include all of the artifacts (2- and 3-D), all of the headers and text, and more than half of the supportive images supplied.

The exhibition must make full use of its shallow space; don't limit yourself to large 2-D panels. Consider how pedestals, cabinets, and other surface changes can be used to articulate the space.

Your final submission will be a 2-D elevation and floor plan (both in color) of your final design, at ¼" scale. These drawings should be done in Illustrator or in a comparable drawing program.

Project 3: Small Museum Exhibition

Objectives: This assignment will allow you to expand on your understanding of three-dimensional space and sculptural form. You will explore methods for presenting information in ways that can promote interactive learning experiences.

Procedure: You will select a topic (from the approved list) for your exhibition that you feel could be effectively presented to children ages six to nine or nine to twelve. You will be responsible for researching the topic, including existing methods for presenting it to children. Look at children's books and instructional materials on the topic. Familiarize yourself with the multiple intelligences of your audience.* You will also need to determine age-appropriate tasks and experiences for your target age group.

The exhibition should not rely on extensive text for interpretation. A young child with limited reading skills should be able to enjoy and learn from it. The content of the exhibit should be structured with a clear hierarchy of information, yet without a rigid sequencing. While much of the information will be presented through two-dimensional surface treatments (images and text), the exhibit itself must be more than a collection of flat surfaces; the articulation of basic design principles in three-dimensional space must be evident and effective.

Design an exhibition which uses a maximum floor space of 8' × 16'. The exhibit must be approachable from all sides, although it can be partially enclosed by wall partitions. The space should allow for several people to interact with it at the same time.

Your primary goal is to promote interaction with the exhibit. Consider visual or conceptual metaphors that could be adapted for your topic. Explore interactive devices and methods for enhancing the learning experience. Carefully determine placement of images, typography, and interactive elements so that they enhance the information hierarchy and are located at appropriate heights for your visitors.

In addition to conceptual and aesthetic aspects, consider the following functional and technical issues: child safety and supervision, minimization of technology within the exhibits, human factors, appropriateness of materials in terms of feasibility, and maintenance requirements.

Develop a content outline that defines the scope of the topic presented, and shows the information hierarchy. Create conceptual drawings that visually interpret your content outline. Follow up on these concepts by constructing rough models (¼" or ½" scale) for review. Rough models will be reviewed in the three phases used in Project 1.

Submission format: Create a final model at ¾" or 1" scale, with accurate text and images. You will be required to have this model photo-documented; submit photos of the model at a variety of angles and distances.

*Refer to supplied reading from *Frames of Mind: The Theory of Multiple Intelligences*, Tenth Edition, Howard Gardner (Basic Books, 1993).

COURSE TITLE _ HISTORY OF DESIGN: TWENTIETH-CENTURY
INFORMATION DESIGN
INSTRUCTOR _ R. Roger Remington
SCHOOL _ Rochester Institute of Technology
FREQUENCY _ Online course, or distance learning course
(There is a weekly online chat session with instructor.)
CREDITS _ Three
LEVEL _ Undergraduate and graduate

purpose

This course provides students with an opportunity to learn about the history of information design in the twentieth century. An interdisciplinary course, it is intended for anyone who is interested in and aspires to process, design, present, and implement message-making through words, text, maps, charts, symbols, pages, signs, screens, and interfaces.

Course content includes definition and anatomy of information design, theories that inform information design, and a review of exemplars and their designers. An in-depth case study will focus on one pioneer of information design, Will Burtin, utilizing resources from RIT's Wallace Library Design Archives.

objectives

When the learner has successfully completed the course, he/she will be able to:

- Recognize what information design is, how it is categorized, its component parts, theories that inform it, and means of evaluating it.
- Understand key designers and seminal projects of information design from the past and present in the context of twentieth-century history.
- Identify, through a study of his life and work, the importance of Will Burtin as a pioneer of information design.
- Compare works of information design and analyze their similarities and differences.
- Apply the content provided in the course to their needs as shapers of information design.
- Evaluate examples of information design as to their effectiveness or ineffectiveness.

- Realize the benefits of participation in course opportunities.
- Perceive, through performance and outcomes, critical thinking skills.

description of classes

- Module One: Overview of information design
- Module Two: Anatomy of information design
- Module Three: Evaluating information design
  Theories that inform information design
  Application of theories
- Module Four: Case study of Will Burtin
  Introduction
  The Man
  The Legacy
  The Work
- Module Five: The design of information design

Assignments

1. Using the provided Anatomy Matrix, logo in examples of information design in your life.
2. Write a critical essay on the processes involved in your ways of evaluating information design.
3. Write a critical essay on effective and less effective examples of information design used in Web sites.
4. Using DesignArchiveOnline, insert examples of Will Burtin's work into the Anatomy Matrix.
5. In a critical essay, suggest topics for a hypothetical conference on Will Burtin.
6. Write a critical essay in response or reaction to Burtin's essay, "Design Responsibility in the Age of Science."

Critique Format

The online version of the course requires a weekly online class meeting for discussion. This "chat" lasts one hour. Each student is required to be present and to participate. The resident version of the course requires a normal in-class discussion based on the writing of critical questions relevant to the class topic. In this format the last class is devoted to a small group "sharing review" in which students are expected to respond in a literate fashion to questions by the instructor. A group discussion follows.

Bibliography

Holmes, Nigel. *Designer's Guide to Creating Charts and Graphs*. New York: Watson Guptill, 1984.

Pedersen, B. Martin, ed. *Diagrams 2*. New York: Graphis Press, 1997.

Tufte, Edward. *The Visual Display of Quantitative Information*, Second Edition. Connecticut: Graphics Press, 2001.

Tufte, Edward. *Visual Explanations: Images and Quantities, Evidence and Narrative*. Connecticut: Graphics Press, 1997.

Tufte, Edward. *Envisioning Information*. Connecticut: Graphics Press, 1990.

Wurman, Richard Saul. *Information Anxiety: What to Do When Information Doesn't Tell You What You Need to Know*. New York: Bantam Doubleday Dell, 1990.

Wurman, Richard Saul. *Information Architects*. New York: Watson Guptill, 1997.

COURSE TITLE _ CRITICAL ISSUES IN DESIGN/CULTURE

INSTRUCTOR _ Ellen McMahon

SCHOOL _ School of Art, University of Arizona, Tucson

FREQUENCY _ One semester, twice weekly

CREDITS _ Three

LEVEL _ Senior undergraduate and graduate students combined

purpose

The main objective of this course is to encourage students to take an analytical
and critical approach to graphic design practice. This involves understanding
the culture of design as well as the complex interrelationships between graphic
design and the culture at large.

description

This senior- and graduate-level seminar combines history, theory, and studio
projects. Students read primary sources that articulate the tenants of modernism and diverse contemporary opinions concerning the relevance of those
ideas today. Readings also examine contemporary strategies in design practice
and put them into a historical context, emphasizing issues such as diversity,
social and personal responsibility, and self-expression. Autobiography is a
thread that runs through all of the topics throughout the semester as we look at
the relationship between the lives of designers and the work they produce.

205

There are two visual projects (one is a self-initiated project inspired by a
local issue and the other is an international postcard exchange with students
from other schools). The latter involves an exchange of written interpretations
of the postcards and a live videoconference.

criteria for evaluation

Attendance is required at all class meetings. Grades will be based on participation in discussions and critiques and all stages of the visual/writing projects.
Grades for the visual project will be based on the extent that students are willing to go to support the internal logic of their solutions. This involves clarity of
concept, the relationship of concept to process and product (use of color, composition, scale, materials, techniques, reproduction methods, and technologies),
attention to detail, care in final execution, and consideration of the client (if
there is one) and the intended audience. I expect students to take risks conceptually and formally.

Students enrolled for 500-level credit will complete three additional readings and prepare a formal presentation for the class.

project descriptions

Visual Project 1: Self-authored Project

You have the knowledge, understanding, and specific technical skills to function as a cultural producer. What does this mean? How do you want to contribute to your visual culture? Initiate a project, or support an existing project in the community, and see what is involved in getting something you want to say out to a mass audience. Where are the opportunities for self-authorship?

The outcomes of these projects will vary tremendously. I will be looking at your intent, the risks you take with the content, your problem solving, commitment, and willingness to embrace the complexity and difficulty of mass distribution. You will present final printed pieces or detailed visual proposals and a written description of your experiences with the project at the end of the semester.

Visual Project 2: Postcard Exchange

This project has been done many times in various forms, as it is continually being modified and refined. The point of the project is to give you a better understanding of how your particular cultural and personal experiences mold your perspectives, create your sense of identity, and influence the way you make and interpret visual material. This semester we will exchange cards with students from two institutions, one in Tlalpan, Mexico, and one in Surrey, Great Britain.

Stage 1

Design and produce a series of three postcards (4" × 6", two-sided) and a package using a combination of text and image. The first card is an exploration of your national heritage and familial past. This may involve research of some kind. Consider the traditions and oral histories of your families and communities. Think about the cultural, social, economic, and political climate in the time and place of your childhood. The second card will address your present situation, daily concerns, and/or subcultural identification. Are you temporarily displaced to attend the university, or is this home? How are aspects of your past evident in your present? The third card will be a venue for visual speculation about your future. This can be personal, about your professional goals and expectations, or you can consider the impact broader social or technological issues have had on you.

The package will serve as an introduction to the project for the intended audience, since it will be the first thing seen or interacted with. It will also contain, protect, and be an extension of the formal and conceptual aspects of the set of three cards.

Stage 2
You will be paired with a student from a design class in Britain and also a student in Mexico. Your cards will be mailed to them and you will receive their cards. After a class discussion you will write an interpretation of each of their cards. They will be interpreting yours in return. These will be e-mailed.

Stage 3
In the final stage of the project you will respond to their interpretations of your cards in "person" via live videoconferencing. In the event that this isn't technically possible, you will respond by e-mail.

Visual Project 3: Deconstructing a Myth
This is an extra-credit project. I will work individually with anyone who wants to do this.

Create a piece of visual communication that deconstructs a cultural myth. We will discuss what this means in connection with the reading, *Six Myths of Our Times*.

There are no restrictions: It can be a game, cards, signage, product, package, interactive process piece, billboard, poster, book, etc.

readings

Required Texts
Maud Lavin, *Clean New World: Culture, Politics and Graphic Design* (Cambridge: MIT Press, 2001).

Marina Warner, *Six Myths of Our Times: Little Angels, Little Monsters, Beautiful Beasts, and More* (New York: Vintage Books, 1995).

Selected readings from: Michael Beirut, et al., eds., *Looking Closer I* (New York: Allworth Press, 1994).

Michael Beirut, et al., eds., *Looking Closer II* (New York: Allworth Press, 1997).

Michael Beirut, et al., eds., *Looking Closer III* (New York: Allworth Press, 1999).

Steven Heller and Marie Fenimore, eds., *Design Culture* (New York: Allworth Press, 1997).

Steven Heller and Elinor Pettit, *Design Dialogues* (New York: Allworth Press, 1998).

Steven Heller and Karen Pomeroy, *Design Literacy* (New York: Allworth Press, 1997).

Ellen Lupton and Abbott Miller, *Design Writing Research* (New York: Phaidon, 1999).

Leslie Savan, *The Sponsored Life* (Temple University Press, 1994). Rudy Vanderlans, ed., *Emigre* 59 (1999).

COURSE TITLE _ PUBLIC GRAPHICS WORKSHOP
INSTRUCTOR _ Stuart Ewen
SCHOOL _ Department of Film & Media Studies, Hunter College, CUNY
FREQUENCY _ Fifteen weeks
CREDITS _ Three
LEVEL _ Upper-level undergraduate and graduate students

purpose

For many years, the Media Studies Program has been committed to expanding the scope of visual communication beyond the conditions of the commercial imperative to explore ways that visual media can be used to offer new ways of seeing, promote public enlightenment, and enhance the quality of public discussion. In this once-a-week workshop, the potential of visual culture to animate thought and to inform public discussion will be applied to the creation of six practical design projects.

expectations

Students are expected to complete a first-week exercise and six complex design projects over the course of the semester. Some projects will be individually conceived and produced, others may be collective efforts.

Beyond attending weekly workshop meetings (Thursdays between 1:00 and 4:00 P.M.), students are also expected to spend a minimum of nine additional hours per week working on their projects. Of these hours, each student may sign up for up to three individual hours per week in the graphics lab, or "G-Lab."

Students in this class will have exclusive access to the G-Lab, and are expected to pay a lab and materials fee of $30.00 for the semester. Checks should be made out to "Hunter College." This fee will cover use of five Macintosh G4 computers, relevant graphics software, three Nikon Coolpix 990 cameras, a Umax flatbed scanner, a Nikon slide scanner, and an Epson Stylus Pro 9000 printer. Graphics files can be very large and you should plan on purchasing Zip disks, as necessary, to store and back up your project work. If you want to store and hold onto digital photographs, you may also wish to purchase a CompactFlash card to use with the Nikon 990s.

We will do our best to provide media (paper, etc.) for printing, and to maintain the printer's ink supply. It may be necessary, however, for you to purchase paper or other materials for your projects.

While working in the G-Lab, you are fully responsible for its security. Never leave the room unlocked or unattended, even for a minute.

appraisal

Student work will be graded on the basis of the following: clarity of conception, skillfulness of execution, originality, visual eloquence, and the force and suggestiveness by which your idea or ideas are communicated. In the case of joint projects, your contributions to a group effort will be considered as well. There will be no incompletes granted in this course.

assignments and projects

First Assignment: Inside/Outside Personal Package

Your assignment is to create an autobiographical object with an inside, an outside, and a route between the two. Think about the experience of the viewers/users as they travel from outside to inside and visa versa. What is communicated or revealed? When, how, and why?

Create a visual metaphor for yourself or some aspect of yourself, using text, image, texture, and materials. Think about the communicative potential of nontraditional (unexpected) materials. Think about ways to represent and suggest intangible qualities. Obviously, think about yourself: how you present yourself to the world, and how you understand your inner or hidden self, how people get beyond the surface to know and understand who you really are.

This is not a self-promotion but a way to expand your thinking about the self and your ability to communicate about yourself. Avoid pictures of yourself and direct descriptions.

209

"Something to Salute" Assignment

With customary beliefs evaporating before our eyes, and a new millennium unfolding, venerable national symbols aren't working the way they used to.

Your assignment is to design a new flag for the United States (or for a future political entity or system that you imagine will take its place), one that is more congruous with the world in which we live, or more suited to the era toward which you think, or hope, we are moving.

Your flag should be visually eloquent, making use of simple and publicly accessible graphic elements, and should symbolize either the (social, economic, cultural, aesthetic, and/or spiritual) values that seem to be prevailing in society today, or the values you would wish to see upheld and promoted in a future society.

Flags will be flown at the March 5th meeting of the Graphics Workshop.

"A thoughtful mind, when it sees a nation's flag, sees not the flag only, but the nation itself; and whatever may be its symbols, its insignia, he reads chiefly in the flag the government, the principles, the truths, the history which belongs to the nation that sets it forth."—Henry Ward Beecher, 1861

"For there to be a sense of reality, there must also be a sense of possibility."
—Robert Musil, 1930

"He had grown up in a country run by politicians who sent the pilots to man the bombers to kill the babies to make the world safer for children to grow up in."—Ursula Le Guin, 1971

"Patriotism is the last refuge of a scoundrel."—Samuel Johnson, 1775

"I will not kiss your fucking flag."—e. e. cummings, 1931

"We're leaving Babylon."—Bob Marley, 1977

"Show Me the Money" Assignment

Unlike land, livestock, food, or mineral resources—which are of material value and can be used directly to provide for people's needs—the worth of money is symbolic and immaterial. It simply represents value. It is a portable concept, a picture that persuasively argues "I am worth such-and-such amount." Simultaneously, it may support and sanctify the values of a particular way of life.

Your assignment is to create a new and expressive design for U.S. money, one that visually communicates and comments upon the prevailing values of society as it is today, or one that communicates the social and economic values that you think ought to be upheld and/or promoted in society.

"Billboards for Democracy" Assignment

This is a collective assignment that will involve collaboration among all members of the workshop. Your assignment is to design, produce, organize, and publicize a large-scale art installation, a colossal enterprise in visual expression that will raise public consciousness regarding the assault on funding for public education and will educate people who see the installation about other imperiled cornerstones of democracy. The installation will be mounted in early May.

1. Will there be a coherent visual theme for the event (gravestones, billboards, three-dimensional constructions, comic strips, etc.)?
2. What are the college's regulations surrounding this event, and how can an effective installation be designed within these guidelines?

3. How will the production of pieces be organized? How can people not in the workshop, or other classes around Hunter or other colleges, be drawn into the creative process to insure a large-scale event? Which classes or departments should be contacted and/or brought in to the planning process?

4. What kinds of structures (t-stands, etc.) need to be built for the event, and how will the construction of the structures be organized?

5. What kinds of publicity need to be distributed or planned in order to insure large-scale participation in the creative process?

6. What kind of publicity needs to be generated in order to encourage media coverage of the event?

7. Who will do what? How will the division of labor be taken care of in the class? Is "from each according to her/his abilities" a good principle in making these determinations?

8. What needs to be done in preparation for the actual installation? This includes materials needed, people needed, and scheduling discussions with administrative people (VP's, Security, Buildings and Grounds, etc.) to insure that no unnecessary friction is generated.

This project will be fun, interesting, educational, and, eventually, very satisfying. It will also demand a great deal of effort and teamwork to pull off successfully. I expect this from all of you.

"Give Away Something You've Created That People Will Want to Keep" Assignment

In the multimedia age, one of the most effective means of capturing the attention of the average passerby is a flyer. Yes, the simple, straightforward, sans-bells-and-whistles sheet of flat or folded paper handed out on the street is the most immediate and interactive of communication forms.

For this project you are required to make a flyer, pamphlet, broadside, or any other kind of handout/give-a-way for street distribution. You can make it as simple or elaborate as you wish, given the following parameters:

1. It must be prepared to be mass-produced in quantities of a minimum of 100 copies, but preferably many more.

2. It must contain a message or information that you intend to convey to a particular audience.

3. You must define and target that audience for yourself, so that it is evident to whoever that audience may be.

4. It must be designed to be kept, maybe not for the ages, but long enough for the message to sink in.

5. It should be designed to effect a response—positive or negative—on the part of the recipient.

6. This process can be achieved either through your choice of one or a combination of: words, pictures, graphic design, or printing techniques. The choice is yours. The possibilities are only limited by the form.
7. Oh yeah, and don't spend any more than $10 on the prototype (original).

If you can attract attention with the most elemental medium, you have scored what the advertising profession once called a "bull's-eye."

part 3

graduate

COURSE TITLE _ FUTURE OF LEARNING WORKSHOP
INSTRUCTOR _ Sharon Poggenpohl
SCHOOL _ Institute of Design, Illinois Institute of Technology
FREQUENCY _ One semester (sixteen weeks)
CREDITS _ Four
LEVEL _ Graduate

purpose

Human-centered or user-centered design begins from observation of people in
situations of action in real life, followed by the interpretation of their satisfac-
tion with a product, communication, or experience. This approach to design
puts people and their needs and pleasures first, rather than the designer's aesthetics, the technologist's technical ability, or business's profit motive. The purpose of this course is to integrate methods and ideas experienced in other
Institute of Design courses, such as Behavioral Observation, or Social and
Cultural Human Factors, into action by tackling a problem related to learning.

Learning is an interesting focus, as virtually all learning is facilitated by
communication. What is at issue is a process in which: observing real people
and the insights derived from observing them feed the design process; building
various kinds of prototypes helps the designer to speculate on the design

possibilities; observing users interacting with the prototypes demonstrates which parts of the design work well (in terms of function and delight) and which parts need further work. This process continues again and again until a good approximation to a design conclusion is achieved—it is an iterative process.

We encourage our graduate students to build on others' research and ideas so that design understanding and development grows in substance and sophistication. Each problem we tackle does not begin naively with the presumption that no previous work has been done on it.

description

The Future of Learning Workshop has worked on several themes (equitable access to technology for inner-city children, tools for teachers, learning games). The theme for the workshop presented here is the field trip. In an earlier Learning Workshop, three students shadowed teachers and their classes in a variety of grades on various field trips. Their observations suggested that little learning was taking place; there was sparse if any preparation in the classroom prior to the field trip, and whatever might have been learned on the trip was not integrated back into the classroom experience. The field trip was a day out of school for both students and teachers. We considered this to be a lost opportunity for children to see information and ideas in another context that extends understanding of its usefulness.

For five years we focused this workshop on the middle school grades, since these are years of transition during which students become more independent as they approach adolescence. If children lose their enthusiasm for learning during these years, they may be lost for a very long time, if not permanently. The workshop continued to work with this age group. Another grounding condition for the workshop was an acceptance of constructivist theories of learning as the basis for our work.

Chicago is a city rich in museum opportunities. One museum that is perhaps not high on the list as a field-trip destination is the Art Institute of Chicago. This was the field-trip site selected by one of the workshop participants, Tania Schlatter. Her task was to situate both the Art Institute as a viable place to learn and to locate the problems associated with it as a field-trip experience from the child's and teacher's point of view. This article focuses on her project, Artifacts, and its development process.

assignments and projects

Project: Artifacts
Artifacts is a Web-based tool that links the preparation, experience, and follow-up of a field trip to the Art Institute of Chicago for middle school children. It

also provides a platform for students to connect the art to their lives through their personal interests and through specific curricular connections. Before a field trip, Artifacts allows students to interact with items from the museum collection and provides leads for exploring cross-curriculum aspects of an artifact. Students pursue Web-based links to information related to a work of art that interests them and log notes about what they find and questions they have in a "Notebook" section on the Artifacts site. Students e-mail questions about "their" works of art to the docent managing the trip. The docent answers e-mails and plans a tour that will allow the students to see the art they researched. Students also read other students' logs about their initial questions and field-trip experiences.

This process encourages students to take an active role in the field trip and alerts the docent to particular interests. In this way, a context for exchange is created before the experience of the trip. Artifacts is unlike the current system, where field trips are pre-set tours, grouped by standard art history criteria. The current system limits the scope of information exchange to art history and constrains the dialogue to art.

With the Artifacts system, students view the works they interacted with on the Web site when they visit the museum and actively present information they gathered to their classmates. Pages printed out from the Notebook section of the Artifacts site help students with their presentations. Docents serve as guides and supplement students' information. This is different from current field trips to the Art Institute, where docents lecture to the students and facilitate questions and answers. After the field trip, students access Artifacts again to log their experiences in the Notebook section and "curate" their own exhibit. Students select three works of art they saw at the museum, "hang" them on a virtual gallery wall, and write why they chose to hang them.

Artifacts was created in response to research conducted by three graduate students (Tim Priebe, Jim Almstron, and Paul Rothstein) at the Institute of Design in the spring of 1997. They observed students on field trips at the Art Institute, the Motorola Museum, and the Field Museum of Natural History, and interviewed teachers in the Chicago area. The Artifacts plan was developed from a list of twelve suggestions for field-trip improvements that emerged as insights from these observations. The insights that this project adopts are:

1. A tool for students to plan and direct the field trip, incorporating the teacher and docents as "nutritionists," affording structure and guidance, but not domination.
2. A pre-visit information system for two-way communication about the site, teachers' goals, and needs regarding the trip.
3. A tool that helps teachers share information about field trips and sites, including experiences and insights.

4. A virtual field trip, which avoids the safety and cost issues associated with traditional field trips.
5. A plan for a new type of experience that promotes active rather than passive learning.

The following summarized weeks of development give only an impression of what was developing from a human-centered design perspective.

Mission Statement (Week 1)

To use art and field trips to engage students in a variety of aspects of learning through a tool that will enhance field trips for seventh and eighth graders to the Art Institute of Chicago.

1. Leverage curiosity as inspiration to expand knowledge.
2. Engage students actively in learning history, literature, social studies, science, and cultural factors through art.
3. Engage students in research, writing, and presentation activities.
4. Promote appreciation for and understanding of art.

Museum Site Visit (Week 2)

The Art Institute has the Robinson Teacher Resource Center to support teacher planning for field trips. This resource has limited hours but has many ways in which to enhance the field-trip experience. Nevertheless, it is up to the teacher with limited time and resources to develop the trip. The collection of lesson plans at the Center tends to focus on a traditional art historical understanding of the museum's artifacts.

Insight: Why not increase accessibility to the Art Institute through the Internet? This could allow students in the classroom to prepare for a field trip. This shifts some of the responsibility from the teacher to the student for field-trip content planning. Teachers can guide student curiosity instead of trying to find ways to stimulate their curiosity.

Observe Children on a Field Trip (Week 3)

"Telling Stories through Art" is an exhibit specially designed for children at the Art Institute. Tania followed several docent-led tours for children through this exhibit. This exhibit was significantly different from those in the main galleries. The physical space was divided for each work of art and its corresponding activities. Scenes from the art were blown up and colorfully displayed. Motifs were picked up and repeated in imaginative ways. Exhibits included places to sit and climb on, and more intimate locations for using a computer or a puppet theater. Some exhibits had sound, multimedia components, or magnets to move. The exhibits tried to engage all senses, including touch.

Insight: Getting beyond passive looking engages the children more deeply; they offered questions and answers enthusiastically here, in contrast to their lack of attention seen in the main galleries. We presume everyone knows how to look carefully and inquisitively, but this is not necessarily an intuitive skill.

Middle School Site Visit (Week 4)

The site for this visit was an advanced technology center (Springman Middle School Communicor) in suburban Chicago. This open-space laboratory had fifty-seven Macs and PCs. All students spent one hour a day in this lab where they worked independently at their own pace on projects. Teacher support consisted of individual or small group coaching and occasional tutorials.

Insight: While not all schools are this sophisticated, this is the direction in which learning is headed—self-paced, project-based, with faculty as coach using technological equipment.

An interruption in the ongoing design process narrative is necessary here. While communication designers are accustomed to developing "look and feel" or appearance prototypes, the development of new information products like Artifacts raises design issues that require other prototyping approaches. We use four different kinds of prototypes to help us develop interactive communication products: conceptual, behavioral, procedural, and appearance. The conceptual prototype is often a diagram or a chart that externalizes what the designer is considering at an early stage in project development. This is useful to formalize one's thoughts and to share them with others for discussion and critique. The behavioral prototype is designed to elicit behavior from users to answer some question or questions the designer thinks are critical to the development of the idea. This prototype often bears little resemblance to subsequent development ideas—it is about getting at certain kinds of behavior, or getting answers easily. Rather than being a sophisticated, digital thing, it is more often like a pop-up book. This is useful in getting spontaneous feedback from users. Because it is not precious, users interact openly and honestly. The procedural prototype is a paper walk-through of an interactive process that allows the designer to check logic and consistency. This can be given to users who will follow different paths through the material and will help to identify dead-ends, loops, or uninteresting—i.e., never-used—options. The appearance prototype usually occurs late in development and explores the aesthetic nature of the solution. None of these prototypes are complete in any sense; they are steps in a developing process.

Our interest in serving people's real needs and interests moves design into its earliest stage of development, where interactive functions are identified, media connections are planned, content is considered, and in this case learning strategies and values are formulated.

The Conceptual Prototype (Week 5)

Plan/Process Diagram: the relationships between the Art Institute, its Web site for students, and the classroom are explored.

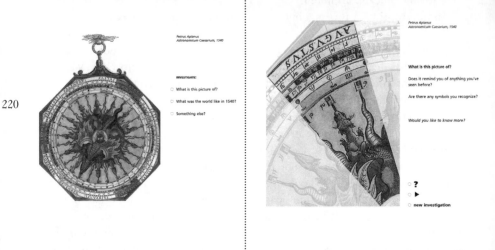

220

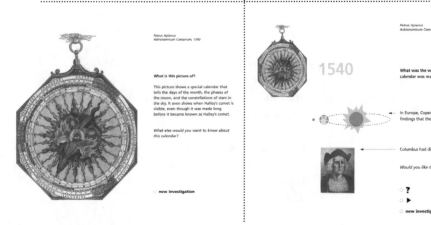

Abbey Church of S. Miniato al Monte, Florence, 1018-62

INVESTIGATE:

- How many different shapes are there in the design of this church?
- Is the design of this church symmetric or asymmetric? What does that mean?
- Something else?

Abbey Church of S. Miniato al Monte, Florence, 1018-62

Is the design of the church symmetric or asymmetric? What does that mean?

Symmetric is a word used to describe something that, when divided into two lengthwise, is the same on both sides.

Asymmetric describes the opposite; something that is not the same when divided into two lengthwise.

Which describes the church?

What everyday examples of symmetry and asymmetry can you find? What about a pencil, a book or a pair of scissors?

?

new investigation

221

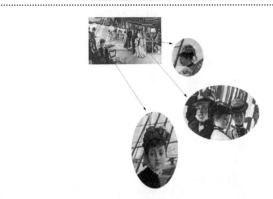

James Tissot
The Ball on Shipboard, 1874

INVESTIGATE:

- Do you recognize any flags?
- Do the partygoers look like they're having fun?
- Something else?

James Tissot
The Ball on Shipboard, 1874

Do the partygoers look like they're having fun?

Is this how you look at parties?

Is this what you wear?

Want to know more?

?

▶

new investigation

Behavioral Prototype (Weeks 6, 7, 8)

The pages below are from the paper prototype developed to see if interacting with art in a decontextualized environment that brought in cross-curriculum aspects of the work would interest students. Three "artifacts" are presented, and each provides two or three different paths to investigate. They take the form of a pop-up book with windows to lift and, like frames from animation, aspects that are hidden and revealed sequentially.

The observation took place in a seventh-grade class in the Newberry Academy of Science and Math (a Chicago Public School) in Chicago's Old Town. Students were in a computer class and were well acquainted with basic computer use. [Editor's Note: Video material that cannot be shown here is used to underscore the points in this part of the syllabus.]

Insights: Students' questions are hard to anticipate; we must offer many threads to follow. Students are fact-focused: state upfront what medium the art is in and show the original in color. Students want context: provide some way to explore the object itself before getting into its details. They seem afraid to make "mistakes"; how can we put them at ease and encourage exploration?

Interactive Digital Prototype Observation (Week 9, 10, 11)

Using the same school and class for observation, a more refined and easily interactive digital prototype was given to students for exploration. [Editor's Note: Video material that cannot be shown here is used to underscore the points in this part of the syllabus.]

Insight: After testing the prototype, Tania redesigned the "instructions," making rollovers to highlight certain information, chunking the process into groups to make the text more accessible, and adding an inventory of function icons with rollovers that tell what they do. The function icons with rollover text become forms of online help for the user.

The "action words"—clickable words that appear when the user has activated a thought-cloud by rolling over areas on the artifacts—were reorganized. Ghosted words and symbols are visible but inactive, providing a clue to the user that if they do something, the words will "light up."

Features were added to the Notebook section, to make it an active part of the site design. Hyperlinks can be accessed, notes can be recorded, questions can be sent to docents, pages can be printed for reference on the field trip. Images that were "grabbed" earlier can be hung by accessing the virtual gallery from the Notebook.

The Final Working Prototype (Week 16)

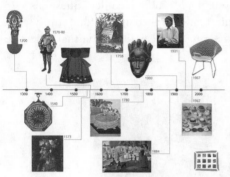

Georges Seurat (French, 1859-1891)
A Sunday on La Grande Jatte, 1884-1886
Oil painting on canvas, 81 3/4 x 121 1/4 inches.

1. Seurat

Georges Seurat (French, 1859-1891)
A Sunday on La Grande Jatte, 1884-1886
Oil painting on canvas, 81 3/4 x 121 1/4 inches.

1. Seurat

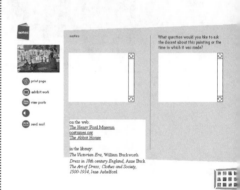

224

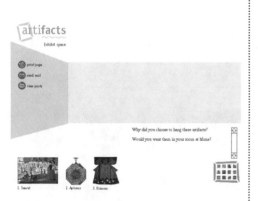

1. Seurat   2. Apianus   3. Kimono

Petrus Apianus
Astronomicum Caesarium, 1540
one of 37 volvelles, approximately 18 x 12 inches

1. Seurat
2. Apianus

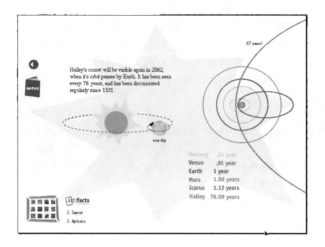

Halley's comet will be visible again in 2062, when it's orbit passes by Earth. It has been seen every 76 years, and has been documented regularly since 1531.

67 years!

one day

notes

Mercury .24 year
Venus .61 year
Earth 1 year
Mars 1.88 years
Icarus 1.12 years
Halley 76.09 years

artifacts
1. Saturn
2. Aptanus

Conclusion

This is a user-centered development process in which the designer seeks to learn about the user, his or her needs, interests, and intuitive cognitive approaches in order to create an information product that fits to their purposes, rather than create one that demands that the user adapt to the product. This requires an affinity for interactive investigation, respect for users, resistance to stereotyping user groups, the ability to forestall making premature judgments and closing down the design process, and an ability to work with complexity and uncertainty. At the Institute of Design, people come first, but this is more easily said than done.

225

Currently this field-trip theme is undergoing renewed investigation at the Institute of Design under the title Informal Learning.

description of classes

The week-by-week description below is quite general, as the projects develop organically and run into problems or opportunities that put them off schedule. As this is a studio course with considerable out-of-studio work (site visits, observation, prototype use, etc.), the participants meet regularly as a group to share progress and problems, but are also coached individually because their projects differ. This workshop met two days a week; one day was generally used for out of class work and the other for studio work and group meetings. Because this is graduate work, independent investigation is expected.

Week 1: Review research and available museum sites, select a museum, and write a mission statement.

Week 2: Museum site visit and amend mission statement if necessary.

Week 3: Observe children on field trip at selected museum and develop design insights from the observations.

Week 4: Middle school site visit of a pertinent class; observe and develop design insights; synthesize information from this and previous weeks.

Week 5: Develop a conceptual prototype and discuss with class.

Week 6: Identify possibilities for a behavioral prototype and present and discuss with class.

Week 7: Develop behavioral prototype further and test with real children.

Week 8: Report to class on insights from testing and changes to the developing design.

Week 9: Develop another behavioral prototype if necessary or go on to an interactive digital prototype.

Week 10: Develop digital prototype and test with real children.

Week 11: Report to class on insights from testing and changes to the developing design.

Week 12: Review all features and procedures for the prototype; be realistic about what you can accomplish; select a path through the experience for development.

Week 13: Develop final prototype.

Week 14: Review operations, aesthetics.

Week 15: Refine.

Week 16: Present final interactive, appearance prototype to class.

readings

General

Bruner, Jerome. *The Culture of Education.* Cambridge: Harvard University Press, 1996. (Required reading for all in the workshop.)

Egan, Kiernan. *The Educated Mind: How Cognitive Tools Shape Our Understanding.* Chicago: University of Chicago Press, 1997. (Reviewed for discussion by the teacher.)

Perry, Deborah L. "Beyond Cognition and Affect: The Anatomy of a Museum Visit," *Visitor Studies: Theory, Research and Practice* 6 (1993). (Required reading.)

Project Specific

Boles, Martha. *The Golden Relationship: Art, Math, and Nature.* Bradford, MA: Pythagorean Press, 1992.

Brown, Peter Lancaster. *Astronomy—The World of Science.* Orbis Publishing, 1984.

Egan, Kiernan and Hunter McEwan, eds. *Narrative in Teaching, Learning, and Research.* Minneapolis, MN: Teachers Press, 1995.

Ettema, Michael. "Instilling Values, Design and Responsible Cultural Institutions," in Williamson, Jack, *Design and Cultural Responsibility.* Bloomfield Hills, MI: Cranbrook Academy of Art, 1997.

Gardner, Howard. *Frames of Mind: The Theory of Multiple Intelligences.* New York: Basic Books, 1983.

Gardner's Art through the Ages, Eighth Edition. New York: Harcourt Brace Jovanovich, 1986.

Goodrum, Charles A. *Treasures of the Library of Congress.* New York: Harry N. Abrams, 1980.

Gowin, D. B. and Joseph D. Novak. *Learning How to Learn.* Cambridge: Cambridge University Press, 1985.

Perkins, David N. *The Intelligent Eye—Learning to Think by Looking at Art.* Pittsburgh, PA: Getty, 1994.

Stafford, Barbara Maria. *Essays on the Virtue of Images.* Cambridge: MIT Press, 1996.

Stafford, Barbara Maria. *Artful Science—Enlightenment Entertainment and the Eclipse of Visual Education.* Cambridge: MIT Press, 1994.

Telling Images, Stories in Art—Family Self-Guide to the Exhibition. Chicago: The Art Institute of Chicago, 1997.

COURSE TITLE _ DESIGN FOR MUSIC

INSTRUCTOR _ Stefan Sagmeister

SCHOOL _ School of Visual Arts/MFA Design

FREQUENCY _ One Semester

CREDITS _ Three

LEVEL _ Graduate

purpose

This class (literally) covers all aspects of graphic design for the music industry. Students will design a complete CD package inside a plastic jewel case, a promotional item (ranging from match book to billboard, from Web site to video), as well as author a design for the same project incorporating a more personal, heart-touching, intuitive vision.

We will concentrate on innovative solutions for the visual design of music.

description

We complete three projects. Most of the time in class is spent for crits with little sermons of mine strewn in.

description of classes

Project 1

Week 1: Introduction; go over assignments; sermon on CD covers

Week 2: Present your favorite design project; bring album title

Week 3: Concept ideas for jewel case CD

Week 4: Developed ideas, comps

Week 5: Review of final presentation of jewel case CD

Project 2

Week 6: Concept for promotional item

Week 7: Rough comps for item

Week 8: Advanced comps

Week 9: Final presentation of promotional item

Project 3

Week 10: Sermon on heart-touching design
Week 11: No class
Week 12: Developed concepts
Week 13: Comps
Week 14: Final presentation of all three projects; review

readings

Debono, Edward. *Thinking Course*. Checkmark Books, 1994.
Eno, Brian. *A Year with Swollen Appendices*. Faber and Faber, 1996.

COURSE TITLE _ THE INTEGRATED STUDIO: ISSUES AND IDEAS
    CRITICAL TO THE PRACTICE OF GRAPHIC DESIGN
INSTRUCTOR _ Véronique Vienne
SCHOOL _ School of Visual Arts (New York, New York)
FREQUENCY _ Once a week for three hours
CREDITS _ Six
LEVEL _ Graduate, second year

purpose

The goal of this second-year course is to introduce students to the complex issues and ideas they will encounter as they progress in their careers. The program is designed to give them the tools they need to decipher the various and often conflicting trends in our culture, and understand how they impact the way we think about design.

The course attempts to map out in broad strokes some of the main historical, social, economic, and political issues that are an integral part of the design practice. Students learn to communicate verbally as well as visually. They collaborate on projects and use brainstorming techniques that show them how ideas can flow back and forth between individuals and groups.

The language we use to talk about what we do is an integral part of the creative process. Words are just as powerful as images—in fact they *are* images. This course helps students understand how, as designers, they not only shape things, they also "name" them.

What we will explore:

- The role of images in our culture (photography, illustrations, etc.— but also the visual content of printed and spoken words)

How you will learn:

- Reading and/or studying graphic material beforehand
    — The *New York Times*
    — *Ways of Seeing,* by John Berger
    — *A World of Ideas/A Dictionary of Important Theories, Concepts, Beliefs, and Thinkers*, by Chris Rohmann
- During the class:
    — Taking quick notes
    — Doing impromptu exercises
    — Tackling spur of the moment assignments
    — Discussing specific chapters from books, articles, news stories

230

What types of assignments to expect:

- Projects that require you to do research
- Working either as an individual or in a team
- Practicing your presentation in advance
- Presenting your work with authority
- Critiquing the work of other students

description of classes

Week 1: The Visual Language

Presentation/Discussion: Introduction to John Berger's Ways of Seeing

- We never look at only one thing; we are always looking at the relationship between things and ourselves. Our vision is continually active, continually moving.
- The world as-it-is is more than pure objective fact, it includes consciousness (an image is a record of how X sees Y).
- The convention of perspective, unique to European art, centers everything on the eye of the beholder. Perspective makes the single eye the center of the visible world.
- The visible world is arranged *for the spectator*, as the universe was once thought to be arranged by God.
- Photography, modern art, and films have tried to overcome this limitation with camera movements, flashbacks, superposition, stream of consciousness, blurs, voice-over, sound effects, etc.

Assignment: Learning from Visual Research

Pick a topic and prepare a three-minute presentation. The following suggestions are inspired by *Ways of Seeing*:

- The Romantic use of nature (leaves, trees, water)
- The mother as Madonna
- Women's legs
- The concept of luxury (luxury versus glamour)
- The concept of virility
- The equation of drinking and success, etc.

Begin to collect images that are available around you in all media, whether in advertising or in editorial material in newspapers and magazines. Come next week with your topic and preliminary findings. Be prepared to address the class to share some of your specific discoveries and yet-to-be-resolved questions. A week later, you will be expected to make a formal ten-minute presentation on your findings, with either slides, power points, or whatever. Make it as visual as possible.

Week 2: The Visual Language (Continued)

Presentation/Discussion

Week one we talked about the invention of perspective: how it transformed the visible world into a spectacle for the benefit of the viewer. Today, in Chapter 3 of *Ways of Seeing*, we are exploring the exception to this rule: how women have been objectified (made into objects), and how, as a result, they see themselves as both spectators and object of the spectacle.

- The social presence of a woman: She is objectified by images. As a result, she is continually accompanied by her own image of herself.
- A woman watches herself being looked at. The surveyor of the woman in herself is male.
- As a consequence, every single one of her actions is motivated by the way she wants to be perceived by her internalized male viewer. She turns herself into an object of vision.
- In Western European paintings, the painted woman (often a nude) is aware of being seen by a spectator. More often, the main spectator is the owner of the painting. The fact that these women look submissive (and are shown as deprived of pubic hair, the symbol of their own sexuality) is a reflection of the desire of the spectator/owner of the painting, rather than a reflection of the subject of the painting.
- In non-European art—Indian, Persian, African, Pre-Columbian—naked women are never submissive. They are sexual objects, but they are equal partners to men.
- Naked versus nude: the difference between nakedness, which implies vulnerability, and nudeness, which implies spectacle. The reason Manet's *Olympia* was such a scandalous painting in its time was the fact that the nude woman was not subservient to the spectator/owner. She made direct eye contact with the viewer, confronting him/her looking at her.
- Proposed experiment: choose an image of a traditional nude from *Ways of Seeing*. Transform the woman into a man. Then notice the violence that transformation creates—not violence to the image, but to the assumptions of the viewer.

232

Presentation by Instructor

A forty-minute slideshow on the visual language used by current magazines on their covers. Some of the findings include:

- A headline can kill an image or make it work.
- The grammatical form used on cover lines is an integral part of the visual message.
- The body language of models is a consistent design element.
- The best covers contain complex narratives.
- On their covers, magazines have an opportunity to define a cultural moment.

Assignment
Students present the topics of visual research they have selected.

Week 3: Students Present the Result of Their Visual Research

Week 4: Introduction to Branding

Presentation/Discussion
Branding was traditionally the domain of advertising agencies. But there has been an evolution in the thinking of what a product is—and, as a result, designers are now involved with designing as well as branding. Why?

- Because the product is no longer considered a tangible thing—or a tangible service. A "product" is now the image of this product in the mind of the consumer.
- Because of the wide range or choices and options on the market-place, people no longer buy things because they need it, but because they want it.
- Because the shift from need to want has spurred a whole new way of thinking about products.

Designers today, because of their inexperience, are approaching branding with-out preconceived ideas. Whereas Procter & Gamble and Young & Rubican are holding on to the concept that branding is a "science," a new generation of designers is reinventing what branding is all about. Instead of defining a brand as an image in the mind of consumers, they are defining it as an experience in the mind of consumers—taking the whole branding phenomenon into a new realm of abstraction.

233

But clients are clients: They want whoever manages their brands to come up with "proofs" that the branding strategy works. So there is an ongoing dia-logue between clients and designers to create a new language of brands.

So, what's a brand?

- "A brand is a set of differentiating promises that link a product or its consumer." (Stuart Agres, from Young & Rubican)
- "A brand is the commodification of a buzz." (Lisa Nugent, from Reverb)

Exercise
Study of charts and diagrams relating to the management of brand equity.

- "Perceived qualities"
- "Brand associations"
- "Key products"
- "Name awareness"
- "Differentiation," etc.

Assignment

Working in teams, students are asked to brand (or rebrand, as the case may be) a company, a product line, or a political personality in the news. They are asked to prepare a pitch as if they were trying to get the account.

Week 5: Brainstorming

Presentation/Discussion

As part of the research for the branding assignment, this class is dedicated to exploring various brainstorming techniques that foster out-of-the-box creative thinking.

- Get into the "wish mode." Give yourself permission to imagine the most satisfying experience.
- Be playful: Have fun toying with your ideas. Speculate. Stretch your imagination.
- Wish for the moon: Don't worry about the feasibility of an invention.
- Headline your ideas: Say, "I would like to propose a revolutionary drink," or "a sugar-free treat" or "a liquid meal" or "an energy pill," etc.
- Learn to support other people's ideas: Show your appreciation, express your support. Smile, clap, cheer.
- Describe the positive: Say, "What I like about this project is. . . ."
- Look for opportunities, not problems: Say, "I wish for. . . ."
- Built on positive aspects: Say, "We could also explore this dimension. . . ."
- Learn to manage your attention span: Drop out and zoom back into the conversation. Let your mind wander for a few seconds (three to five seconds) . . . and then bring it back to the conversation.

Exercise

- Introduce yourself: Write your name on a nametag with a symbol that tells how you see your role today.
- Interact with the group: Play "keep the ball in the air" with other members of the group.
- Create a headline: What result do you expect from this session? Write the headline you will read in a newspaper next week (month, year . . .) about this new product on the market.
- Put your ego aside: Two people draw a face, taking turns making a stroke to create the face. You stop when someone hesitates.
- Get excited about an idea you don't like: Pick an idea you are not particularly excited about, and turn it around into a great concept.
- Doodle: Draw and scribble while you listen and participate.
- Beat the clock: Break into small teams and develop a branding positioning in twenty minutes (on a topic relating to the assignment).

— Headline
— Name
— Benefits
— Packaging
— Audience

Week 6: Students Present the Results of Their Branding Campaigns

Formal pitch by the various teams, followed by a critique by an invited guest who acts as the "client."

Week 7: Verbal Communication

Presentation/Discussion

How to make effective presentations:

- Selecting key messages
- How to determine appropriate support material for the key messages
- Structuring your presentation:
    1. What: Defining the topic and "naming" it
    2. How: Defining the action necessary to develop the project
    3. Why: Defining the expected result

How to establish your authority:

- Basic elements of personal presence and style
- Methods and techniques for answering questions
- Importance of choosing the right words

Exercise

Explaining what "it" is. As graphic designers—and image-makers—you will often be called upon to describe something that doesn't exist yet, or something that is still in the developmental stage.

The "what" exercise: What a thing is is always the most difficult thing to explain. To enrich your own vision and deepen your understanding of what you are talking about, find as many ways as possible to describe a "simple" thing. For example:

What's a car?

- A gas guzzler
- A powerful stereo system on wheels
- A moving meditation space
- A major contributor to global warming
- A private mode of transportation
- A design icon
- A delivery system for speeding tickets, etc.

What's a road?

- A ribbon of asphalt
- A life line
- A symbol of hope
- An escape route
- A connector, etc.

What's a man?

- A creature with a very long childhood
- A hairless primate
- The owner of a sophisticated cortex
- A biped who can talk
- The male of the species
- A chap
- An organism with XX chromosomes, etc.

Each description conjures up different images—and enriches the meaning of the word.

Week 8: Visual/Written Communication

Presentation/Discussion

How the *New York Times* structures captions to describe a photograph:

- Who, what, where, when?
- What's the subject and what's the object of each sentence?
- What happens when you switch subject and object around? How does it affect the way you look at the photograph?

Exercise 1

Students are given current photographs from the *NYT* without their captions and are asked:

1. To look at the images and figure out their narrative
2. To write captions using the who-what-where-when formula
3. To write captions describing the why of the images

Exercise 2

Deconstructing photographs from the *NYT* (a Dada-inspired tic-tac-toe game):

1. Draw a grid over the photograph
2. Look at the image as an assemblage of nine squares
3. Name each square to describe what you see in it

Week 9: Mapping Out the Language of Signs

Presentation by Instructor

The instructor gives a quick overview of the main concepts behind semiotics, structuralism, post-structuralism, and deconstruction—and the contribution of the following philosophers to the idea of language.

- Plato: the allegory of the cave. The platonic ideal as a "meta-narrative."
- Ferdinand de Saussure: language as a series of arbitrary signs. Signifiers and signifieds. How linguistic signs gain meaning through the contrast of their differences (what they aren't).
- Ludwig Wittgenstein: how language both shapes and limits what we want to say (which explains why we experience frustrations when describing what a thing is).
- Claude Levi-Strauss: human society as the constant interplay of means of communication. Mental systems of classification operating according to binary oppositions.
- Roland Barthes: the idea of the "Text" as a self-contained system of signs whose meaning arises from their interrelations, not from authorial intent or historical context. "The Death of the Author"—the end of authorial intention as a prime focus of criticism.
- Michel Foucault: the notion of "discourse"—or current ideology.
- Noam Chomsky: the idea of "universal grammar"—our innate ability to understand hidden grammatical rules as children.
- Jean Baudrillard: the argument that artists put self-reference at the center of their creation.
- Jacques Derrida: a view of "deconstruction" as a method for exposing the inconsistencies and contradictions in the "text." The idea that the "text" outlasts its author and the particular context in which it was created, with the reader bringing as much to the "text" as its author.

Exercise
Students are asked to place the topic of their theses within a larger "discourse."

- Deconstruct its "text."
- Expose its inconsistencies.
- Focus on what is left out, covered up, glossed over.

Week 10: Principles of Deconstruction
(the "Said" and the "Non-Said")

Discussion
Review of Jacques Derida's idea that deconstructing a text means figuring out what's left out of the discussion, what's deliberately or inadvertently covered up, and what's glossed over or misrepresented.

- What people/clients are not talking about
- What people/clients are saying by leaving out details
- The truth that lies reveal

Example: Analyze a current *NYT* article and define what the writer is *not* talking about (due to focus of the article, lack of space, political bias, etc.).

Exercise
Each student is given a graphic artifact (self-promotion, catalogues, brochures, etc.) and asked to "deconstruct" it (expose its visual inconsistencies, contradictions, omissions, lies, untruths, etc.).

Week 11: What's a Text?

Discussion
A text is a large object that can be described as a cultural artifact or document. As such, it is "read" by people who want to understand its role, its importance, its meaning, etc. A "text" is something that attracts critics, commentators, observers, or pundits.
   Examples of a "text":

   • The front page of the *New York Times*
   • Street fashion
   • The Internet
   • The first Gulf War
   • *I Love Lucy*
   • Times Square

Assignment
Explore Times Square and deconstruct its text using images/film/poetry/art. Each student is assigned a particular aspect of Times Square to study. Specific topics include:

   • Pedestrian traffic
   • Noise levels
   • Ticker tapes
   • Danger zones/comfort zones
   • East versus west side of Broadway, etc.

Week 12: The Death of the Author

Presentation/Discussion
How to use the dialectic approach to map out the role of the designer as author, and the overarching theme of "authorship" proposed by the MFA program.
   This discussion is based on the famous example by Hegel:
   Master (thesis) >>>> Slave (antithesis)
   But the master needs the slave in order to be the master. In other words (synthesis), the slave makes the master.

Applying this to the problem of "authorship":

- Thesis (pro): the designer as author
- Antithesis (con): the client as author
- Synthesis (the larger picture): the user as author

Exercise

Describe your thesis project from the point of view of a potential user. Tell us what it is as if you were at a party and wanted to explain its advantages and benefits to a casual listener.

Week 13: Introduction to Situationist Theories

Presentation by Instructor

The Situationist movement, a short-lived phenomenon (1957–1972) was influenced by:

- Deutscher Werkbund
- Expressionism
- Cubism
- Futurism
- Constructivism
- De Stijl
- Bauhaus
- Dada/Surrealism
- Baudelaire
- Lettrists International
- COBRA group (Copenhagen, Brussels, Amsterdam)
- Imagist Bauhaus

239

Off-shoots:

- Pro-situs
- Structuralism
- Anti-design
- Pop Art
- Postmodernism
- Provo groups
- Beat generation
- *Adbusters* magazine
- "Buy Nothing Day"
- Anti-WTO/anti-globalization demonstrators

The following is a list of Situationists definitions:

Situationist: Someone who constructs the situation of his or her life to release his or her own potential.

Spectacle: The collapse of reality into a stream of images, products, and activities sanctioned by business.

Détournement: Rerouting of events or images—hijacking, misappropriation, corruption of preexisting aesthetic elements.

Dérive: Drifting through the city without destination—momentarily defying the white patriarchy of urban space-time.

Psychogeography: How constructed or unconstructed space affects our behavior.

Discussion

Why did Situationists take over the negotiation between reason and imagination and promoted a sense of spontaneity, playfulness, and open-ended experiments designed to undermine cultural imperialism and elitism?

Week 14: Deconstructing Times Square
Student presentations of the "Times Square as a Text" project.

Week 15: Final Review

Exercise
Students choose one of the topics below and prepare five-minute presentations, explaining:

1. What it is
2. How it can be helpful
3. Why it is relevant

- Headlining: To choose the most important aspect of an idea and present it in a few words, like a newspaper headline.
- Text: A self-contained system of signs whose meaning arises from their interrelations, not from authorial intent or historical context (Roland Barthes).
- Ways of seeing: Being aware that the way we see things is affected by what we know and what we believe (John Berger).
- Spectacle: The collapse of reality into a stream of images, products, and activities sanctioned by business (Situationists).
- Deconstruction: Analysis that exposes the inconsistencies and contradictions of a "text" by focusing on what's left out, covered up, glossed over (Jacques Derrida).
- Signifier and signified: Acknowledging the difference between a word and its meaning, between the container and the content (Ferdinand de Saussure).

- Drift/derive: Drifting through the city without destination (psycho-geographical drift: to "momentarily defy the white patriarchy of urban time-space") (Situationists).
- Meta-narrative: Myths taken for granted by a large number of people who do not question its philosophical premises (postmodernism).
- Binary oppositions: Describing communication as a constant interplay of what is and what is not (Levi-Strauss).
- Discourse: Current ideology that serves as a platform for new ideas (Michel Foucault).
- Brand equity: The sum total of perceived and real qualities that define a product or a service in the mind of consumers (David Aaker).
- The wish mode: Giving yourself permission to imagine the most satisfying experience (brainstorming).
- Death of the author: The end of authorial intention as a prime focus of criticism (Roland Barthes).
- What, how, why: The three things you need to describe in order to build an image in the mind of your listener.

purpose

To develop an integrated approach to form and content.

assignments and projects

Project: You Are An Animal

This is not a how-to project. It is an exercise that asks the students to develop their conceptual understanding and technical abilities to make meaning with images. The final results are not as important as the experience of discovering meaning through form-making or thinking by making. This project is not content driven; the goal is to integrate conceptualization with creation. This is a very demanding project, an excessive number of iterations is necessary to get the student past preconceptions, and to promote productivity and confidence in form-making. There are four parts to the project: Form, Image, Methodology, and Experimentation. Each exercise emphasizes a different aspect of form-making in four consecutive weeks.

Form

This very specific but simple part of the exercise reveals each student's personal style. By limiting the media to black ink on white paper, the student's degree of sophistication in seeing and drawing becomes obvious. Issues raised in critique are: What is the relation of formal, technical, and conceptual ability to style? What is the difference between a symbol and an illustration, drawing, or mark? What kinds of words lend themselves to a literal/visual translation, and which ones do not? How would you describe and evaluate your visual language or style? What is the structural syntax of each style that makes them intelligible?

Methodology

This part of the exercise demonstrates how different working methods generate different results. The methodologies are very simple and direct as opposed to vague notions of "brainstorming." Methodologies, systems, and processes are

242

very appealing to students because they offer a system for logical problem solving, and they guarantee that *something* will happen. However, that *something* may or may not be relevant or of value. Methodology is a pedagogical tool and should not become a substitute for real thinking. It is the critical and inventive application of methodologies and process that make them valuable.

Issues raised in critique are: What is the relationship between methodologies and their outcome? To what extent does following a system bypass your preconceptions, and promote or inhibit creativity? What makes a good or bad methodology?

This step in the exercise looks at the difference between drawn or self-generated images, and photographic or "found" images. Issues raised in critique are: Photographic images carry a lot of specific and extraneous information; how do you use it? What is the difference between making and "taking" an image? How is the photographic image's relationship to meaning different than a drawing or symbol?

Experimentation

The student designs three different methodologies to try and discover the best way to edit and synthesize all of the visual information they have generated. An additional step to this project is to design a Web site that explains the various methodologies and the project as a whole.

Assignment: You Are an Animal 243

Form (Week 1)

1. Select an animal that you find interesting (non-human). Research the animal and choose five descriptive words that describe and relate to the animal, ranging from the obvious to the oblique. Consider mythology, legend, folklore, and fables, as well as contemporary issues like ecology/conservation, and scientific research.
2. Write each word at the top of three 8½" × 11" pages of white paper. Divide each page into four sections with a one-point rule line.
3. Create "original" (unique) symbols that represent the words and put them in the middle of the empty spaces (approximately two inches in diameter.) You will have twelve symbols on three pages for each word (sixty symbols total).

No illustrations, photos, or collages. All symbols will be in black ink on white paper. No computer. Have fun!

Methodology (Week 2)

1. Combine your symbols from the previous exercise using the following methodologies. Final symbols must be Postscript drawings (Illustrator, Freehand, or Fontographer), black-and-white laserprint. Appropriate solutions:

Expose Group

244

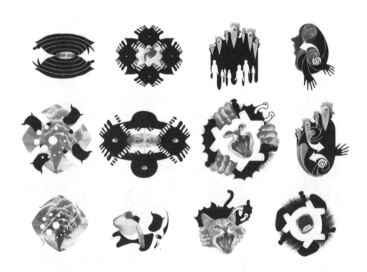

Analyze Synth

245

Image symbols grey

a. Analyze your words and create three groups of two or three words that work well together. Next, select two or three symbols from each of the word groups that create the best literal/conceptual combinations, and then synthesize them into a new symbol. Make three refined symbols. Combine the three symbols to make one final symbol.

b. Select the three most successful word/symbol groups in terms of visual quality. Combine two of the best symbols from each group to make three "best symbols." Combine two of the three "best symbols" to make one final symbol.

2. Process of elimination and incorporation.

Select two pages from each of your five word groups (eliminate one page in each word group). Combine all four symbols on each page into one symbol, so you now have ten symbols. Eliminate one of the words (and its two symbols) that is the least successful. You now have four words with two symbols each. Divide the four words into two groups of two words. Combine the four symbols in each of the two groups into one symbol, so you now have two symbols total. Combine the two symbols into one final symbol.

3. Chance process.

Assign a letter to each of your five words from A to E. Then number all of the symbols in each word group from one to twelve. Pick, at random, three letters from A through E (draw from a hat?). Then select three numbers from one to twelve at random. Put one number with one letter, then combine the three designated symbols into one. Combine the final symbol (Appropriate Solutions exercise b) with B4. Combine your C10 with E3 from the person to the right of you in the last crit.

Image (Week 3)

1. Using the same five words, repeat the first exercise. This time use photographs (that you take and "make") as well as found images using collage techniques to generate sixty images. No *drawing*. The image symbols do not all have to be based on the exact same ideas as before. Create "original" (unique) images that represent the words and put them in the middle of the empty spaces (approximately two inches in diameter). You will have twelve images on three pages for each word (sixty images total).

Experimentation (Week 4)

Devise three different methods for synthesizing *all* of your symbols and images. Create ten examples using each method for a total of thirty refined symbols. Present three large posters that incorporate all ten symbols and a written description of the method used. The posters design should demonstrate its particular methodology. All three posters must be the smartest, and most beautifully complex posters, produced in the past decade.

COURSE TITLE _ CRITICAL INTERSECTIONS: THE DIALOGUE OF
    MODERN ART AND DESIGN
INSTRUCTOR _ Johanna Drucker
SCHOOL _ Yale University
FREQUENCY _ One semester
CREDITS _ Three
LEVEL _ Graduate and undergraduate students in design, art,
    and art history

purpose

There have been numerous moments when the formal and theoretical innovations in modern art and graphic design were integrated—either through the
work of specific individuals or through institutional developments (the
Bauhaus, De Stijl, Vkhutemas, etc.). This course examines the generative dialogue between the visual forms of fine art and design—as in the work of the
Arts and Crafts Movement, Soviet Constructivism, Surrealist photography,
Dada photomontage, and so forth, up through and including postmodern and
contemporary work. The fields of graphic design and fine art will serve as parallel arenas for examination and discussion (with the assumption that students
will be more familiar with the history of fine art in the modern period and need
greater exposure to the history of design). The course is organized chronologically and includes such fundamental concepts as the creation of the public
sphere, the idea of the avant-garde, the concept of the spectacle, simulacrum,
and the influence of technology on visual form.

This course revolves around two central issues. The first is the assertion
that graphic print media are a significant element of modern visual culture
and that an acquaintance with these forms is fundamental to an understanding of modernity. Comprehending the various "rhetorics" by which they
function in the public sphere requires a familiarity with typographic, linguistic, technological, and pictorial conventions that have emerged in the
modern period. The second question guiding this course is that of how this
understanding will shed light on the dialogue of fine art and mass media in
this period.

requirements

1. Research focus project: Each student will be responsible for review-
    ing one book and/or issue of a journal in a Yale collection (a large

percentage are in the Art of the Book collection in Sterling). The object will be analyzed according to style, content, thematic, and critical concerns pursued in the class.

2. Critical paper: A single work analyzed in relation to its historical context, design concerns, relation to visual fine art of the period, and with an analysis of the typographic, linguistic, and visual "rhetoric" of the piece.

3. and 4. Midterm and Final: Basic ideas and images from readings and lectures.

description of classes

(with assigned readings)

Session 1
Introduction: Working questions, issues, and concerns of the class. Modernity, secularization of artistic practice, distinction of artist and artisan, demarcation of private/public zones, "rhetorics" of visual/verbal art and their historical and theoretical articulation.

Session 2

Visual modernity: Modernity and culture, art and signage, the transformation of the public sphere. The history of the public notice. Technologies of type and pictorial reproduction.

Perfect/Austen, "The Story of Typography," and sections up to and including "Modern" and "Slab Serif" faces. From *The Complete Typographer*, First Edition (New York: Prentice Hall, 1992).

Jürgen Habermas, "Introduction: Preliminary Demarcation of a Type of Bourgeois Public Sphere," in *The Structural Transformation of the Public Sphere* (Cambridge: MIT Press, 1986), pp. 1–35.

Raymond Williams, "When Was Modernism," "The Emergence of Modernism," in *The Politics of Modernism* (London: Verso, 1989), pp. 31–48.

Session 3
Graphic modernism: Techniques of production and style in modern typography, pictoriality. The concept of the "autonomous" art object and the production-based identity of fine art. Private and public rhetorics in print media versus fine art media.

Robin Kinross, "Modern Typography," "Enlightenment Origins," and "The Nineteenth-Century Complex," in *Modern Typography* (London: Hyphen Press, 1992), pp. 7–24.

Estelle Jussim, "The Major Codes of the Graphic Arts: Theory and History," in *Visual Communication and the Graphic Arts* (New York and London: R. R. Bowker, 1983), pp. 19–44.

Recommended: William M. Ivins, *Prints and Visual Communication* (Cambridge: MIT Press, 1969).

Charles Baudelaire, "The Painter of Modern Life," in *The Painter of Modern Life*, Jonathan Mayne, trans. (New York: DaCapo, 1986), pp. 1–40.

Session 4

Industrialization of printing processes: The effects of industrialization, mass-production, photographic-based reproductive technology.

Estelle Jussim, "The Major Codes of Photo-technology and their Development as Publishing Media," in *Visual Communication and the Graphic Arts* (New York and London: R. R. Bowker, 1983), pp. 45–76 (plus notes: pp. 312–316).

Recommended: Thomas Crow, "Modernism and Mass Culture in the Visual Arts," in *Pollock and After: The Critical Debate*, Francis Frascina, ed. (New York: Harper & Row, 1986), pp. 233–266.

Session 5

Poster art and the artist's poster: Lithography's capacity to reproduce the artistic "touch" with a minimum of mediation or transformation opened the possibility for artists to produce work in a reproductive medium that blurred the boundaries of commercial and fine art.

Michele Bogart, Chapter 2, "Posters vs. Billboards," in *Artists, Advertising, and the Border of Art* (Chicago: University of Chicago Press, 1995).

Richard Hollis, "Graphic Design from 1890 to 1914: The Art Poster," in *A Concise History of Graphic Design*, Second Edition (Thames & Hudson, 2002).

Recommended: Walter Benjamin, "The Work of Art in the Age of Mechanical Reproduction," in *Illuminations* (New York: Schocken Books, 1977), pp. 217–251.

Session 6

The Arts and Crafts Movement, Morris in particular: William Morris's approach to the applied and graphic arts synthesized a political conviction, highly influential stylistic formal innovation, and a hybrid of fine art and commercial work.

William Morris, "Note by William Morris on his Aims in Founding the Kelmscott Press," in *The Ideal Book*, William S. Peterson, ed. (Berkeley: University of California Press, 1982), pp.76–78.

William Morris, "Art, Labor, and Socialism," in *Marxism and Art*, Maynard Solomon, ed. (Detroit: Wayne State University Books, 1979), pp. 79–90.

Session 7

The Viennese Secession and Jugendstijl: The influence of the Arts and Crafts Movement, particularly the Glasgow School, on Viennese and German graphic arts laid the foundation for later modern innovations.

R. Hollis, "The Beginnings of Design in Europe," in *A Concise History of Graphic Design*, Second Edition (Thames & Hudson, 2002).

Session 8

Radical modernism, typography, and design: Futurism in Italy and Russia, Dada and Switzerland, Germany, and elsewhere all generated radical typographic modes in their independent publications. Much of the stylistic influence on these works was from advertising graphics, but crossing into the domain of fine art and literature made a significant impact.

R. Hollis, "The Avant-Garde and the Origins of Modernism," in *A Concise History of Graphic Design*, Second Edition (Thames & Hudson, 2002).

Victor Margolin, "Visions of the Future," (excerpts) in *The Struggle for Utopia* (Chicago: The University of Chicago Press, 1997), pp. 8–29, 123–135.

Raymond Williams, "The Language of the Avant-Garde," in *The Politics of Modernism* (London: Verso, 1989), pp. 65–80.

Session 9

Radical modernism, photomontage: The disjunctive properties of photomontage served the radical agenda of avant-garde artists looking to revolutionize the visual terms of "subjectivity."

Douglas Kahn, "The Tiger Montage," in *John Heartfield: Art and Mass Media* (New York: Tanam Press, 1985), pp. 73–85.

Session 10

Constructivism, design, and media: In the context of the post-revolutionary Soviet Union, graphic and applied arts took on a significant role in reshaping the emerging society. Debates about revolutionary versus proletariat aesthetics were played out in visual and graphic form in the 1920s within a context of rapidly changing political forces.

Leah Dickerman, "Building the Collective," in *Building the Collective* (Princeton: Kiosk, Princeton University Press, 1996), pp. 11–38.

Session 11

Bauhaus Design to Neue Typographie: German and Swiss and Russian designers, artists, and theorists transformed the graphic look of modern art, typography, and graphic design: Moholy-Nagy, Piet Zwart, Herbert Matter, and Jan Tschichold.

R. Hollis, "National Tendencies until 1940," in *A Concise History of Graphic Design*, Second Edition (Thames & Hudson), 2002.

H. L. C. Jaffe, "De Stijl as Signpost," in *DeStijl* (Cambridge: Harvard, Belknap Press, 1986), pp. 202–208.

Johanna Drucker, "Critical History: The Demise of Typographic Experiment," and "Turning the Page on the Hard Edge of Modernism," in *The Visible Word* (Chicago: The University of Chicago Press, 1994).

Session 12

American context—arts and crafts to the culture of consumption: Developments in an American context in the early twentieth century paralleled those in Europe and the Soviet Union in certain respects, but not in others.

Richard Hollis, "The United States in the 1930s," in *A Concise History of Graphic Design*, Second Edition (Thames & Hudson, 2002).

M. Bogart, Chapter 5, "Promotion and Painting," in *Artists, Advertising, and the Border of Art* (Chicago: University of Chicago Press, 1995).

Roland Marchand, "The Consumption Ethic: Strategies of Art and Style," in *Advertising the American Dream* (Berkeley: University of California Press, 1985), pp.117–162 (plus notes, pp. 387–393).

Stuart Ewen, "The Social Crisis of the Mass Culture," in *Captains of Consciousness* (New York: McGraw-Hill, 1976), pp. 187–220 (plus notes, pp. 240–241).

T. Jackson Lears, "From Salvation to Self-Realization, Advertising and the Therapeutic Roots of the Consumer Culture, 1880–1930," in *The Culture of Consumption*, Richard W. Fox and T. Jackson Lears, eds. (New York: Pantheon, 1983), pp. 3–37.

Session 13

Swiss Design and the Neue Graphik: The emergence of an international-style Swiss design. The concept of the grid within modern art and graphic design.

R. Hollis, "Switzerland and Neue Graphik," in *A Concise History of Graphic Design*, Second Edition (Thames & Hudson, 2002).

Frances Butler, "Reading Outside the Grid: Designers and Society," in *Looking Closer*, Beirut, et al., eds. (New York: Allworth Press, 1994), pp. 91–96.

Recommended: Rosalind Krauss, "Grids," *The Originality of the Avant-Garde and Other Modernist Myths* (Cambridge, MIT University Press, 1986), pp. 9–22.

Midterm

Session 14

European design in America—focus on Surrealism: Surrealism, particularly the photographic manipulation of imagery, became a major motif of American graphic design with the influx of European emigré artists and designers in the 1930s. The contrast between this and the influences in painting and fine art are striking on formal as well as conceptual terms. Surrealist visual vocabulary was also adopted for many war-time posters and graphics.

M. Bogart, Chapter 6, *Artists, Advertising, and the Border of Art* (Chicago: University of Chicago Press, 1995), pp. 256–280.

R. Hollis, "The War and Propaganda," in *A Concise History of Graphic Design*, Second Edition (Thames & Hudson, 2002).

Mike Mills, "Herbert Bayer's Universal Type in Its Historical Contexts," in *The Abc's of the Bauhaus and Design Theory* (New York: Herb Lubalin Ctr., Cooper Union, 1991), pp. 38–45.

Neil Harris, Chapter 17, "Designs on Demand: Art and the Modern Corporation," in *Cultural Excursions* (Chicago: University of Chicago Press, 1990); pp. 349–378 (plus notes, pp. 420–431).

Session 15

Corporate culture comes of age—image and identity: The relation of graphic design to corporate identity solidified in the post-World War II period.

M. Bogart, Chapter 6, from *Artists, Advertising, and the Border of Art* (Chicago: University of Chicago Press, 1995), pp. 280–302.

R. Hollis, "The United States 1945 to the 1960s," in *A Concise History of Graphic Design*, Second Edition (Thames & Hudson, 2002).

Paul Rand, "Logos, Flags and Escutcheons," in *Looking Closer*, Beirut et al., eds. (New York: Allworth Press, 1994), pp. 88–90.

Herbert Marcuse, "One Dimensional Man," in *One Dimensional Man* (Boston: Beacon Press, 1964), pp. 84–120.

Session 16

Consumerism in a mass scale: Mass-circulation magazines, billboards, posters, and in-print advertising proliferated in the post-war economic boom as interest on the part of the art community in the visual potency of such designs and imagery intensified.

R. Hollis, "Italy and the Milanese Style," "France," and "Northern Europe," in *A Concise History of Graphic Design*, Second Edition (Thames & Hudson, 2002).

Roland Marchand, "The Consumption Ethic," in *Advertising the American Dream* (Berkeley: University of California Press, 1985), pp. 117–162 (plus notes).

Marshall McLuhan, "Preface," and miscellaneous excerpts from *The Mechanical Bride* (Boston: Beacon Press, 1951), pp. v–vi, 5–7, 14–15, 23–26, 98–101.

Session 17

The impact of mass media on print media: The reciprocity between mass broadcast media (television and film in particular) and print media in the post-war period. Demise of illustration. Photo-offset as the industry standard for reproduction. The demise of the public sphere.

Marshall McLuhan, *Understanding Media: The Extensions of Man* (Cambridge: MIT Press, 1994).

Stuart Ewen, "Youth as an Industrial Ideal," and "The Social Crisis of Mass Culture," in *The Captains of Consciousness* (New York: McGraw-Hill, 1976), pp. 139–149 and pp. 187–220.

Session 18

Pop Art and design

The interconnections of fine art and graphic design became extremely close in the 1950s and 1960s as artists took up the visual vocabulary of graphic design and commercial media.

Andreas Huyssen, "Mass Culture as Woman: Modernism's Other," in *After the Great Divide* (Bloomington: Indiana University Press, 1986), pp. 44–62.

Ellen Lupton and Abbott Miller, "Line Art: Andy Warhol and the Commercial Design of the 1950s," in *Design/Writing/Research* (New York: Princeton Architectural Press, 1996), pp. 73–89.

Roland Barthes, "The Rhetoric of the Image," in *Image/Music/Text* (New York: Hill and Wang, 1977), pp. 32–51.

Session 19

The concept of the spectacle: Guy Debord and the artists/theorists of the Situationist International put forth a description of the conditions of contemporary life that moved beyond the earlier paradigms of modernity into a sharp-edged, if still potentially optimistic, critique.

Guy DeBord, "Separation Perfected," in *Society of the Spectacle* (Detroit: Red and Black, 1983).

Greil Marcus, "Legends of Freedom," in *Lipstick Traces* (Cambridge: Harvard University Press, 1989), pp. 163–185.

Session 20

Psychedelic style and the counterculture: Nineteen sixties graphic style developed a striking visual and verbal form in the context of the counterculture. The question arises as to the extent to which style articulates a politics through symbolic form in the public arena and/or signifies a sense of alternative community.

R. Hollis, "The Late 1960s," in *A Concise History of Graphic Design*, Second Edition (Thames & Hudson, 2002).

Dick Hebdige, Chapter 1 and Chapter 8, in *Subcultures* (New York: Methuen & Co., New York, 1979), pp. 5–19, pp. 113–127.

Session 21

Activism and graphic arts: The disillusionment with modernism in the fine arts that arose in the 1970s is in part linked to the frustration felt in attempting to use the radical formal innovations of the early twentieth century in an art of contemporary protest. Graphic artists also searched for effective means of visual/verbal communication that could communicate within the public sphere.

Steven Heller, "Hit and Run," in *Angry Graphics*, (Layton, Utah: Gibbs Smith, 1992), pp. 2–7.

Session 22

Postmodernism, mass media, and appropriation: Fine art strategies of appropriation carried the conviction of a critique in the late 1970s and early 1980s but the increased sophistication of advertising techniques and aesthetic sensibilities and production values raises questions about the capacity of fine art to effect any radical transformation within these strategies.

R. Hollis, "New Waves: Electronic Technology: The 1970s and After," in *A Concise History of Graphic Design*, Second Edition (Thames & Hudson, 2002).

Paul Jobling and David Crowley, "Graphic Design in a Postmodern Context: The Beginning *and* the End?" in *Graphic Design: Reproduction and Representation*. (Manchester: Manchester University Press, 1996), pp. 271–290.

Mary Jane Jacob, "Art in the Age of Reagan: 1980–1988," in *A Forest of Signs* (Cambridge: MIT University Press, 1989), pp. 15–20.

Hal Foster, "Re: Post," in *Art After Modernism*, Brian Wallis, ed. (Cambridge: MIT/Godine, 1984); pp. 189–201.

Session 23

Postmodernism and graphic style: The impact of new technology, particularly the desktop computer, transformed the visual style of 1980s graphic design, typestyle, and print media. Appropriation, pastiche, and various modes of visual sampling, morphing, and mutation all became conspicuous elements of visual style in fine arts and design. Anti-tech, 'zine-style, independent design came into being in contrast to the slicker manipulations of desktop work and industry output.

Maud Lavin, "Design in the Service of Commerce," in *Graphic Design in America* (New York: Walker Art Center/Abrams, 1987), pp. 127–143.

Zuzana Licko, "Discovery by Design," in *Looking Closer 2*, Beirut et al., eds. (New York: Allworth Press, 1997), pp. 46–48.

Session 24

Electronic tools and graphic design: Tools of design and conditions for production changed the designer's role from that of a producer of organized display materials to an engineer of portals onto information that is structured for vari-

ous kinds of manipulation. Time-based elements of media as well as navigational and orientation devices are regularly incorporated into information
design, and the designer often works with information architects and program-
mers rather than printers and photo technicians in the creation of the final
output. Design for the print medium continues to be a crucial part of design
activity, but the coordination of materials across a range of new media also
creates new requirements and demands. The aesthetic manipulation of information depends upon an understanding of knowledge-as-data and of electronic
media as a cultural form and force.

Jessica Helfand, "The Pleasure of the Text(ure)," in *Six (+2) Essays on
Design and New Media* (New York: William Drenntell, 1997), pp. 21–36.

Jessica Helfand, "Electronic Typography," in *Looking Closer 2*, Beirut, et al.,
eds. (New York: Allworth Press, 1997), pp. 49–53.

Johanna Drucker, "Information in Your Face: The Interface Challenge," in
AIGA Journal of Graphic Design 16, no. 2 (1998).

Timothy Durfee, "The Architecture of Electronic Space," in *AIGA Journal
of Graphic Design* 16, no. 2 (1998), pp. 23–26.

Recommended: Jean Baudrillard, *Simulations* (New York, Semiotexte, 1983),
pp. 1–13.

Session 25

Electronic environments and the challenge of art and design now: Theories of
reading that derive from film and television offer concepts like "flow" and
"frame" as fundamental to the understanding of the media experience.
Information visualization blurs the boundaries between graphic design and user
interface in the design-for-the-screen sensibility that dominates contemporary
Web-site work.

Ben Shneiderman, et al., *Readings in Information Visualization* (San
Francisco: Morgan Kaufmann, Publishers, 1999).

Edward Tufte, *Envisioning Information* (Chesire, CT: Graphics Press, 1990).

Edward Tufte, *The Visual Display of Quantitative Information* (Chesire, CT:
Graphics Press, 2001).

Richard Saul Wurman, *Information Architects* (New York: Graphis Inc., 1997).

Required Texts

Bogart, Michele. *Artists, Advertising, and the Border of Art*. Chicago:
University of Chicago Press, 1995.

Hollis, Richard. *A Concise History of Graphic Design*, Second Edition. London:
Thames & Hudson, 2002.]

Perfect, Christopher and Jeremy Austen. *The Complete Typographer*, First
Edition. New York: Prentice Hall, 1992.

(Additional readings as per week-by-week assignments.)

Recommended Texts

Ivins, William. *Prints and Visual Communication*. Cambridge: MIT Press, 1969.

McLuhan, Marshall. *Understanding Media: The Extensions of Man*. MIT Press, 1994.

256

COURSE TITLE _ DESIGNING WITH LIVE ACTION AND
        TYPOGRAPHY: A PROCESS
INSTRUCTOR _ Anne Saint-Pierre
SCHOOL _ School of Visual Arts
FREQUENCY _ Fifteen weeks
CREDITS _ Three
LEVEL _ Graduate

purpose

To provide a conceptual framework for students, exploring ways to integrate live action and typography into meaningful and functional design projects; to raise methodology and logistics issues from a real-life perspective, and equip future designers/art directors with the proper tools to produce their projects successfully.

description

A project-based course meets three hours weekly for one semester; through examples in the television and film industries, and a variety of assignments, students develop their own creative methodology as designers and directors, and gain thorough experience with motion graphics design and production issues.

Students are encouraged to think out of the box; each week early in the semester, they research and make a short presentation of a different animation concept inspired by daily life, literature, movies, or fine art; emphasis is placed on language as well as design skills.

Each student is also assigned a semester-long motion graphics project— either a television image campaign or a feature main title, requiring a conceptual presentation, storyboards, a shoot and post-production; each phase is approached from a real-life point of view, and professionals are invited to share their experiences through concrete examples and documents.

A collaborative attitude between students is encouraged.

Assignments: Short weekly presentations to the class; one semester-long project, at industry level.

description of classes

Week 1
Presentation of class, overview of curriculum.

The components of motion graphics: live action, design, typography, and sound. Outstanding visual concepts.

Budget matters and aesthetic choices, in class and real life.

Assignments: weekly concept search, and choice of a semester-long project.

Week 2
Creative direction 1: authorship, responsibilities, communication with clients and creative team.

Thinking strategically and intuitively. Outstanding examples.

Logo design, function, and existence on-screen.

Assignments: weekly concept search, strategy and conceptual treatment for student project.

Week 3
Creative direction 2: individual work student/teacher on conceptual treatment.

Functions of words on screen: information, word play, narration, design component. Outstanding examples.

Assignments: weekly concept search, finalize conceptual treatment, write copy if applicable.

Week 4
Storyboarding 1: planning without stifling; style sheets, drawings, photography, video; great presentation skills.

Music and sound design in motion graphics. Outstanding examples.

Assignments: weekly concept search, choose music and start storyboarding, using digital camera or mini-DV when applicable.

Week 5
Storyboarding 2: individual work, student/teacher.

Live action as design component: aesthetic and practical choices.

Outstanding film, video, and photographic treatments.

Assignments: weekly concept search, continue storyboarding.

Week 6
Typography 1: typography and logo design.

Word play, calligraphy, and many other ways to push the envelope. Outstanding examples.

Assignments: weekly concept search, text, typography, and/or logo design.

Week 7

Typography 2: individual work, student/teacher (text, typography, and/or logo design).

Assignments: weekly concept search, finalize typography design, and incorporate into storyboard.

Week 8

Pre-production: people and logistics; budget, schedule, shoot, and post-production planning; lecture by a producer.

Assignments: budget, plan shoot and post-production of semester project; decide on collaborations for parts of production (help on camera work, music search, etc.).

Week 9

Directing tabletop and talent for motion graphics. Good tips.

Lecture by a director of photography. Outstanding examples.

Individual work, student/teacher.

Assignment: shoot project in mini-DV.

Week 10

View footage and work in progress.

Lecture by a colorist. Outstanding examples.

Assignment: finish shooting.

Week 11

View footage.

Post-production 1: lecture by an editor. Planning. Good tips.

Outstanding examples.

Individual work, student/teacher.

Assignment: plan and start post-production with After Effects/Final Cut Pro.

Week 12

Post-production 2: present work in progress.

Individual work, student/teacher.

Assignment: pursue post-production.

Week 13

Post-production 3: present work in progress.

Individual work, student/teacher.

Assignment: pursue post-production.

Week 14
Post-production 4: present work in progress.
  Individual work, student/teacher.
  Assignment: complete post-production.

Week 15
Presentation and discussion of completed projects.

readings

Steve Curran, *Motion Graphics: Graphic Design for Broadcast and Film* (Rockport, MA: Rockport Publishers, 2000).
  Brody Neuenschwander, Leonard Currie, David Quay, *Letterwork: Creative Letterforms in Graphic Design* (London/New York: Phaidon Press, 1993).
  Paul Wheeler, *Digital Cinematography* (Focal Press, 2001).
  Matt Woolman and Jeffery Bellantoni, *Type in Motion: Innovations in Digital Graphics* (New York: Rizzoli International Publications, 1999).

conclusion

In addition to a project they can include in their portfolios, students will acquire a practical sense of the process and players involved, and an understanding of authorship in a collaborative setting.
  This class can also provide a foundation for a thesis project in motion graphics, broadcast design, or a related field.

purpose

The best title sequences are complete mini-movies with a beginning, middle, and end. They communicate quickly and effectively—sometimes directly and sometimes subliminally. And they usually (but not always) incorporate the use of text. We will review historical examples of title design. We will create several projects, including storyboards, animatics, and one full-motion sequence. The course is about ideas—not so much about technique.

projects

We will go through the various stages of creating a title sequence for a film. You can choose a real film (how about a new title sequence for *Psycho?*) or an imaginary one. Your sequence should contain approximately ten title "cards," or credits, and should have a running time of one to two minutes. The point of all of this is that a great title sequence should have an *idea* behind it. Not just decoration, not just getting through the credits. A real little movie, with a beginning, middle, and end.

Parallel to this course, you will be getting an introduction to Adobe After Effects, which has become the "Swiss Army knife" of motion graphics. By the time we are working on *moving* graphics, you should have sufficient skills in After Effects to complete these projects. But I'd like to emphasize that After Effects is not the only way to accomplish the goals of this course. In fact, I'll try to talk about as many different ways to create motion graphics as possible. If you can find a technique that better serves the *idea*, by all means use it!

Presenting Ideas: Storyboards

You may have imagined a fabulous title sequence, but unless you can communicate that vision, no one is going to ask you to produce it. Very few people (especially clients) have a good visual imagination. You have to show them what you're talking about. You also have to think about what the goal of the sequence is. Do you want to create a mood; transmit information; tell a story; create a sense of geography, of history, or time period? Do you just want to assault the viewers' eyes and make them crazy? Any of these are valid goals, so choose one and make sure your proposal accomplishes it. Choose an imaginary or real film, and create a short title sequence for it (no more than ten credits). These are to be presented on paper, and the group will critique them. You will have three weeks to "deliver" your storyboards.

Developing Ideas: The Animatic

The next step in developing a sequence is to begin connecting the significant moments or "key frames" in time. One goal of the animatic is to begin to bring the sequence to "life." The other goal is to better communicate (or "sell") the idea of the sequence to others. An animatic can be as simple as a sequence of static storyboard frames cut to a voice or music track. A variation on animatics is the "ripamatic." In a ripamatic, you steal images or scenes from other films to serve as stand-ins for original material that you plan to create. In this way, you can get a feel for how your sequence might work, before you actually produce anything. The animatic helps you pre-edit your film before you shoot or create it. In our class, you will make an animatic of your storyboard project. It can be presented on video or on a computer (i.e., Quicktime movie). You can use whatever means are most appropriate to create a moving sketch of your idea, with sound and image. You will have four weeks to create your animatic.

Completing the Idea: The Finished Project

You will now complete the production of your title sequence. Shoot video, create animation, composite images, and create a soundtrack. You will deliver the project on videotape, and it will be a full-motion (24 or 30 fps) movie with final production values, including audio. You will have six weeks to complete your sequence.

grading

Your grade in this course will be primarily (75 percent) based on your projects, and heavily weighted toward the final project, as it represents almost half of your work. I'm looking for originality of thought and effort. Production values are nice, but not the primary goal. The other 25 percent will be based on your participation in and contributions to class discussions. As this is a course about ideas, I am most interested in hearing your reactions to what you see. This is subjective territory; no absolute rights or wrongs. Controversial views are encouraged.

required reading

Matt Woolman and Jeffery Bellantoni, *Type in Motion: Innovations in Digital Graphics* (New York: Rizzoli International Publications, 1999).

COURSE TITLE _ GAME-DESIGN WORKSHOP
INSTRUCTOR _ Eric Zimmerman
SCHOOL _ School of Visual Arts, MFA/Design
FREQUENCY _ Four classes on consecutive weeks
CREDIT _ One
LEVEL _ second-year MFA students

purpose

Games represent some of the most ancient forms of designed interactivity. And computer and video games are certainly among the most complex and sophisticated artifacts of digital culture today. Yet game design as a design discipline remains largely unexplored. How do games work? What are the unique qualities of games? What makes game interaction meaningful? How does the cultural status of games impact the design of games? And what can games teach us about interactive design?

This course will introduce students to these questions in a workshop format, focusing on the creation of non-digital games. Projects and discussions in the class will present formal, social, and cultural frameworks for understanding game play and game design. Using these discussions as a starting point, students will collaboratively create games. Rather than a course on software, the focus of the course is critical thinking. The goal of the class is for students to develop a sophisticated understanding of how games function. Key skills that will be taught include critical analysis of game design, the ability to rapidly prototype an idea, dynamic systems thinking, and an understanding of games as pop culture. And we'll be playing a lot of games too.

conceptual model

The course utilizes a conceptual model that considers games as three different kinds of dynamic systems: Games as Rules, Games as Play, and Games as Culture. This Rules/Play/Culture model will be discussed throughout the semester, but in summary:

- Games as Rules means considering games as formal systems of logical and mathematical rules.
- Games as Play means considering games as experience, including the physical, psychological, and social aspects of experience.

- Games as Culture means understanding as cultural phenomena and how they fit into larger cultural contexts.

design methodology

The focus of this course is the creation of playable games. While a number of small game projects will take place in class, your design focus will be a single game completed over the four weeks. The design methodology used in the class is an iterative, prototype-and-testing process. This means that you will be creating playable prototype versions of your games as soon as possible after a project is assigned and you will make most of your design decisions based on actual play testing.

For your game-design assignments, you will not be graded on the finished quality of the cards, game pieces, and other materials you create. Instead, the focus of the grading will be on the game design: the underlying game logic, the designed interactivity that the players enact in the game, and the overall play experience.

One of the primary contexts for the work we do in this class is digital game design. However, you will not be creating digital games as part of this course. The games you create in this class will be implemented using non-digital materials. There are several reasons for this. First of all, creating even the simplest digital game project would be far too time-intensive for such a short workshop. In addition, digital development would involve a great deal of coding, de-bugging, and asset creation—tasks that are not central to the game design itself, which is the main focus of this class. Finally, whether it's digital or not, a game is an interactive system. Creating non-digital games is a valuable exercise in thinking about the fundamental principles of interactivity outside the immediate context of computer technology.

grading

During the workshop, you will be completing two formal assignments that will be graded: a game design and a short game analysis. Each assignment will be graded and given a written evaluation. Each assignment is worth a certain amount of points. Students that come to each of the four evenings and participate in discussions should receive full credit for attendance/participation.

Attendance/participation (including in-class projects)	40 percent
Short papers/presentations	20 percent
Game design project	40 percent

These points add up to 100 percent. Final letter grades are given on the following scale:

98–100	A+
93–97	A
90–91	A-
88–89	B+
82–87	B
80–81	B-
etc.	

description of classes

Week 1: Introduction

Talk and discussion (forty-five minutes)
- Introductions
- Overview of workshop
- Rules, Play, and Culture
- Games as systems

Play and analyze games (forty-five minutes)
- Students will split up and play board games.
- Reconvene, and each group will give an analysis of its game.

In-class formal design exercise (forty-five minutes)
- Each group will be given a simple game (Tic-Tac-Toe, War, Rock/Paper/Scissors, etc.).
- Groups will play the game and then make formal changes to the rules in order to enrich the play.
- Groups reconvene to share and critique designs.

End (fifteen minutes)
- Assign four-week game-design project.
- Assign short analyses (groups of two).

Week 2: Rules and Play

Talk and discussion (thirty minutes)
- How rules become play.
- Designing choices for meaningful play.

Formal analyses (thirty minutes)
- Analyses presented and discussed.

In-class play design exercise (one hour)
- Each group comes up with a single activity that is not normally part of a game experience.

- Each group takes another group's activity and designs a simple game that incorporates the activity into the game experience.
- Groups reconvene to share and critique designs.

Work on game project (thirty minutes)
- Groups have brought in prototype of four-week game project.
- Groups work on their own to refine prototype.

Week 3: Designing Meaningful Play

Experiential analyses (thirty minutes)
- Analyses presented and discussed.

Talk and discussion (one hour)
- The computer game industry.
- Digital game-development process.
- Discuss gameLab game projects.

Work on four-week game project (one hour)
- Groups play each others' games and critique.

Week 4: Game Culture

Cultural analyses (forty-five minutes)
- Analyses presented and discussed.
- Final game project presentations (one and a half hours).
- Final presentation of game projects.
- Guest game-design critics will come to class for critique.

Final discussion (fifteen minutes)

assignments

Game Analyses (20 points)

Each student will complete a single analysis over the course of the workshop. Students will work in pairs to write a short analysis (three to five pages) and give a five-minute presentation to the class for discussion. The grade for the analysis will be based on the written paper and not on the presentation. The paper should not just summarize the game (it's O.K. to summarize on the first page), but the paper needs to be a critical analysis of some aspect of the game design. If possible, bring in the game you are analyzing to share with the class. Depending on when you are presenting your analysis in class, you will be given a conceptual focus to help structure your thinking—either formal, experiential, or cultural. Analyses will be completed outside of workshop time.

Game-Design Project (40 points)

In small groups, students will create a finished, playable game based on criteria given during the first workshop meeting. The following week, students will bring in a playable prototype of the game. During weeks two and three, students will have in-class time to work on their games; however, students will be expected to spend time designing outside of the workshop as well. During the final class, the finished designs will be presented and critiqued by visiting game-design critics.

contributor biographies

Sean Adams is a partner at AdamsMorioka in Los Angeles. He currently teaches Typography and Design Issues at California Institute of the Arts.

Susan Agre-Kippenhan is a professor at Portland State University, where she teaches courses in graphic design and media literacy. She is a former president of the Portland/AIGA. She writes and presents widely on the subject of linking community needs and educational objectives.

Hans Allemann joined the faculty of the University of the Arts in 1973. Both his work as a professional practitioner and educator have been recognized internationally. He is a member of the Alliance Graphique Internationale and a fellow of the American Institute of Graphic Arts.

Cristina de Almeida has practiced graphic design in both Brazil and the United States. She is currently an associate professor of graphic design at Western Washington University, in Bellingham, Washington.

Bob Aufuldish is a partner in Aufuldish & Warinner and an associate professor at the California College of Arts and Crafts, where he has taught since 1991. fontBoy (*www.fontboy.com*), a digital type foundry, was launched in 1995 to manufacture and distribute his fonts. His work has been included in competitions and publications in the United States and internationally.

Randall Balsmeyer is the creative director and president of Big Film Design, New York. For fifteen years he headed Balsmeyer & Everett, Inc., which established a worldwide reputation for creativity in both the design of title sequences and visual effects. His company has designed titles for thirteen of Spike Lee's features and six of the Coen Brothers' films. The directors he's worked with include Altman, Bertolucci, Cronenberg, Hartley, Scorsese, and Solondz. His company has produced visual effects for films ranging from independent features such as Todd Solondz's "Storytelling" to studio pictures like Harold Ramis's *Analyze This*. In addition to his design work, Randy has also been the visual effects supervisor for many films, including three Woody Allen pictures. He pioneered the use of location motion control photography for David Cronenberg's *Dead Ringers*. He is also a director of photography in Local 600.

Leslie Becker is professor and chair of graphic design at the California College of Arts and Crafts, where she has taught Typography and Thesis, and overseen curriculum development. She has maintained a multidisciplinary design practice, Becker Design, since 1973, including print graphics, custom furniture, pro bono work, and consulting. Among the publications she has written for are *Print* magazine, *Graphis New Talent*, and *Design Book Review* and has lectured at AIGA National and AICAD conferences. Leslie has a BFA from the Cooper Union and an MA from UC Berkeley and has been a practicing, multidisciplinary designer for over thirty years and a design educator for twenty-five years.

Roy R. Behrens is a professor of art at the University of Northern Iowa, where he teaches graphic design, illustration, and design history. He also edits *Ballast Quarterly Review*, art directs the *North American Review*, and is a contributing editor to *Print* magazine. His most recent book is *False Colors: Art, Design and Modern Camouflage* (Dysart, IA: Bobolink Books, 2002).

Cheryl Brzezinski-Beckett is the area coordinator and associate professor of graphic communications at the University of Houston. Beckett also serves as creative director of Minor Design Group. Fifteen years later, she's still in Texas.

John Calvelli is a designer and educator living in Portland, Oregon. He has also lived and worked in San Francisco, where he was a brand strategy manager for an Internet subsidiary of KPMG Consulting; and New York, where he directed the department of graphic design for the Museum of Modern Art. He has an MFA from CalArts in visual communication.

Elisabeth Charman teaches graphic design at Portland State University.

Jan Conradi is currently associate professor of graphic design at SUNY (State University of New York), Fredonia. She is education editor for Visual Arts Trends and is a member of AIGA, SoTA (Society of Typographic Aficionados) and Typocrafters. She maintains a freelance consulting practice and is the founder of ComingHome Press, a venture dedicated to producing limited-edition letterpress books.

Johanna Drucker is Robertson Professor and director of media studies at the University of Virginia. She has published and lectured widely on the history of the book, twentieth-century typography and design, and contemporary art and theory. She also publishes artists' books.

Inge Druckrey is a professor at the University of the Arts and has taught at Yale University, the Rhode Island School of Design, the Kunstgewerbeschule Krefeld, Germany, and the Kansas City Art Institute. Her work for clients in this country and Europe, as well as her writings on design, have been widely published in the international design community. Her work is included in the permanent collections of the Cooper-Hewitt Museum for Design and the Museum of Modern Art in New York City.

Stuart Ewen is Distinguished Professor in film and media studies at Hunter College and in history, sociology, and American studies at Hunter College. He is the author of numerous influential books including: *All Consuming Images, Captains of Consciousness*, and *PR! A Social History of Spin*. Under the nom de plume Archie Bishop, he has been a photographer, graphic artist, media prankster, and political situationist for nearly thirty years.

Karen A. Fiss received her Ph.D. from Yale University in 1995 and is assistant professor of visual culture and design at the California College of Arts and Crafts, San Francisco. Her recent publications include "The Emperor's New Graphics," *Print* magazine (Fall 2002), and "In Hitler's Salon," *Art, Culture, and Media under the Third Reich* (University of Chicago Press, 2002). She was co-editor of *Discourses: Conversations in Postmodern Art and Culture* (M.I.T. Press and The New Museum, 1990) and is currently completing a book manuscript entitled *Grand Illusion: France, the Third Reich, and Cultural Politics, ca. 1937*. She has received fellowships from the Getty Grant Program, the National Endowment for the Humanities, and the Center for Advanced Study in the Visual Arts.

Lisa Fontaine is an associate professor of graphic design at Iowa State University. She received both BFA and MFA degrees in graphic design from Boston University. Her client work includes both print design, exhibit design, and environmental graphics.

Mark Fox is an associate professor and the assistant chair of design at the California College of Arts and Crafts in San Francisco, where he has taught courses in graphic design since 1993. He served as president of the San Francisco chapter of the American Institute of Graphic Arts from 1995 to 1996, and has operated his studio practice, BlackDog, since 1986. His most recent article on design, "*Logos=God,*" was published by *Communication Arts* in 1999.

Annabelle Gould is a freelance designer and educator in Los Angeles. She has a BFA in graphic design from North Carolina State University and an MFA from Cranbrook Academy of Art.

Sondra Graff is an adjunct assistant professor in the communication design department at the Fashion Institute of Technology. She came to design circuitously through the world of dance. She is an art director at Pentacle, collaborating with multimedia artist Venantius J. Pinto. They specialize in designing promotional graphics for performing artists, dance, and theater companies. Sondra graduated with honors from Parson's School of Design. Prior to that she attended Interlochen Arts Academy and has both performed and taught dance professionally in New York City. When not teaching or designing she can be found on the rock face in the Gunks dangling from a cliff.

Susan Harris has been specializing in multimedia since 1995. She studied design and later taught, at the California College of Arts and Crafts (CCAC) in San Francisco. After working for various designers, and then freelance, Susan founded Fluent Studios (originally known as Slow Clouds Design). Fluent Studio's clients include Autodesk, KQED, marchFIRST, Macromedia, Sumitomo, Red Advertising, and Studio eg. Susan has co-authored *HTML and Web Artistry 2*, which will be published this fall. A full client list and portfolio can be viewed at *www.fluentstudios.com*.

Charles Hively is vice president, creative director at Greco Ethridge Group. He teaches at Parsons School of Design and has worked at a number of national agencies, including Lowe & Partners and Mullen/Long Haymes Carr. In addition, he has founded and run two full-service creative advertising agencies in Texas.

Deborah Huelsbergen is an assistant professor at the University of Missouri, Columbia, where she teaches all levels of graphic design and calligraphy. She has two separate undergraduate degrees from the University of Kansas, a BGS in acting and directing and a BFA in visual communications. She holds a MFA from Iowa State University.

Sunghyun Kang received a BFA in the field of applied art in 1980 from Ewha Womens University in Korea. She earned a MFA in graphic communication in 1986 from the University of Houston, and has taught graphic design in Korea for nine years. She earned a MA in graphic design in 1999 from Iowa State University, and joined as a faculty of the department of art and design at Iowa State University in fall 2000.

Joel Katz is an information architect working in print, wayfinding, and the Web. He is the founding president of AIGA/Philadelphia, the first chapter of AIGA, and has served on AIGA's national board of directors. His work is widely published, most recently in the books *Information Architects* and *UnderStAnding*, and he is an active exhibitor of his photography and photographic assemblages.

Jeffery Keedy is a designer, writer, type designer, and educator who has been teaching in the graphic design program at California Institute of the Arts since 1985. He was the director of the design program at CalArts between 1991 and 1995. His designs and essays have been published in *Eye, I.D., Emigre, Critique, Idea, Looking Closer One, Two* and *Four, Faces on the Edge: Type in the Digital Age, New Design: Los Angeles,* and *The Education of a Graphic Designer* (Allworth Press).

Cedomir Kostovic earned his BFA and MFA degrees from the Sarajevo Academy of Fine Arts (Bosnia), where he taught graphic design until 1991. Invited as an Artist in Residence, he spent one year at Old Dominion University in Norfolk, Virginia. Since 1992 he has been teaching graphic design and illustration classes in the art and design department at Southwest Missouri State University, where he now holds the position of professor.

Maud Lavin, associate professor of visual and critical studies and art history, is the author of the recently published *Clean New World: Culture, Politics, and Graphic Design* (MIT Press) and a monograph on the Berlin Dada artist Hannah Hoech, *Cut with the Kitchen Knife* (Yale University Press), named a *New York Times* notable book for 1993. Her writings on design, politics, and related cultural issues have appeared in *Print, I.D., Art in America, Artforum, Interiors, inform,* the *New York Times Book Review, Graphic Design in America* (Abrams/Walker Art Center), *Montage and Modern Life* (MIT Press/Boston ICA), and other publications.

Sherry Lefevre teaches film writing and English at the University of the Arts. She has taught English literature for twenty-five years, interrupted by five years of writing, editing, and producing documentary films.

Joan Lombardi is an associate professor in the communication design department of the BFA graphic design program at the Fashion Institute of Technology, where she has served as assistant chair of the department. Her professional design career began at CBS, Inc. and Columbia Records, and was followed by a multidisciplinary performing arts career with Nova Arts Inc., where she served as creative director, choreographer, and performer. As chair of the Curriculum committee at FIT, Joan has created, inspired, and implemented many course outlines for the BFA Graphic Design Program.

Ellen Lupton is the director of design studies at Maryland Institute College of Art in Baltimore. She is also curator of contemporary design at Cooper-Hewitt, National Design Museum, Smithsonian Institution in New York City.

Julie Mader-Meersman is a graphic designer, visual artist, and assistant professor in the department of art and design at Minnesota State University, Moorhead. She earned her MFA in graphic design from the University of Washington.

Nancy Mayer is an information designer with over twenty years experience in the field. Her work has been recognized in both Europe and the United States. She has taught design history at Otis College of Art and Design in Los Angeles and has recently begun research in archaeology, specializing in upper-paleolithic symbology.

Katherine McCoy is a senior lecturer at Illinois Institute of Technology's Institute of Design in Chicago, after co-chairing the department of design at Cranbrook Academy of Art for twenty-four years. As partner of McCoy & McCoy Associates, she consults in communications design, design marketing, and interior design for cultural, educational, and corporate clients. Recently she has formed, with partner and husband, Michael, High Ground Tools and Strategies for Design, to offer continuing professional education seminars and workshops for designers.

Ellen McMahon is an associate professor and co-chair of the Studio Division of the School of Art at the University of Arizona in Tucson. She teaches Critical Issues in Design/Culture, Typography, Illustration II, and Portfolio Preparation. Her work, which combines writing and visual art, explores the politics of intimacy within the family.

Anna McMillan is a partner in Red Industries, a Web design firm based in San Francisco. Prior to starting Red Industries, she worked for *WIRED* designing many sites for their online magazine, *HotWired,* including the *HotWired* homepage, *RGB Gallery, The Netizen,* and *Animation Express, HotWired*'s animation channel—the creation of which was inspired by Anna's speech at Seybold on animation. She has been featured in *I.D.* magazine, O'Reilly's *Photoshop for the Web, Mastering Photoshop 5 for the Web,* and *HotWired Style.* Currently Anna is Red Industries' animation and motion design director, creating animations for Lucasfilm's Star Wars and ONE Media.

Jennifer Morla is president and creative director of Morla Design, San Francisco. Her work is represented in the permanent collections of the Museum of Modern Art and the San Francisco Museum of Modern Art. In addition, she has had solo exhibitions at SFMoMA and DDD Gallery in Japan. Ms. Morla is an adjunct professor at California College of Arts and Crafts, where she teaches the senior-level thesis.

Chris Myers has over fifteen years experience teaching at California Institute of the Arts and the University of the Arts, where he served as chairman of the graphic design department for seven years. His work has been recognized in both Europe and the United States. He currently serves on the board of trustees of the American Center for Design and is an on-site accreditation evaluator for the National Association of Schools of Art and Design.

Martha Nichols teaches writing at the University of the Arts. She has an extensive background in painting, drawing, and literature, and has exhibited her work widely in Pennsylvania. Her experience as a practicing artist brings a unique editorial perspective to these projects and the many art/literature courses she has led at both the undergraduate and graduate levels throughout the Philadelphia area.

Kali Nikitas is the principal of Graphic Design for Love (+$), which serves cultural institutions and nonprofits. Her work has been recognized by *I.D.,* the AIGA, the (former) ACD, and the Type Directors Club. She has curated two international shows including: "And She Told 2 Friends." In addition to her practice, she is chair of the design department at the Minneapolis College of Art and Design.

Christopher Ozubko is a professor of design, and director of the School of Art at the University of Washington in Seattle, where he has taught since 1981. His work has been published and exhibited in all of the major design periodicals, annuals, and venues internationally. Christopher is a member of ATypI and was past president of the Seattle Chapter of AIGA. In 1994, Ozubko was selected for the international review of Who's Who in Graphic Design, and in 2002 he was recognized as an AIGA Fellow.

Sharon Helmer Poggenpohl teaches in the masters and doctoral program in design at the Institute of Design, Illinois Institute of Technology, which focuses on developing methods and human-centered approaches to design. She also edits and publishes *Visible Language*, an international journal concerned with the communication transition from print to screen.

R. Roger Remington is a professor of graphic design at Rochester Institute of Technology, visiting professor at Hochschule Anhalt in Dessau, Germany, and lecturer at Hochschule für Gestaltung in Schwäbisch Gmünd, Germany. His teaching, research, and writing is primarily about the history of graphic design, with a focus on the period of 1930–1950 in American graphic design. He was co-author of *Nine Pioneers in American Graphic Design* and author of *Lester Beall-Trailblazer of American Graphic Design*. In 2003 his new book on *American Modernism* will be available from Laurence King Publishers in London.

Elizabeth Resnick is the chair of the communication design department at the Massachusetts College of Art, Boston. She is the principal in Elizabeth Resnick Design and currently serving as the co-art director for *Art New England* magazine, a regional arts publication. She serves on the Board of Directors of AIGA Boston chapter.

Joseph Roberts is a graduate of the School of Visual Arts and is president of Klauber & Roberts. His clients include AT&T, CIGNA, Ortho Pharmaceuticals, The Josef & Anni Albers Foundation, Yale University Press, Aperture, The Starr Foundation, and Boscobel Restoration. He is currently the Chairman of the Communications Design Department, Pratt Institute, Brooklyn, New York.

Stefan Sagmeister is the principal of Sagmeister Design in New York. He teaches music design in the School of Visual Arts MFA design program. His own music clients include The Rolling Stones, David Byrne, Lou Reed, Aerosmith, and Pat Metheny.

Anne Saint-Pierre is a New York-based creative director. She currently consults for broadcast design clients and advocacy groups through her own company, Design Asylum. She previously served as staff art director for Telezign, Post-Perfect, and Caesar Video Graphics. She holds an MA from the École Nationale Supérieure des Arts Decoratifs, Paris, and has lectured at the School of Visual Arts, New York, and Broadcast Design Association conferences.

Louise Sandhaus is co-director of the graphic design program at CalArts and part of the design collective, Durfee Regn Sandhaus, a multidisciplinary design entity that produces material and electronic "information spaces." Recently, she helped organize the design education conference, "Schools of Thoughts." Her writings have appeared in *Eye* and *Émigré*, *The Education of an E-Designer* (Allworth Press), and she has edited several publications. Her work has been recognized in *AIGA 365* and *I.D. Design Review* and is in the permanent collection of San Francisco Museum of Modern Art.

Sol Sender is director of brand strategy at Design Kitchen, Inc. Corporate clients have included, and continue to include, Motorola and The Nutrasweet Company. Pro bono work for the Abraham Lincoln Brigade Archives will result in a catalog of children's drawings from the Spanish Civil War, *They Still Draw Pictures*, to be published in 2001. Areas of independent research and writing include twentieth-century European design and politics and hippie communes of the 1960s and 1970s. Sol's essay, "Design and Complicity: Herbert Bayer's Silent Legacy," appeared in the winter 2000 AIGA Chicago *inform* journal. Sol studied at Bowdoin College and the School of the Art Institute of Chicago.

R. Brian Stone teaches visual communication in the department of design at the Ohio State University. Prior to joining the faculty at OSU, he taught for several years at the University of the Arts. He is a frequent speaker at conferences and universities, and maintains professional activities in the areas of interactive visual communication, screen-based interface design, and Web usability.

Terry Stone has over twenty years experience in design management. Her areas of expertise include: strategic development, client relationships, management of creative people, and marketing of creative services. She is currently strategy director for AdamsMorioka, Inc. Teaching at CalArts for four years, her classes "Design Issues" and "Professional Practice for Graphic Designers" are required courses for undergrads. Terry has been on the Board of Directors of the AIGA in Los Angeles, Atlanta, and Miami, where she served as president.

Taylor, perhaps better known as the Captain Cursor, the Orange Terror, fights a never-ending battle for truth, justice, and reliable Internet standards. During a freak accident involving runaway JavaScript code, downloadable fonts, and a bright orange cover of *Wired* magazine, mild-mannered technologist Taylor was transformed into Captain Cursor. Captain Cursor now maintains this double identity, Internet Super Hero by night, but by day he disguises himself as a freelance technologist, to better find trouble spots online. Whether it happens to be the evil Dr. JavaScript, Professor Plugin, or any of the other nefarious supervillains that plague Web developers across the globe, Captain Cursor is there to help fight the menace. *www.captaincursor.com.*

Stephanie Tevonian received her BA in French literature from Vassar College and her MFA in graphic design from Yale School of Art and Architecture. She has worked primarily in two-dimensional design with an emphasis on book design and promotion, primarily in the nonprofit sector. Stephanie has had her own company since 1972, with an eight-year diversion from 1980–1988 as partner in the design group Works. She has participated in the AIGA as a member of the New York Chapter Executive Committee and as chair of a subcommitttee about the environment. During this time she produced three evening events with national participants about the design process and environmentally responsible design. At present, she continues as a designer and design consultant and as a teacher of graphic design and typography for the Fashion Institute of Technology.

Josh Ulm is director of ioResearch, a studio specializing in interactive design, installation, and storytelling. His clients have included Lucas Films, Nike, National Geographic, DreamWorks, Intel, General Motors, NBC, and the International Olympic Committee. He currently teaches at the Academy of Art in San Francisco, has taught in the past for Lynda.com, and has spoken at numerous Web and Internet conferences. *www.ioresearch.com.*

Michael Vanderbyl has gained international prominence in the design field as a practitioner, educator, critic, and advocate. Since being established in San Francisco in 1973, his firm, Vanderbyl Design, has evolved into a multidisciplinary studio with expertise in graphics, packaging, signage, interiors, showrooms, retail spaces, furniture, textiles, and fashion apparel. Michael is the recipient of the Gold Medal award from the American Institute of Graphic Arts; he is a member of the Alliance Graphique Internationale (AGI) and presides as Dean of Design at the California College of Arts and Crafts.

Véronique Vienne is the author of *The Art of Doing Nothing*, published by Clarkson Potter. Her other books in that series include *The Art of Imperfection* and *The Art of The Moment*. She also writes about design, fashion, and cultural trends for magazines and corporate clients. Her general-interest articles have been published in *Martha Stewart Living, Town & Country, House & Garden, InStyle, Redbook, Real Simple*, and more. A selection of her critical essays on design, originally published in *Metropolis, Graphis, Print, Communication Arts, Eye, American Photo*, and *AIGA Journal*, are available in a book, *Something To Be Desired*, published by Graphis.

Douglas Wadden is professor of design and chair of the division of design in the School of Art at the University of Washington in Seattle, where he has taught since 1970. He has extensive experience in communications design for museums, institutions, and corporations, and has won numerous awards throughout his career. He has been a lecturer, juror, and national board member for both the AIGA in New York and the ACD in Chicago. His teaching interests are in typography, photography, information design, publications, and design history. In 1998 he was elected into the Alliance Graphique Internationale.

Ric Wilson is a designer and art director with the IDPgroup, in Columbia, Missouri, an advertising, design, and Internet-marketing firm. Wilson received his MFA from the University of Missouri, where he is a visiting faculty member. Wilson developed this course as part of a five-course sequence for the University of Missouri Extensions program to serve as a minor emphasis area for the Bachelors of General Studies degree at the University.

Rob Wittig cofounded IN.S.OMNIA, a literary electronic bulletin board system, and later wrote *Invisible Rendezvous* (Wesleyan University Press, 1994), as an analysis of this spirited project. Rob subsequently won a 1987 Fulbright Scholarship to Paris to study technical, artistic, and theoretical aspects of creating visual/verbal literary works with online publishing technologies, on the invitation of Jacques Derrida, Jean-Francois Lyotard, and the Centre Georges Pompidou. Rob now directs TANK20_language_arts (*www.tank20.com*), an electronic literature publisher, and teaches in both literature and graphic design programs.

Michael Worthington is the co-director of the graphic design program at California Institute of the Arts. His writing has been published in *Eye* magazine, the *AIGA Journal, Education of a Graphic Designer, Sex Appeal,* and *Restart: New Systems in Graphic Design.* He runs Worthington Design in Los Angeles, and his design has received awards from the ACD, the AIGA, *ID* magazine, and the New York Art Directors Club, and has appeared in various publications including *Typography Now 2, Type In Motion, Typographics,* and *New Design Los Angeles.* He was a recently recipient of a City of Los Angeles Fellowship (COLA).

Natalie Zee is an interactive designer and author based in San Francisco. Specializing in Rich Media, Natalie has amassed years of experience building leading-edge interactive projects for such top clients as Mattel, Levi's, 3Com, Visa, Apple, and Macromedia. As an award-winning designer, she has worked for Macromedia, frog design, and marchFIRST (starting back with CKS). She is currently the co-author of two books: *The Last Mile: Broadband and the Next Internet Revolution,* published by McGraw-Hill, and *HTML Artistry: More than Code,* published by New Riders. A regular speaker at Web conferences around the country, Natalie holds a degree in mass communications and technology from the University of California at Berkeley. She is currently the Rich Media Creative Director at SBI and Company in San Francisco, *www.avantmedia.com.*

Eric Zimmerman is CEO and cofounder of gameLab, a game development company based in New York City. GameLab creates digital games for publishers, including LEGO, Shockwave.com, and Mattel Interactive. GameLab game titles, including BLiX, LOOP, and Junkbot, have won gameLab Webby Award nominations and a nomination for a GDC Game Developers Choice award. Zimmerman teaches game design at various schools including the Schoo of Visual Arts MFA/Design program and Parsons. Information on gameLab, as well as links to the games, can be found *www.gmlb.com.*

index

281

283

285

286

289

Books from Allworth Press

Allworth Press is an imprint of Allworth Communications, Inc. Selected titles are listed below.

The Education of a Graphic Designer
edited by Steven Heller (paperback, 6¾ × 9⅞, 288 pages, $18.95)

The Education of an Illustrator
edited by Steven Heller and Marshall Arisman (paperback, 6¾ × 9⅞, 288 pages, $19.95)

The Education of an E-Designer
edited by Steven Heller (paperback, 6¾ × 9⅞, 352 pages, $21.95)

Graphic Design History
edited by Steven Heller and Georgette Balance (paperback, 6¾ × 9⅞, 352 pages, $21.95)

Texts on Type
edited by Steven Heller and Philip B. Meggs (paperback, 6¾ × 9⅞, 288 pages, $19.95)

Editing by Design, Third Edition
by Jan V. White (paperback, 8½ × 11, 256 pages, $29.95)

Design Issues: How Graphic Design Informs Society
edited by DK Holland (paperback, 6¾ × 9⅞, 288 pages, $21.95)

Citizen Designer: Perspectives on Design Responsibility
edited by Steven Heller and Véronique Vienne (paperback, 6 × 9, 272 pages, $19.95)

Inside the Business of Graphic Design: 60 Leaders Share Their Secrets of Success
by Catharine Fishel (paperback, 6 × 9, 288 pages, $19.95)

Looking Closer 4: Critical Writings on Graphic Design
edited by Michael Bierut, William Drenttel, and Steven Heller (paperback, 6¾ × 9⅞, 304 pages, $21.95)

Please write to request our free catalog. To order by credit card, call 1-800-491-2808 or send a check or money order to Helios Press, 10 East 23rd Street, Suite 510, New York, NY 10010. Include $5 for shipping and handling for the first book ordered and $1 for each additional book. Ten dollars plus $1 for each additional book if ordering from Canada. New York State residents must add sales tax.

To see our complete catalog on the World Wide Web, or to order online, you can find us at
www.heliospress.com.